THE WORLD HELD HOSTAGE

The Brighton bombing of the Conservative Party Conference Hotel on 12th October 1984 came within a hair's breadth of eliminating the British government, something neither the Kaiser nor Hitler could achieve. There are strong links to suggest that Gadhafi was involved with the Irish terrorist movement in the execution of this bombing as a way of taking revenge and salvaging some national pride from the humiliation of the Libyan People's Bureau siege following the murder of W.P.C. Fletcher (see page 124).   *Press Association Ltd*

Did you know...

that there are nearly two million trained and dedicated terrorists throughout the world? (p 233)

that Lord Mountbatten was murdered by a terrorist trained in Libya? (p. 106)

that the Brighton bombing of the UK Cabinet was intended to be a direct reprisal for the expulsion of Libyan 'diplomats' following the killing of WPC Fletcher, and was identical to the later attempt on the Chad Cabinet? (pp 124, 144)

that Col. Gadhafi spends 70 per cent of his oil revenues bolstering terrorist groups? (p 146)

that the IRA use former French collaborators with the Germans to bring arms into the British Isles? (p 194)

that the UN and its agencies have actively supported the PLO? (pp 205–207)

that major Western governments have accommodated terrorists and reached 'understandings' with them? (p 213)

that European businessmen and companies give assistance to terrorists in the quest for greater profits? (pp 151, 215)

that US army personnel and other US government employees have actively participated in the training of terrorists in Libya? (p 134)

that Carlos is a KGB agent? (p 99)

that George Blake, the MI6 spy, is the cousin of the world's greatest terrorist organiser? (p 100) that Palestinian terrorists were instrumental in overthrowing the Shah of Iran and took over the US Embassy in Teheran? (pp 127, 66)

that the Provisional IRA gave tactical advice on the escalation of picket-line violence during the British miners' strike? (p 149)

that European neo-Fascist groups have received money and support directly from Gadhafi? (pp 90, 130)

that the US government has, for more than 25 years, allowed Irish-Americans to subsidise the IRA with both weapons and money and has refused to allow the extradition of IRA members? (pp 106, 223)

that Col. Gadhafi and other Palestinians are using former SS concentration camp officers to train terrorists? (p 96)

that with German help Col. Gadhafi is manufacturing a nuclear warhead with an existing range of Cairo and Tel Aviv and a potential range of Paris, Bonn and London? (pp 150–3)

that Col. Gadhafi's terms for peace include the forced repatriation of most of the Jewish Israeli population? (p 60)

THE
WORLD HELD
HOSTAGE

The War waged by International Terrorism

DESMOND McFORAN

St. Martin's Press
New York

First published in the United States of America in 1987

Printed in Great Britain

ISBN 0–312–00835–X

Library of Congress Cataloging-in-Publication Data

McForan, Desmond.
The world held hostage.

Bibliography: p.
Includes index.
1. Terrorism. 2. Terrorism—Arab countries.
3. Fedayeen. 4. Jewish–Arab relations—1949–
I. Title.
JX5420.M34 1987   341.7'7   87–4776
ISBN 0–312–00835–X

CONTENTS

ix

LIST OF TABLES

LIST OF DIAGRAMS

LIST OF ILLUSTRATIONS

ACKNOWLEDGEMENTS

There are many people to whom I am indebted for their help, support, assistance and advice, both in this country and throughout Europe. It is impossible to name them all here, and many of them would not wish me to do so for reasons of security and safety. Without their help this book would not have been possible. All of them, I am sure, know the extent of my deep-felt gratitude and I only hope that with the publication of this work they will judge that the risks they took were justified.

There are, however, some people whose help has been utterly invaluable throughout all the preparations of this manuscript: the late Hon. Terence Prittie gave encouragement and support; Dr Walter G. Hankins in California gave me the benefit of his wisdom; my parents have been a well-spring of solace and inspiration, providing that very special sort of comfort that can quickly heal a battered and bruised soul—to them I am and always will be eternally grateful; without the love and help of my wife, Cecily, the project would never have seen fruition. She endured much during the whole process, assisting me with many aspects of the book, always remaining completely and totally supportive. Finally, my thanks go to Nicholas Hagger, not only for his clarity of vision and staunchly pro-Western stance, but also for accepting the burden of seeing this project into print.

DEDICATION

This book is dedicated to all those brave and selfless men and women who daily risk their lives to protect us from the menace of terrorism. To these unsung heroes of democracy, I, for one, am eternally grateful.

INTRODUCTION

The Soviet advance into Eastern Europe during 1944 was only the beginning of the struggle for existence now faced by the Western democracies against those who seek their annihilation, a struggle which has reached global proportions. Anarchists with nothing in common save their desire to overthrow democracy have joined forces to provide a constant threat to the Western nations; their expertise comes from Moscow, their finance from the oil wealth of the Arab States. This international network of terror cares nothing for innocent victims sacrificed in its quest for the eventual eradication of democracy. Its ultimate battleground: a Third World War.

The Soviet Union, Libya and Cuba are the training grounds for ruthless terrorists of all nationalities and extremist ideologies; the funding for their atrocities results from the Western World's self-destructive need for oil to maintain its civilisation. These opportunistic purveyors of violence make it their business to wreak havoc and despair wherever they can, aided by the free publicity they get from the media of the very nations which they intend to destroy, and supported always by the USSR. In every democratic country of the world, Soviet KGB agents are organising and manipulating this alliance of terror. No other area exemplifies this explosive situation more graphically than the Middle East. Since 1948, when the infant state of Israel defeated the united armies of the Arab world, Palestinian refugees have been subjected to the odious but importunate rhetoric of the Arab leadership. Preferring to keep the refugees in tented and prefabricated cities as a reminder of Arab defeat, rather than make any attempt to integrate them into their societies, the Arab states have effectively abandoned the refugees to their fate. The Arab armies were again defeated in 1956 and crushingly so in 1967.

In their desire for political expression, the refugees found an outlet in the *fedayeen* bands of insurgents, who made every effort to take their hopelessness and despair and direct it in violence against the people of Israel. The Arab oil states, eager to encourage them in these ventures to prevent the refugees directing their frustrations against the governments who had abandoned them, provided the *fedayeen* with weapons and money. As the voice of Palestinian nationalism grew louder and the demands of the terrorists waxed, the Arab governments began to feel more insecure: their carefully nurtured worm had begun to turn. Jordan nearly became the terrorists' first victim and had to use force to get them out of the country. And so they turned to Lebanon. The other Arab states took fright. But instead of following King Hussein's example, they curried the terrorists' favour by lavishing extravagant sums of money on them—sums in excess of the gross national product of some smaller states. This money was available due to the quadrupling of the oil price, particularly after 1973, and has kept pace ever since.

The Palestinian terrorists, now securely funded, followed the dictates of their Marxist-oriented political consciences and turned to the USSR for specialised assistance. Happy to accommodate the PLO and its constituent groups because they were a strong destabilising influence in this strategically important region, the Soviet Union provided the Palestinians with support and weaponry. As the Palestinians took their battle against the Israelis and the Jews of Europe, further assistance was afforded them by European Marxist-oriented groups. (Baader Meinhof, INLA, ETA and the Red Brigades just to name a few.) Once these links were established and utilised by the Palestinians, they began to provide both money and weapons as well as training facilities for other disaffected groups, and individuals, from all over the world. **The funding for these activities came from the Arab oil-producing states—the expertise came from the Soviet Union and its satellites,** with the result that **now some 50 terrorist organisations are centrally co-ordinated and under the influence of the Soviet Union.**

It is this relationship between oil and terror that this book seeks to analyse and draw attention to. **It is a relationship that has not been exposed until now.** All previous studies of terrorism have concentrated on either the political effect of terrorism or the danger it heralds. Some have provided an analysis of individual operations and groups, whereas others have concentrated upon the ideological links with either Nazism or Marxism.

I hope that a clear revelation of the facts, which have not been put together in this form before, will alert the West to the grave situation that confronts it, and to the dangers that lie ahead.

Desmond McForan

PART ONE

The growth of Palestinian nationalism and the Palestine movement

THE BASIS OF all discontent in the Middle East can be traced to the emergence of Arab nationalism in the latter years of the Ottoman Empire. This movement was allowed some degree of open self-expession until 1914, when in order to ensure its survival, the nationalists organised themselves into secret societies. Somewhat appeased by the creation of states such as Iraq, Syria, Lebanon and others in the aftermath of the conflict, Arab nationalism was severely repressed in certain countries of the region, while on the other hand having its attention focussed on the problems inherent in Mandatory Palestine. Following the creation of Israel and the refugee problem in 1948, a few better-educated Palestinians began to pick up the mantle of nationalism again.[1]

The result was 'Harakat al-Qawmiyyin al-Arab, the Arab Nationalists' Movement, founded by a group of Palestinian students at the American University of Beirut in the early 1950s. Its four leaders were George Habash and Wadi Haddad, Hani al-Hindi, a Syrian and Naif Hawatima, a Jordanian. Initially, the ANM masqueraded as a literary club while in reality it was a secret society organised into cells. ANM's numbers were never large as its members preferred to regard themselves as an élite who would achieve their ends by influencing Arab governments. Cells were established in most Arab states by Palestinians working abroad or nationals from those states, recruited when they came to Beirut to study. The ANM was primarily concerned with the unification of Arab lands and restoring the Arab nation to its former glory. This was to be achieved by political integration of all the Arab countries, the subjugation of Israel, the eradication of Western imperialist influence from the region, and the social and economic regeneration of the Arab people. The first objective was to

3

subjugate Israel and, in this context, no distinction was made between Israelis and Jews. The Arab people were called to wage a war of vengeance on Israel for her 'rape' of Palestine, '... and to confront her Jewish inhabitants eventually with a choice between expulsion and extermination.'[2] Other political groupings like the *Ba'ath* and the Moslem Brotherhood, whose main programmes were Pan-Arab, also began to establish branches among the displaced Palestinian *fedayeen* as well as amongst the more educated Palestinians who had migrated to other lands. Thus a pattern had begun to emerge, whereby Palestinians were depending not only on other Arab political groupings but also on other Arab governments and states.

By 1955 the Palestinian refugees who had been displaced to camps in Gaza, the West Bank and Lebanon began to feel the first stirrings of reaction to the Israeli State, which took the form of military action. In March of that year, *fedayeen* commandos operating out of Egyptian-controlled Gaza began attacking people and settlements in southern Israel and, by the summer, were joined by *fedayeen* from the West Bank who began sabotage raids under Jordanian and Lebanese auspices.

By the autumn, this guerrilla activity was sharply increased by *fedayeen* attacks and cross-border raids from Lebanon. However, it is essential to remember that all Palestinian anti-Israeli activity was purely of a military nature prior to 1962.

From about 1960 the ANM began to drift leftwards, with Naif Hawatima and the Lebanese Muhsin Ibrahim, arguing that the movement should concentrate on the social and economic regeneration of the people as the first prerequisite towards unity. They asserted that this could be achieved by enlisting the support of the Arab masses against capitalism, feudalism and reaction, which would result in the overthrow of the traditionally conservative Arab regimes. To this end, the ANM increased recruitment of foreign nationals in order to expand its network of cells throughout the region. In late 1960 it helped in the foundation of the National Front for the Liberation of Saudi Arabia which by early the following year had allied itself with the dissident members of the house of Saud led by Talal ibn Abdul Aziz and was the recipient of Soviet funding. The reasons behind this move was derived from King Saud's attempt in 1958 to torpedo the newly created United Arab Republic, comprising of Egypt and Syria, by means of bribery and

4

attempted assassination.[3]

By 1964, several insurgent and clandestine guerrilla groups had begun to operate in the Arabian peninsula and one of those was the Yemen-based Arabian Peninsula Peoples Union, a Nasserist group. Yet another important group firmly allied to Habash's ANM was the National Liberation Front of South Yemen, based in Aden. This latter organisation reflected the growing rift within the leadership of the ANM. The NLFSY wanted both to destroy the traditional authority of the *daulahs* in Aden as well as discredit its ideological adversaries, thus securing recognition in Cairo, Baghdad and Damascus. To this end, four delegates were sent to the ANM conference in Beirut under Qahtan al-Sha'abi, where they sided with the pro-Nasserists, Habash, Haddad and al-Hindi, against the Marxists led by Ibrahim and Hawatima. On their return to South Yemen in May 1964, the split within the leadership became more obvious. However, it did not prevent them from waging a campaign of terror in Aden in August of that year.

At the May 1964 ANM conference in Beirut, the conflict within the leadership came out into the open. The Nasserists wanted the ANM kept as an elite group wedded to Nasserism while the Marxists wanted to seek mass support for a sweeping social revolution which would incorporate both the destruction of Israel and the elimination of Western influence from the region. In order to counter Hawatima and Ibrahim's influence, George Habash organised the Palestinian members of the ANM into the National Front for the Liberation of Palestine. This served yet another purpose—to detract from the Arab League's formation of the Palestine Liberation Organisation by creating a radical, grass roots organisation which would have its base amongst the displaced refugees.[4]

I   YASSER ARAFAT'S RISE TO POWER

The PLO was essentially a kind of Arab agency created by the Arab states. It grew out of the Alexandria Summit Conference of 15 September 1963 and was financed by the Arab League. In spring 1964, about 400 Palestinians met in Jerusalem to form the Palestine National Congress and King Hussein of Jordan, who opened the meeting, resolved to establish a Palestine Liberation Organisation and to open camps to train guerrillas. A former Saudi Arabian diplomat, Ahmed Shukhairy, was

5

chosen as chairman and leader of the PLO and a standing army was created by the organisation, called the Palestine Liberation Army.

Since the success of the Algerian revolution, politically-conscious Palestinians had sought advice and tutelage from Algerian instructors. These Algerians were instrumental in the early formation of the PLO. However there was another oganisation which helped and they were known as *Harakat at-Tahrir al-Falastini*, the capital letters of which, in reverse, form the arabic word *fatah*—to conquer. Fatah was created as a clandestine organisation and was led by a former President of the Palestine Students Federation in Cairo, Yasser Arafat.

Arafat was born in Gaza in 1929. His full name, Abd el-Rahman Abd el-Rauf Arafat el-Qudwa el-Husseini, reveals his family tie to the late fanatical pro-Nazi, anti-Semitic, Grand Mufti of Jerusalem, Haj Amin el-Husseini. In order to protect his position, Arafat has threatened death to any Arab journalist revealing his blood-tie to the former Grand Mufti. In his younger days he tried to bury this family connexion to prevent being tainted by the loss of status which the Husseini family had undergone. Had this connexion become widely known, he would have been viewed with deep suspicion by his underground comrades.

Following his admission as an Engineering student at Cairo University in 1951, he and other students were active in anti-British irregular operations in the Canal zone. When he became President of the Palestine Students Federation in 1952, he initiated close contacts with the extreme Moslem Brotherhood, which was to stand him in good stead later. In 1956 he was a junior officer in the Egyptian army where, it has been suggested, he saw action during the Suez crisis. Shortly after his demobilisation, he left Egypt and set up as a building contractor in Kuwait. While there, however, he spent most of his time touring the Palestinian *diaspora*, recruiting members for Fatah. He was not—as he claims—the sole inspiration behind the concept of Fatah. The credit for that must go to two other *diaspora* Palestinians (of whom more will be written later), Khalid al-Hassan and Khalid al-Wazir. Together with Arafat these two organised the setting up of cells in Kuwait and West Germany among Palestinian students as well as starting a guerrilla training camp in Algeria.[5]

Following the formation of the PLO in 1964, Palestinian activities throughout the Middle East became more conspicuous. In the Gulf Sheikhdoms, Arafat, along with al-Hassan, al-Wazir and other Palestinian leaders like the PLO chairman Shukhairy, were fêted and given large subventions by the sheikhs. This generosity had as much to do with dissuading Palestinian radicals from threatening the conservative, traditional feudalism as it had with supporting anti-Israeli operations. In the latter context, the Gulf sheikhs happily welcomed the opening of the Arab boycott of Israel's offices in their principalities. However, this was due much more to the covert machinations of the ANM in the region than anything the PLO was threatening.

Arafat had also managed to work out an agreement with Colonel Ahmed Suwaidani, who was in charge of Syria's security and Head of Military Intelligence. This agreement was made possible by the active intervention, on Arafat's behalf, of Palestinian officers in Syria's Deuxième Bureau and ensured Arafat of success in securing himself as the leader of Fatah as well as securing Fatah's rise in importance in the Palestinian *diaspora*. The Arafat–Suwaidani agreement ensured cooperation between Fatah and Syria's military intelligence network, to the extent that the personal details of known *fedayeen* saboteurs on Syrian Deuxième Bureau files were opened for Arafat's inspecton.[6] From this point onwards he began to actively seek control of the PLO by exercising coercion and terrorism.

II THE PLO/FATAH LINK

Fatah's main source of recruitment was the Union of Palestine students in Cairo. This had a long-term effect on the future leadership of the PLO cells which ensured that senior positions would fall to former students of a lower middle or middle class background, thus breaking with tradition and the feudal Arab concept of leadership. While this recruitment was underway, however, relations between Fatah leaders and the Arab governments became troubled. The whole concept of Palestinian nationalism ran counter to the currently accepted trend of Arab unity, espoused by Nasser and his adherents, which had taken effect in 1957–8, and resulted in the ill-fated United Arab Republic. During the lifetime of the UAR many Palestinians who espoused the cause of Palestinian nationalism were imprisoned, refused travel permits and muzzled in other ways by various Arab governments—in some cases until 1967.[7]

Between the establishment of the PLO and the fateful Six-Day War of June 1967, Arafat did everything that he could to consolidate his position within Fatah, and Fatah's position within the emerging Palestinian resistance movement. He desperately tried to remain independent of other Arab influences, particularly Arab governments. This was a pipe-dream, however, as without the support of Arab governments he would not have been able to finance Fatah's activities or to achieve the much needed legitimacy within the Palestinian *diaspora*, since most Palestinians still looked to the traditional leadership as embodied within their governments. Yet Fatah was not reticent about proclaiming its true aims. In June 1965, Fatah delegates to the Palestinian National Congress meeting in Cairo expressed their policy bluntly at their first meeting with the world's press: 'To entangle the Arab Nations in a war with Israel'.[8]

III   THE ARAB STATES' CONNEXION
WITH TERRORISTS—EARLY DEVELOPMENTS

Fatah, however, was much less of a headache to the Arab states than the ANM with its transnational Arab connexions. Immediately following Habash's creation of the National Front for the Liberation of Palestine, the parent organisation, the ANM, orchestrated limited terrorism and insurgency against the weaker monarchies in the Gulf region. From 1964 onwards, the ANM founded its own cells in Saudi Arabia by converting graduates who were returning home. At the same time, it encouraged the Federation of Democratic Forces of the Arabian Peninsula and its rival group the Arabian Peninsula Peoples Union to step up activity against the House of Saud. Over the next few years both organisations were responsible for a number of intermittent bombings in several towns throughout Saudi Arabia. The ANM regarded the Saudi monarchy as being anti-Nasserist and an obstacle towards Arab unity, as well as being both traditional and conservative which made them a legitimate target for those who wished for sweeping revolution.

Following the defeat and humiliation of the Arab forces against Israel in June 1967, Saudi Arabia was able to end official Egyptian interference within its internal affairs by offering to save Nasser from disgrace by financially underwriting Egypt on condition that the latter withdrew its forces from Yemen. Nasser immediately agreed, his armies were reequipped and his economy heavily subsidised. King Feisal also trumpeted his suspension of oil shipments to both the United States of America and Britain; this was done to prevent any insurrection occurring among the large numbers of Palestinian workers in the oil fields. Feisal's actions, together with Saudi Arabia's strategic power and preponderance in the Gulf region, ensured that the sheikhdoms would follow suit.[9]

The post-1967 radicals gave the Arab world the twin hopes of Palestinian liberation and Pan-Arab unity. They rejected, however, the old methods espoused within Nasserism. Instead they urged that the battle be carried to the enemy—Israel. In rejecting Nasserism they were also rejecting Nasser himself since he was the personification of the cause of defeat. Ibrahim and Hawatima's arguments for widening the ANM's aims to include overthrowing capitalism and the traditional Arab social order now convinced George Habash, who declared that the ANM would lead the struggle against capitalism, imperialism, Zionism and Arab reaction. In almost the same breath, Nasser and the other 'progressive' régimes in power were labelled 'petty-bourgeois' [sic] and worse.[10] This new stance, however, required a reorganisation and rationalisation of ANM.

In the autumn of 1967, George Habash began negotiations with various extremist-minded cliques and committees to thrash out a workable alliance. Naif Hawatima controlled a group centred on the American University of Beirut, the Vengeance Youth, which quickly agreed to the alliance. Two other small groups of some significance were Wajih al-Madani's Abtal al-Awda (Heroes of the Return) and the Palestine Liberation Front led by Ahmed Jibril. Jibril had been a captain in the Syrian army and in 1958, together with 20 fellow officers, formed the PLF. In 1964 the group began to mount raids across both the Syrian and Lebanese borders into Israel and by June 1967, 95 missions had been completed. These were the components of a new adumbrative organisation that came into being in

9

December 1967 under the leadership of George Habash—the Popular Front for the Liberation of Palestine. Each group retained its own identity and source of support, but each agreed to act in concert with other groups and to lend support wherever needed.

The most important member of this nebulous movement was the ANM with all its transnational contacts, and it now turned its attention away from Nasserist Arab unification and aimed to regain Palestine. However, it was not long before it returned to the problem of Pan-Arab unity with a fresh, radical and socialist ideology which both Fatah and the PLO still reject.

At the same time as Habash began his negotiations between Palestinian groups, the Syrian Ba'athist régime decided to sponsor its own Palestinian group, closely directed by the Syrian army, and active on the Syrian and River Jordan fronts. This group came into being in the spring of 1968 and was called Sa'iqa (Thunderbolt) or Vanguard of the Popular Liberation War. Not to be outdone, the Iraqi Ba'athists simultaneously founded their own Palestinian group known as the Arab Liberation Front. So the scene was set for a period of direct involvement by Arab states in Palestinian affairs. Now that Fatah was based in Jordan and attracting increasing numbers of young Palestinians; they also began to receive substantial financial support from other Arab governments.

Fatah's growth had much to do with the Arab defeat in the Six-Day War which had shown that the Arab states were inherently weak and therefore unequal to the task of defeating Israel. The defeat had produced 1,375,915 refugees registered with UNRWA and had allowed Israel to acquire a strategically secure frontier but within these new borders was now a strategically insecure population. These factors ensured that the concept of Arab unity could by more achievable through the vehicle of Palestinian liberation.[11]

IV   THE STRUGGLE WITHIN THE
PALESTINIAN RESISTANCE MOVEMENT

During 1968, changes continued to happen in the evolution of the Palestinian resistance. In January at the ANM conference, an announcement was made of the formation of the PFLP and this was followed by depriving the Kuwait branch of the ANM of control over subversive activities in the Gulf region because it had ostensibly shown 'bourgeois tendencies'. The reality was that Habash wanted direct control. Six months later, the entire membership of the ANM Kuwait branch was suspended, probably because it had undergone significant Fatah and anti-PFLP infiltration.[12] In March 1968, George Habash was forced to flee Jordan into Syria where he was immediately incarcerated for nearly eight months. During his absence, an ideological rift appeared between the PFLP groups over the questions of terrorism, mass political education in the revolutionary struggle, the problem of nationalism as opposed to socialism, and the rôle of the *petite bourgeoisie*. Ahmed Jibril and his Palestine Liberation Front had begun experimenting with various forms of paramilitary activity including the hijacking of airliners. The quest for ideological and organisational purity became necessary because of the endemic fear of double-agents. Hence small, tightly-knit and well-financed groups became the norm, exacerbating and reinforcing political differences particularly in philosophy and tactics. Although Habash escaped from Syria in November 1968 and directly challenged his *de facto* successor Hawatima for the leadership, it was a lost cause. The more extreme Jibril was happy to part company with Habash in January 1969, since he regarded the latter as talking too much and doing too little about the Palestinian cause. The following month, Hawatima defected together with his supporters to form the Popular Democratic Front for the Liberation of Palestine (PDFLP). At the same time, Jibril transformed his PLF into the Popular Front for the Liberation of Palestine—General Command (PFLP–GC). The schism spread rapidly throughout the entire organisational structure of the ANM. In every Arab country its branches split, destroying any cohesion previously possessed. Whereas the PDFLP applied for and was granted constituent membership of the PLO, Habash and Jibril rejected Arafat and all that he stood for, remaining singularly independent for some time.[13]

In May 1968 a new Palestine National Congress was called for July, to be held in Cairo. Fatah managed to gain a third of the seats on the Council, giving Arafat a strong claim on the leadership. Following months of negotiations with other resistance groups, Arafat felt strong enough to call for a fifth PLO Congress in Cairo for February 1969. Out of the 105 seats,

Fatah gained 33 and Sa'iqa and the PFLP (who boycotted the conference) won 12 each. Thus Fatah emerged with a status approaching that of a government in exile. Having achieved this, Fatah strengthened its organisation by setting up a central committee and a political bureau. These co-ordinated the regional Fatah committees which were newly established in all the areas where refugees lived. Fatah transformed itself into a clandestine politico-military organisation, with code-named cells, security procedures, communications links and couriers all overseen by the Regional Committees. This further strengthened Arafat's hand and he was elected as Chairman of the PLO to replace the impotent Shukhairy, while the eleven-man executive of the PLO fell under the control of Fatah. Immediately, Arafat created the Palestine Armed Struggle Command in an effort to co-ordinate the military activities of PLO member groups and so make them subservient to Fatah's aims, objectives and politics. By July 1969, eight Palestinian groups were represented on the PASC with the exception of those within the PFLP. Arafat's intention seems to have been to use the group's struggle against Israel to ensure internal Palestinian unity rather than to create or impose a unity based on ideology or some other means.[14]

Two factors concerning the rapidity of Fatah's rise are important here which previously have not been given due weight. Firstly, the Arab states have always been prepared to use the Palestinians for their own ends and following the humiliating defeat of 1967 they feared insurrection. In order to counter this, the Arab governments were happy to channel this despair by overtly supporting the PLO, PFLP, and in some cases their own Palestinian groups, in the hope that they could weather the storm. Secondly, Fatah capitalised on the fact that many of the elderly Palestinians still deferred to their traditional leadership and maintained provincial loyalties. Through the Regional Committees, Fatah could identify with such loyalty assuming that the host country supported them, which it invariably did. Similarly, Fatah wooed the youth of the camps and the *diaspora* community, presenting the perpetrators of terrorist crimes as heroes. Even so, the links between the Arab states and the Palestinians were always tenuous. Apart from the first factor, many Arab states gave aid and support to the Palestinians either to embarrass other states or to put pressure on front-line states like Jordan, to relieve the pressure on their own battlefronts.

Thus the Palestinian resistance grew apace but in two very distinct directions. Arafat's Fatah represents a consensus of very narrow nationalistic views, whereas Habash's PFLP was much more radical and prefers Pan-Arab secular change. These differences stem from the personalities and backgrounds of the leaders. Arafat's grouping attracts Sunni Moslems whereas Habash appeals to non-Sunni Palestinians. Habash and Hawatima are both Greek Orthodox Christians as are many of their supporters and, since the PFLP is arguably the only real opposition to Fatah, it also attracts other minorities such as Shia Moslems, Armenians and Alawites. The importance of Habash, however, lies in another direction. Quite simply, he broke with Arab tradition. As a physician he should have become rich through dealing with private matters. Being an ideologically committed person, he dealt with public matters, rising to power via the street and clandestine cell—in the event, he remained poor. By choosing to break with tradition he created new possibilities for his people, the Palestinian refugees.

Habash's Pan-Arab aspirations were still to the fore even during the internal PFLP problems in 1968–9. Since 1965, the ANM had had close ties with the Arabian Peninsula People's Union and had strengthened its own ANM cells. These two merged to form the Popular Democratic Front (PDF) which was billed as a workers revolutionary movement 'embracing the path of mass violence'. With its strong links to the PFLP, and committed to the overthrow of the House of Saud, it concentrated its recruitment drive on army and airforce personnel in Saudi Arabia. It had close working links with the two other clandestine organisations which it had helped to form and support, namely the Federation of Democratic Forces of the Arabian Peninsula and the much smaller National Front for the Liberation of Saudi Arabia. In June and July 1969 these three organisations joined together in two separate conspiracies.

May 1970 was an exciting month for the Palestinian *fedayeen* groups. On 20 May 1970, Ahmed Jibril sent a commando squad of the PFLP–GC into Israel, near Kibbutz Moshav Arivim. They fired a rocket at an Israeli school bus and killed nine children.[15] The same month, Habash was forced to take shelter

13

under the PLO umbrella due to the latter's power in making financial disbursements given by the oil-exporting states of Libya and Saudi Arabia through the PLO to the various terrorist groups. Finally, at the PLO Congress that month, it was realised that the only obstacle which lay in the path of Palestinian unification was the Jordanian Hashemite monarchy. The PLO were determined that it should be overthrown. King Hussein of Jordan did not oblige.

King Hussein's reply to the PLO came in two stages: 'Green June' and 'Black September'. In June King Hussein acceded to the PLO's demands but stated that he would tolerate no more. As the *New York Times* put it: 'The pact King Hussein has signed with guerrilla leader Yasser Arafat comes close to granting the Palestinian militants full partnership in Jordanian affairs.'[16] In September, following ten weeks of uneasy truce, Habash and his PFLP co-ordinated the hijacking of a Swissair DC8, a TWA 707 and a PanAm 704 on 7 September, and on the 9 September a BOAC VC10. The PFLP blew up the planes on Jordanian soil, and King Hussein determined to rid Jordan of the terrorists. On 15 September he appointed a military government to restore the state's authority. This was followed by unleashing Bedouin troops who inflicted carnage on the PLO. Casualties have been estimated at 8,000. But the real significance of Hussein's move was not so much its success but that no Arab state lifted a finger to help the PLO. Jordan's victory was a victory for the traditional and conservative Arab leadership. As Fouad Ajami points out:

The audacious radicals had to be taught a lesson; the Arab world had to be purged of Marxists; free-lance guerrillas had to be disciplined if the states were to negotiate with Israel or to respond to the diplomatic initiatives offered by outsiders.[17]

In defeat the veneer of unity was further exposed by the Action Organisation for the Liberation of Palestine. When President Nasser agreed to a truce with Israel, the AOLP also accepted a cease-fire, whereas the PLO broadcast vehement criticisms of both Nasser and his régime over Radio Cairo. The extent of the PLO's fragmentation was further seen in the open acknowledgement that they were vulnerable to Israeli counter-intelligence and counter-insurgency operations.

The ejection of the PLO from Jordan was a considerable blow

to both Arafat and Habash, not simply as a personal affront but because their organisational structure had been destroyed. In 1968, Jordan had assisted Abu Daoud to set up a central intelligence body, being completed by December, called Jihaz al-Rasd (Surveillance-Apparatus). This body took over all aspects of intelligence, counter-intelligence and disinformation work, exclusively for Fatah. Apart from anything else, Arafat had to organise the resettlement of the 'Rasd' as well as repair the damage done to its internal structure. However, in response to King Hussein's 'Black September', a new organ was created which became attached to the Rasd-Jihaz al-Amaliyat al-Khassa, colloquially known as the Black September Organisation.[18]

Black September was created at a meeting between the leaders of Fatah and PFLP held at the offices of the PLFP's newspaper *al-Hadaf*, in Beirut. The founding members consisted of Ghassan Khanafani, Bassan Abu-Sharif and Wadi Haddad of the PFLP and Hassan Salameh, Abu Daoud, Abu Yussef and Abu Jihad of Fatah. The link between Rasd and this Special Operations Apparatus was Fatah's Head of Intelligence, Abu Daoud.[19] Many of the resistance members had already been trained in terrorist and guerrilla techniques at the Patrice Lumumba University near Moscow.

The creation of Black September was the final act by the Palestinian resistance groups, in the acknowledgement that they were operating according to the Ishutin concept. That Palestinian *fedayeen* groups embraced Ishutinism is obvious from their structure—that of an open, overt political arm or wing, whose sole task is to manufacture and disseminate propaganda of an insurrectionist nature, together with a clandestine, covert, underground military wing, formed out of groups of terrorist bands. This fitted in neatly with the existing structure. Although the original Russian exponents of Ishutinism argued that the movement should be led by academic luminaries, this was not applicable in the Middle East. The personality cults surrounding people like Arafat and Habash sufficed. Palestinian adherence to Ishutinism has developed the *fedayeen* terrorist organisations into full-scale urban guerrilla movements having a strong territorial base.[20]

Unity between the various groups remained a veneer. The sponsorship provided by governments such as Iraq, Syria and the new young leader of the officers' coup in Libya, Colonel Muammar Gadhafi, created widespread rivalry. On numerous occasions this resulted in running street battles in which hundreds of Palestinian members of *fedayeen* groups were killed together with innocent bystanders. This situation was exacerbated by the propensity of other Arab governments to embroil themselves in the internal affairs of fellow states who did not ascribe to their own political interpretations. In November 1972, for example a plot was hatched to assassinate both King Hussein of Jordan and his brother Crown Prince Hassan ibn Tallal. The plot was led by Major Rafa el-Hindawi of the Jordanian Armoured Corps (together with Fatah), whom Libya paid 20,000 Jordanian Dinars for his part in the failed assassination. The Jordanians replied with bombs directed at PLO nerve-centres in Beirut.[21]

Following the partial restoration of Arab honour in the 1973 October War and the implementation of the boycott by the oil-producing states, a Rejection Front was created amongst some of the more fanatically Marxist revolutionaries in the Palestinian refugee resistance. Heavily supported by Moscow, the Rejection Front was also financed and assisted by Syria, Iraq, South Yemen, Libya and Algeria. Libya, which had previously been financing 'black' terror groups in Europe, turned to Moscow to acquire sophisticated weaponry. This was then apportioned out to the various Rejection Front groups. The leader of the Front was George Habash and the inner council consisted of him, Ahmed Jibril, Naif Hawatima and Abu Nidal. The latter was wholly sponsored by Iraq and organised his groups out of offices in Baghdad. Similarly, links began to be forged with militant Islamic groups, particularly those which emanated from Egypt.

V   THE RISE OF THE MOSLEM BROTHERHOOD—
PAN-ARAB UNITY

Post-1967 Egypt had seen a return to the popularity of the Moslem Brotherhood; they were regarded by some as being neither purist—in adhering to the tenets of Islam—nor revolutionary enough in their desire to remove the decadence of Westernisation. This stimulated the formation of more radical groups which wanted a return to Islamic fundamentalism and to be rid of degenerate and decadent personifications of Islamic failure—namely the royal sheikhdoms and monarchs of Jordan, Saudi Arabia, the Gulf region and Morocco. These groups also extended Nasserist Pan-Arab ideas on unification, imbuing them with a certain religious idealism that desired the return of the region to the unity experienced under the Prophet. To do this, however, meant ridding the area of its nationalistic rulers.

Although Palestinian nationalism ran counter to the fundamentalists' ideas, expediency makes for strange bedfellows and, since the Rejection Front wanted to topple the existing régime in order to expedite their sweeping socialist revolution, both groups could work together to achieve at least part of their overall aims. Accordingly, in April 1974, Anwar Sadat, the Egyptian President, faced a *coup d'état* engineered by one of the larger extremist groups, the Islamic Liberation Organisation. Although it was unsuccessful, the government began to clamp down severely on Islamic fundamentalism and other groups, already established, began to achieve prominency on the Islamic extremist scene. The more formidable of these groups included Al-Jihad (Holy War), Jund Allah (Soldiers of God), Jawa'at al Muslimin (The Moslem Group) and Jama'at al-Takfir w'al Hijra (Repentance and Holy Flight). The RHF had considerable links in other countries, particularly amongst expatriate Egyptians in the Gulf oil states. Their rise to prominence was assured when, in July 1977, the RHF kidnapped and executed Sheikh Ahmed Hassan al Dhahabi, a former cabinet minister under Sadat. At that time the RHF's strength was conservatively estimated at 4,000 and its network was transnational and well-organised.[22]

The Rabat Summit, held by the Arab League in October 1974, agreed to the elevation of the PLO, which became the twenty-third member of the League. Henceforth, the PLO under Arafat's chairmanship was to be recognised by the Arab League as being the sole legitimate representative of the Palestinian people. This was a great political victory for Arafat and followed a move within the PLO to make his position unassailable. The same year at the Palestine National Congress, the

17

Executive Council was increased to fourteen. Apart from four seats allocated to representatives from the refugee camps, who were in any case usually Arafat–Fatah supporters, the remaining ten seats were allotted to various terrorist groups reflecting the enormous differences of opinion inherent within the whole Palestinian movement. Fatah, led by Arafat, was given two seats including his own, while Habash's PFLP, Hawatima's PDFLP and Jibril's PFLP–GC were each allocated only one seat each. Sa'iqa, under the leadership of Zohair Mohsin until his assassination, and the Syrian sponsored Palestine Liberation Army were also allotted one seat each. The remaining three seats were distributed as follows: the Iraqi sponsored ALF received one, while all the remaining independent splinter groups and factions were allotted two seats between them. At first glance, the composition of the Council seems to fairly reflect the wide spectrum of Palestinian opinion on the means to be adopted for the recovery of Palestine. A closer inspection, however, reveals that Arafat and Fatah would still retain control over the Council. Apart from Fatah's two votes, the four votes allocated to West Bank exiles would inevitably fall to Fatah since Fatah's control of the refugee camps had tightened due to more cells being organised by Regional Committees. Thus, candidates from the camps would in all likelihood, be Fatah's personnel who, because of their membership of the organisation, were assured of selection. Similarly, Fatah could use financial inducements to secure the support of the independent groups' two representatives, thus retaining a majority on the Council over the Rejection Front of Habash, Hawatima and Jibril.

By mid-1975, however, the relative success of Black September required that the Rasd be further developed, and it was agreed that an umbrella intelligence organisation would be set up for all guerrilla groups in the movement. This organisation was known as the United Security Apparatus of the Palestine Revolution and was headed by 'Abu Iyad', the code-name of Salah Khalef. It became particularly useful during the next few years when Palestinian-exported terrorism grew dramatically.[23]

The Lebanese conflict of 1975–6 was a turning point in the PLO's fortunes. The Palestinians *were not* and *are not* Lebanese. The arrogance they displayed with regard to Lebanese

18

Moslems and Christians and the very defiance of the legitimate Lebanese government was breathtaking. The situation was exacerbated by the fact that the Arab states pumped both arms and money into Lebanon to supply their chosen faction and to appease the Fatah-controlled PLO.[24] Initially, worried by what might ensue if the Palestinians won control over the country, the Syrian government utilised both Sa'iqa and the PLA against the remainder of the Palestinian terrorists. Only when Syria realised that the situation could not be resolved by this method did it send its regular army in. The two Arab summits in Riyadh and Cairo, both endorsed the presence of 20,000 Syrian troops and in order to assist Syria financially in its policing of Lebanon, agreed to provide the urgently needed subsidies.[25]

The ferment within the Arab world was not to leave Saudi Arabia untouched. Saudi Arabia was now beginning to face the problems of internal strife brought about by terrorism.

The turning point was 20 November 1979 when the most sacred of Islamic sites fell into the hands of rebels. It would appear that much of the planning and organisation was undertaken by members of the RHF active in Saudi Arabia who, arranged for financing through ANM–PFLP sponsored groups. Tension and revolt simmered underneath the surface of Saudi society and broke out in 1976, 1979 and again in August 1982 when a large cache of Soviet-made weapons was unearthed. This cache resulted in the dismissal of the then Saudi Minister of Information, Dr Mohammed Yamani.[26]

Thus, with the increasing unrest in Iran which dominated the Gulf region in 1979, the amalgam of Islamic fundamentalism and radical political views was overtly on view. From Lebanon to South Yemen, the ideological alchemy was and still is, provided by Palestinian extremist groups led by George Habash's PFLP.

As the Palestinians regained strength in Lebanon they began to win the international propaganda game hands down. Young and disillusioned Palestinians were persuaded, bribed or blackmailed to join one of the various groups. By 1978 there were more than 14,000 'freedom' fighters in Palestine *fedayeen* units, double that of four years before.

1980 was a time of mixed fortunes for the Palestinian movement. Early in the year, Libyan-backed dissidents with

19

Palestinian support attacked and seized government buildings in the small Tunisian town of Gafsa. They hoped that the ageing President Bourghiba would be forced to take a hard-line stance against the implementation of the Camp David Peace Treaty between Israel and Egypt. The revolt was quickly put down.[27] This was followed by a rift which developed between the PFLP leaders—especially Habash—and the Iraqi government. Habash saw Ayatollah Khomeini's revolution with the overthrow of the Shah as exactly what he and his adherents sought in the Arab world. Thus the PFLP, together with Arafat and other senior members of Fatah and the Executive Council of the PLO, trumpeted their support for Khomeini. The Iraqi government, under President Saddam Hussein, did not take kindly to this as the Iranian Shia revolution had created disturbances amongst the large Shia community in Iraq. Thus, on 25 April 1980 the entire PFLP staff of 32 were expelled from Iraq and their offices permanently closed.

The PLO and Fatah did not escape dissension either. In May 1980, Salah Khalaf—code-named 'Abu Iyad'—was ousted from the Palestine National Council. He was the former operational head of Black September who had always been allied with the anti-Arafat forces in the Arab world, particularly Syria and Libya. Following his expulsion, he made a five-month tour of Eastern Europe, the Emirates, Kuwait, Tunisia and Libya. Having extracted US$40m. to finance independent actions, he proceeded to support the Lebanese Shia Amal terrorists and, in the following year, allied himself with his loyal followers, Taysir Hassan, Abdul Karim and Hamdi Abdul Said, who led Al-Thawra (The Revolution), a small but deadly terrorist group.

In an attempt to nullify Khalaf's influence, Fatah arranged for the PFLP to be readmitted to the Palestine National Council in April 1981. At the same time, however, entrance to the PNC was refused to two smaller independent Iraqi-backed groups, the Palestine Liberation Front and Dr Samir Ghoushi's Popular Struggle Front. The Israeli invasion of Lebanon, prompted by indiscriminate acts of terror in 1982, drove a wedge between many of the Palestinian terrorist alignments bringing to the fore the question of the PLO's legitimacy. First, it is necessary to note that the PLO *was created* by the Arab states and not by *demand* of the Palestinian Arabs. As one eminent scholar in the field has remarked,

What is brutally exposed is the absence of a PLO base amongst the Palestinian masses. The PLO is expressed not as a national movement but as a series of intricate in-fights among a few personalities who became ever more unscrupulous as they lost their toeholds in one Arab capital after another.[28]

A former Israeli Intelligence Chief, Yehoshofat Harkabi noted that the PLO at one time or another has opposed the policies of every Arab state. However, without Arab finance and support, the PLO would be 'practically powerless' and thus is dependent on retaining the status quo.[29]

Conversely, the PLO argues that the Palestine National Council of one hundred members are drawn from all walks of life, proof, they say, that the PLO is speaking for all Palestinians. Constitutionally, the Council is supposedly the supreme authority, formulating policies and programmes for the PLO; however, it only meets twice a year! Its usefulness is that it allows the Arab world to recognise the PLO as the only legitimate representative of the Palestinian people. The truth is very different.

In fact, the PLO controls the Palestine National Council as the Council itself is only elected by the executive for cosmetic reasons. The members of the Council do not form groups, factions or alliances, nor indeed do they act in any way hostile to the PLO Executive. Therefore, there is no real contender for the post of chairman other than Arafat. (Through the network of cells and Regional Committees, Fatah usually chooses or 'selects' the membership as direct elections have never been held.) The fact that the Council is controlled by the PLO and is indeed, within the structure of the PLO, was finally admitted in 1981. A remark contained within the PLO journal *Free Palestine* revealed the connexion. 'The Palestine National Council is the most important of the institutions within the PLO, and is widely seen as being the Palestinian parliament.'[30] By electing such people as Abdul Rahim Ahmad of the ALF, Yasir Abd Rabbuh (PDFLP), Talal Naji (PFLP-GC) and Abd al-Muhsin Abu Mayser of the PNF to the Executive, the PLO cannot be expected to represent the genuine interests of the Palestinian people. As Professor Laqueur points out, the Palestinians in their struggle for independence have won the sympathy of

21

major international powers, public opinion and the support of the 'puppeteers of international terrorism', Libya and Algeria.[31] The PLO and its adherents are terrorists. They are not guerrillas or partisans, and because they are terrorists there can be no question concerning their illegitimacy. Terrorists are not legitimate. Therefore the PLO is illegitimate irrespective of what one thinks of the larger Arab–Israeli problem.[32]

Finally, at no time have Palestinian Arabs ever risen in revolt in support of attacking Arab armies whilst under Israeli domination. In 1956 there was not one Arab attack inside Israel during the Sinai–Suez campaign. In 1967, it can be argued that the humiliating defeat inflicted by Israel on the armies of Egypt, Jordan and Syria paralysed the Palestinians on the West Bank. But in 1973, when both the Syrians and Egyptians were pressing their advance against a surprised and reeling Israeli force and when, for a few days, it seemed as though Israel would be vanquished, the Palestinians of Gaza, the West Bank, Golan and pre-1967 Israel remained at their jobs, ensuring that the state ran smoothly. They did not commit one act of resistance against Israel. Thus, the PLO cannot and does not speak for the masses of Palestinians—only for itself.

PART TWO

Arab support for Palestinian terrorism: the Pan-Arab Axis

THE MIDDLE EAST is a volatile powder-keg; its history reflects an instability that was caused by the arbitrary way in which France and the United Kingdom carved up the Ottoman Empire and created states which took little or no account of natural tribal lands, people or geography. Now nearly every government in the region is trying to weaken or destabilise some other régime with which it is at variance, or from which it senses a threat. In recent years this has been aggravated by a shift in the regional power constellation, resulting in the stability of the traditional oil monarchies being further threatened, particularly by the Iranian revolution. The situation is not made any easier by the activities of the various Palestinian terrorist groups.

Abu Iyad, Yasser Arafat's deputy within the Palestine Liberation Organisation, conceded as recently as 1981 that many Arab governments regarded armed Palestinians not only as a threat to their own security, but also as criminals. These same governments, however, were prepared to supply them with arms, provided that they did not operate within the financing country.[1] Besides providing arms and finance as well as other types of support, each Arab state has infiltrated its own agents into various Palestinian terrorist groups, including their international branches. This infiltration is not surprising, as several of these groups have threatened the oil-producing states in particular to prevent—or at least try to—any dialogue or initiative with the USA concerning the Palestinian question. It was therefore to be expected that the same Arab states showed almost total unconcern for the PLO's predicament when the Israeli forces invaded Lebanon in June 1982. Such was the indifference that several Arab heads of state did not even alter their holiday plans.[2] This suggests that the commitment of the Arab states to the PLO has been greatly exaggerated; a suggestion reinforced by the same states' original reluctance to receive PLO forces into their territories. When they did eventu-

25

ally agree to do so, it was only on terms that ensured the PLO's complete subjugation to the host state. The abandonment of the PLO also showed that as far as the Arab states were concerned, the interests of the Palestinians had become subordinate to those of their own states. The only Arab government which gave anything like the support the PLO had come to expect was Syria; she alone pressed continually for the restoration of the Lebanese situation prior to the Israeli invasion, while taking part in military operations against the Israelis, but only in limited low-risk containment.[3]

This lack of political, military or economic support for the PLO contrasted sharply with the pre-1982 situation. Then, all the Arab states—with the exception of Egypt after 1978—gave the PLO full backing and assistance, allowing them complete freedom of action and providing them with whatever they needed. The generous aid lavished on the PLO ensured that the organisation and its off-shoots were kept well away from the donor Arab states. These same Arab countries allowed the PLO to impose themselves on Lebanon, realising that the Lebanon was weak and would therefore be unable to bear either the human or material costs involved in containing the PLO. Without exception, the Arab world permitted this to occur whilst pursuing a policy that instead of weakening the Israeli position, permitted Israel to resort, almost exclusively, to military methods and thus ignore—however temporarily—political solutions to the Palestinian problem.[4]

It is the oil-producing states which are the largest financial backers of the Palestinian terrorists, and the Gulf Sheikhdoms—with the sole exception of Oman—have financed purchases of arms by the PLO. They have felt it advisable to do so to prevent the Palestinian terrorist groups from turning their attention towards fomenting insurrection within these tiny countries. As Walter Nelson pointed out in an interview,

Every gallon of petrol we buy finances the PLO, because a portion of the income of the Arab OPEC countries goes to Arafat's group. His annual income runs into countless millions.[5]

Part Two attempts to itemise how this income is accrued and to determine exactly what support the various Arab states have given to the PLO, whether singly or as a group.

26

Shortly after Fatah and Arafat took control of the PLO, the Arab League summit meeting at Rabat in Morocco decided to allocate £26m. to meet the financial commitments of the PLO for the coming year. Out of that sum £12m. was for the support of the Palestine revolution and £11m. for the support of the citizens of the occupied territories of the West Bank and Gaza Strip. The remainder was assigned to cover administration costs incurred by the PLO.

Five years later, on 26 October 1974 at the Rabat Summit, the Arab League recognised the PLO as the sole representative of the Palestinian people. Accordingly, the financial contributions of the Arab League were reordered. For the year 1974–5, the oil-producing countries pledged US$2,500m. in grant aid for Syria, Egypt, Jordan, the PLO and the People's Democratic Republic of Yemen. The PLO received a US$50m. subsidy as well as a share of the US$1b. per annum fighting fund which the League established. The People's Democratic Republic of Yemen were allotted US$70m. per annum to establish a major Arab military base on the Bab el Mandeb Straits which command the southern entrance to the Red Sea. The oil-producing states, flush with money following the quadrupling of oil prices after the 1973 October War, were able to lavish the confrontation states and the PLO with money enough to purchase all the sophisticated weaponry they desired. The contributing countries to the US$2,500m. grant were as follows:

	US$
Saudi Arabia	400m
Kuwait	400m
UAE	300m
Qatar	150m
Iraq	100m
Oman	15m
Bahrain	4m
	1370m

It was agreed that the balance should be made up by Algeria, Tunisia, Morocco and Libya.[6]

From 1968 to 1977 inclusive, the Arab League earmarked US$29m. per annum for the PLO, irrespective of any money de-

27

cided upon at Arab League Summit meetings. In November
1977 at the Baghdad Summit, the Arab League pledged
US$3.5b. in grant aid to Syria, US$1,250m. for Jordan and
US$250m. for the PLO. A further US$150m. was distributed to
the PLO for apportionment amongst Palestinians in the West
Bank and Gaza Strip, to ease the occupation and support their
perseverance.[7]

The following year at the annual Arab League Summit,
again in Baghdad, a US$3.5b. fund was established in an
attempt to consolidate the various forces in the Arab world following Sadat and Begin's signing of the 'Framework for Peace'
at Camp David that same month. Saudi Arabia contributed
US$1b. with Kuwait and Libya each contributing US$550m.,
Iraq US$520m., Algeria US$450m., the UAE US$400m., and
Qatar US$220m. Again it was to be divided between Syria,
Jordan and the PLO, but Lebanon was also granted US$100m.
for reconstruction. This donation, however, had certain strings
attached. The money for Lebanon was only to become available
following an internal resolution of the Lebanese conflict, thus
preventing Lebanon from seeking Western or non-Arab assistance in resolving its internecine conflict. Consequently it
ensured Lebanon's continued helplessness in the face of the
Palestinian terrorist groups. The PLO received US$250m. from
the Summit fund and Jordan was given US$60m. to administer
within the occupied West Bank *via* the 'open bridges'. In the
same year, Arafat and the PLO together with other terrorist
groups, were in receipt of sums totalling US$100m. per annum
received from various Arab governments completely indepen-
dently of the Arab League contributions.[8]

Apart from purely financial support, most Arab governments
gave logistic support to the Palestinian terrorists. An example
of this is that these governments allowed their diplomats to
smuggle arms and equipment abroad for the Palestinians. By
1976, the Palestinian terrorists had been provided with their
own well-stocked armouries inside the Lebanese refugee
camps, paid for by Syria, Iraq and Libya. The latter, due to
spiralling oil prices, acquired almost unlimited scope for
trading in arms, while Syria financed the Palestinians out of
the generous aid it received from Saudi Arabia. The arms were
unloaded in Lebanon in the ports of Tyre and Sidon which
handled the replenishments from Libya, while stocks from

Syria flowed across the countries' common border. In all cases the Arab states purchased the arms on the Palestinians' behalf from the USSR and Eastern Europe. The arms supplied to the PLO were primarily used in Lebanon.

Libya and South Yemen (PDRY) together with Syria, all afforded the Palestinians military bases within their borders, although under strict government control. With the advent of the Khomeini regime in Iran a boost was given to PLO and allied Palestinian operations due to the granting of extra-territorial status following the seizure of the US Embassy in Teheran. This status along with the other Arab countries' largesse, allowed the Palestinians to maintain operational headquarters, training camps and political propaganda offices, as well as ensuring asylum and a safe-haven.[9]

Apart from financial aid, armaments, training camps and logistical support granted by them to the PLO and other Palestinian terrorist organisations, the Arab states fulfilled yet a further function. Many Palestinian refugees sought employment in the oil-rich Arab states. In order not to leave this political source untapped, the PLO managed to persuade the Arab League states to allow them to raise funds among the expatriate Palestinian communities. Fearful of the repercussions which granting such permission might result in, the Arab states themselves agreed to collect such contributions. It was resolved that the governments would introduce a PLO income tax, compulsorily payable by each income-earning Palestinian working within the public sector of each Arab state. This 'liberation' tax was deducted at source. Hence, Palestinian communities throughout the Gulf region pay a tax of 3 per cent of gross earnings on low incomes and 5 per cent and more on higher incomes. In 1977, when the scheme first started, total receipts amounted to some US$10m. Most of the Palestinians working in the oil-rich Gulf states pay the higher rates, since the oil-sector is regarded as public sector service. Those who work in private businesses are expected to make similar-sized 'voluntary' contributions. All tax levies are paid into the Palestine National Fund which is the controlling agency for the PLO's finances.[10]

Thus, when blame and liability are spoken of with regard to the Palestinian issue, the role of the Arab states should not be forgotten. The generous financial aid given to the PLO must be tempered by the fact that these same states have kept the Palestinian refugees, *en masse*, well away from their own territories. In addition, they have allowed the smallest Arab state to shatter due to the burden of absorbing what the remainder of the Arab world had created—human flotsam. Below, is a consideration of the support granted to the Palestinian rejectionist-terrorists by the Arab states.

I   JORDAN

The Hashemite Kingdom of Jordan was, between 1948–67, the major Arab state concerned with the Palestinian refugees. As Jordan was carved out of the original League of Nations Palestine Mandate by Great Britain and granted independence in 1946, natural links existed between the peoples dwelling on both sides of the River Jordan. In 1948, Jordanian troops managed to control and hold that area of Palestine known as Judea and Samaria and now referred to as the West Bank. It was this area which absorbed most of the Palestinian refugees following the Arab defeat in 1948.

The origins of the refugee problem have been acknowledged by both sides as originating from the Arab states. Abu Mazen, writing in the official PLO newspaper *Falastin ath Thawra*, stated bluntly that:

The Arab armies entered Palestine to protect the Palestinians from the Zionist tyranny but, instead, they abandoned them, forced them to emigrate and to leave their homeland, imposed upon them a political and ideological blockade and threw them into prisons similar to the ghettos in which the Jews used to live in Eastern Europe .... The Arab states succeeded in scattering the Palestinian people and in destroying their unity. They did not recognise them as a unified people until the states of the world did so, and this is regrettable.[11]

The same sentiment is echoed in the writings in 1973, of the Syrian Prime Minister Haled al-Azm, on his years in government, 1948–9:

Since 1948 we have been demanding the return of the refugees to their homes. But we ourselves are the ones who encouraged them to leave. Only a few months separated ... our call to them to leave and our appeal to the United Nations to resolve on their return .... We have brought destruction upon a million Arab refugees, by calling upon them and pleading with them to leave their land, their homes, their work and their business, and we have caused them to be barren and unemployed though each one of them had been working and qualified in a trade from which he could make a living. In addition, we accustomed them to begging for hand-outs and to suffice with what little the UN organisation would allocate them.[12]

Sabri Jiryis, an internationally-known Palestinian researcher at the Institute of Palestine Studies in Beirut, regards what occurred after the 1948 war as a kind of 'population and property exchange' between the Palestinian Arabs of Israel and the Jews of the Arab lands. The Arab states expelled most of their Jews, deporting them to Israel after confiscating their property or buying it for the lowest possible price. Jiryis remarked that,

Israel is absorbing the Jews of the Arab States; the Arab States, for their part, must settle the Palestinians in their own midst and solve their problems.[13]

Jordan had done its best to absorb the refugees who fled into the West Bank before, during and after the 1948 fighting and after 1967. Jordan is widely regarded as a Palestinian entity not only by most Arab States but by many Palestinians and Jordanians. On 12 April 1948, at the Arab League meeting in Cairo, King Abdullah stated quite categorically that, 'Palestine and Transjordan are one, for Palestine is the coastline and Transjordan the hinterland of the same country'.[14] Since then, King Hussein, Crown Prince Hassan, the government-controlled Jordanian press and Jordanian Government spokesmen have all reiterated the 'oneness' of Palestine and Jordan. So, too, have Palestinian terrorists as politically far apart as Habash and Farouk Khaddoumi, and Palestinian leaders from the West Bank.

The population of Jordan comprises of between 60 per cent and 70 per cent West Bank Palestinians who control more than 70 per cent of the Jordanian economy. Thus the West Bank refugees proved to be resourceful and did not reflect their reputation for being impoverished and unemployed, apathetic and destitute, relying on external support. That they felt distress is certain, but even after 1967, this distress centred around the problem of social status, many complaints referring directly to

31

their social position. In this context, the only country which made any attempt to alleviate it was Jordan.

Jordan, being the state most directly concerned with the Palestinian problem, has also been the most realistic with regard to the political situation. Prior to the 1967 Six-Day War, the Hashemite régime had been active in impeding *fedayeen* operations against Israel as well as arresting several insurgents. By the same token, King Hussein had positively indicated a willingness to accept Israel's existence, endorsed by the Security Council Resolution no. 242, and had held anything up to twelve secret meetings with Israeli officials, covering both the pre- and post-war periods.[15]

Prior to ejecting the Palestinian terrorists from Jordanian territory in 1970–1, Jordan although extending moral support for the Palestinian cause, had never endorsed either the liquidation of Israel or the idea of a PLO-dominated state on the West Bank. Neither did the Hashemite Kingdom give unconditional military support to the terrorists. Apart from providing periodic intelligence concerning the state of Israel's forces and occasionally giving covering-fire for some cross-border operations, no substantial financial support or large bequests of weapons, ammunition or medical supplies were granted. Instead, as relations grew worse between the Jordanian authorities and the terrorists towards the close of the decade of the Six-Day War, the former significantly reduced what little assistance it was already providing.

By 1970, intelligence cooperation had ceased, as had artillery support for cross-border actions. In the following year, with the terrorists defeated, the Jordanian army was continuously confiscating *fedayeen* arms and ammunition, thus significantly *reducing* the terrorists' existing armoury. But arguably the greatest service the Jordanians could have provided the terrorists with, was that of a sanctuary embodying freedom of movement.

There are perhaps three basic reasons for the Hashemite Monarchy deliberately denying the Palestinian terrorists this advantage and they reflect the decidedly different attitude that this régime has in comparison with other Arab states. Firstly, the Israeli response to cross-border insurgency from Jordan was to mount search and destroy operations, commando raids and air strikes against refugee bases housing the terrorists.

This resulted in a measurable dislocation of the Jordanian economy which was further exacerbated by an almost constant stream of refugees towards the Jordanian hinterland. Thus, by 1970–1, Jordanian troops were actively involved in intercepting and detaining *fedayeen* units *en route* for Israel.

Secondly, by 1969–70 the Palestinian terrorists were emerging as a significant challenge and thus posed a very real threat to Jordanian sovereignty. Lastly, this latter threat was compounded as terrorist organisations such as the PFLP and PDFLP openly declared their animosity towards King Hussein, while the ALF and Sa'iqa were terrorist units sponsored by régimes almost endemically hostile to Jordan.

In September 1970, the Jordanian army, almost exclusively staffed by apolitical bedouin tribesmen fiercely loyal to King Hussein, pressured him to let them loose on the strutting and domineering terrorists. The resultant fighting was so ferocious and intense that more than 90 terrorists fled into the hands of the Israel Defence Forces to avoid being slaughtered by their Arab brothers, whom previously they had jeeringly humiliated.

What Jordan managed to do in 1970, Lebanon failed to do in 1976 and the lesson for Jordan in the Lebanese solution has recently been very forcefully put:

Whether radicals of the 'rejection front' or moderates, the Arab oil states are prepared to sacrifice a small Arab country, and to withhold significant help from it, if that enables them to curry favour with the PLO and at the same time to keep its activities confined to territories other than their own.[16]

Jordan itself has learned to its advantage what the PLO's absence from within a country can mean to economic expansion and growth. King Hussein is still aware, however, of the way in which the Palestinian terrorist leaders threaten both his throne and his kingdom and furthermore he cannot rely on Arab support to assist him if the terrorists make a direct attack. Having always acknowledged that his country would do all that it could to help Palestinian refugees, the Jordanian King is now faced with Israeli statements that Jordan constitutes the Arab state of Palestine and PLO statements that it is their intention to liberate the whole of Mandatory Palestine. The sad truth is that, should Jordan become the acknowledged Palestinian state, the PLO and its constituent groups would have no room at all for the Hashemite throne.[17]

The legitimacy upon which the PLO rests in its drive towards statehood, is that its organisation is the sole legitimate representative of the Palestinian people. This, however, includes the basic assumption that the PLO represents the will of the Palestinians in the occupied territories which we have already proved is not the case. But to many governments, groups and individuals in the West, this is accepted wholeheartedly, as one reputable commentator on the Middle East points out, 'a considerable exaggeration of the reality'. Surprisingly enough, King Hussein shares the same viewpoint. In 1977, in the West German newspaper *Die Zeit*, King Hussein argued that,

The PLO must not be forced upon the Palestinians because this people has not yet had a chance to exercise its right to self-determination.[18]

More than three and a half years later, his view has hardened. In reply to a question concerning the legitimacy of the PLO as the sole representative of the Palestinians, the King remarked:

Ridiculous! How can half a dozen splintered organisations—partly ruled by criminals who quarrel amongst themselves about radical ideologies—make such a claim? What they call representation, or war of liberation, is nothing but terror.[19]

But the PLO since 1967 has been a fact of life for Palestinians living within the West Bank and Gaza Strip; it is uninterested in fostering local leadership and makes every attempt to impose itself upon the indigenous Palestinians.

One of the reasons for the PLO's continued stipulation that any representative of the Palestinians must be a PLO official, is that it is very wary of 'substitute leadership'. In mid–1970, for example, Bassam Shaka'a, Mayor of Nablus, helped to initiate a West Bank National Guidance Committee. The PLO official in Amman promptly ordered the Mayor to appear before him to explain himself and when Shaka'a did so, he was informed that the PLO executive had ordered the Committee to be dissolved. On his return to Nablus, Shaka'a was instrumental in its dissolution. In the same year, Mohammed Abu-Warda, a prominent Palestinian politician and deputy chairman of the local council of Jabalya Camp north of Gaza, was shot at point-blank range by a terrorist. Abu-Warda had been an outspoken supporter of Camp David and, as such, the PLO considered him dangerous.

It is small wonder, then, that the PLO and its terrorist members could not command popular support in either Gaza or the West Bank, let alone Jordan. So hated and despised were the terrorists that after 1967, ordinary West Bank and Gaza Strip Arabs actively assisted the Israeli authorities in hunting down individual terrorists. Searches for a reason reveal the following compelling statistics: **Between June 1967 and June 1971, Palestinian terrorist attempts to intimidate the Arab population of the Gaza Strip alone, resulted in the deaths of 138 local Arabs with 1,199 wounded.**[20]

Following the occupation of the West Bank, after 1967, many influential people remained who were loyal to Jordan, and two very interesting patterns of life emerged. Firstly, the West Bank refugees totally rejected the pressure brought to bear by both the leadership of the PLO and that of the Arab states by refusing to bow to them and in turn accepted employment from the Israelis. It is well known that political intimidation is easier to manipulate and control than the economic sort and, almost overnight the West Bank unemployment problem was eradicated. Secondly, parents encouraged their children to take advantage of the opportunities made available to them by the Israeli administration to learn vocational skills and undertake training. Such training became orientated towards emigration, mainly to the oil-rich Arab states. This second trend also indicated that a return to the original family villages was not contemplated as there has been a sizeable drop in demand for Arab agricultural training. Such actions run directly counter to the desires of the PLO.

The same is true for the West Bank merchants, bankers and traders, although many have subscribed to the emotional appeals of the Palestinian terrorist groups. They do not relish the end of the Israeli occupation if, in its wake, it is to bring the imposition of a régime controlled or directed by Arafat, Habash and/or Hawatima. They have seen the Palestinian terrorists in operation in Lebanon and watched that country's dramatic decline from its former vibrant, successful entrepreneurial economy to become a graveyard littered with the waste and destruction of war. Thus the interests of commercial notables in the West Bank would seem to be better served by a continu-

35

ation of Israeli occupation, and their leaders have been astute enough to realise that if the PLO continues its armed struggle so much strife and tribulation will be caused that complete Israeli assimilation would probably be the result.[21]

But support for the PLO does exist. The PLO's emotional appeals for a homeland does find Arab accord but at the same time the people are prepared to face the economic reality of the situation. However, some individually wealthy merchants and local Chambers of Commerce habitually pay the fines of demonstrators and curfew violators. But such support for the PLO is not whole-hearted and many look instead to Jordan.

Jordan receives a copious flow of financial aid from Saudi Arabia and other Arab oil-producing countries including Kuwait. A sizeable proportion of this aid is voluntarily redirected to support Palestinians in the West Bank. This is quite separate from funds emanating from the Arab League and disbursed by the monarchy. The recipients of this aid are former civil servants or employees of the kingdom and they act as conduits for its disbursement. Not all the money, however, is earmarked for individuals, much of it goes into West Bank municipality treasuries with the full knowledge and blessing of Israel. Aside from this type of aid, King Hussein has also authorised grants of between 200,000 to 300,000 Jordanian dinars and 6m. Israeli shekels. Interruptions in the granting of aid have been caused by Jordan withholding them as a mark of displeasure for extremist West Bank notables who have publicly gone too far. By the same token, the amounts of aid have fluctuated, particularly up to the time of Camp David. More recently, Jordan has entered into negotiations with Israel, through its West Bank intermediaries, to reopen its West Bank Passport Office as well as the establishment of another West Bank University in Jerusalem. The Jordanian government has also contributed large but unspecified amounts of money for the building of hospitals in Nablus and Ramallah and for the creation of cooperatives in the Nablus region to provide electricity, water, health and education services. Apart from such specific grants, Jordan pays yearly some US$15m. into the West Bank economy of which about US$8. takes the form of salaries and pensions to former servants of the kingdom.[22]

According to international law, Israel can continue to settle the West Bank until Jordan and Israel sign a Peace Treaty agreeing on common borders. Interestingly enough, when King Abdullah appropriated the West Bank into his kingdom after the 1948 war, not one Arab state recognised his sovereignty over the area and this still poses a considerable problem for his son, King Hussein. His one hope is for a federal link of some kind between Jordan and the West Bank as, indeed, he has repeatedly suggested. Provided that Israel could be offered secure borders, a real basis for negotiation might lie in some form of compromise between Hussein's 1972 Autonomy plan and the Israeli Allon plan.[23]

Whatever happens, King Hussein has shown that he and his country are the only Arab nation concerned with the well-being of the ordinary Palestinian. Jordan provides Palestinian refugees with a nationality and a home. By contrast, oil-rich Arab states have lavishly funded the Palestine terrorists to the almost total exclusion of the ordinary law-abiding Palestinian refugees, financing death and destruction. Significantly, Jordan is the only Arab state to shoulder its responsibilities *voluntarily*, while at the same time denying a haven to those merchants of death—the Palestinian terrorists.

II EGYPT

Following the humiliating defeat of her forces in the 1948 war, Egypt allowed Palestinians fleeing from the fledgling state of Israel to gather in refugee camps organised in the Gaza Strip. From there, Egyptian officers organised *fedayeen* incursion raids into Israel. These raids continued unabated until the 1956 Sinai campaign. Thereafter they were dramatically reduced. Although Egypt administered the Gaza district it was not incorporated into her sovereign territory, and she was prepared to encourage PLO activities from the refugee camps.

Within Egypt itself, however, only a limited and government-controlled armed Palestinian presence was allowed; but withdrawn from 1967. Egypt provided military training for considerable numbers of Palestinian terrorists at specialist army camps and continued to do so until 1978. The Egyptian authorities also provided them with a safe haven, generous amounts of weaponry of varying types and financial

37

assistance as well as logistical support including the use of their diplomatic pouch.

Cairo was proud to be the headquarters of the various Palestinian organisations as well as the Arab League and, as such, was the hub of anti-Israeli–Arab activity. It is therefore not surprising that the Egyptian authorities allowed Palestinian terrorists to conduct negotiations with foreign powers from their Cairo offices.

The provision of intelligence concerning the deployment of Israeli troops was made freely available to the Palestinians, and close liaison existed between the Egyptian secret services and some of the Palestinian terrorists which proved invaluable to the terrorists on a number of occasions. It was supplemented by other types of assistance given to terrorists which led to Egypt's direct involvement in their activities.

Nasser, in a conversation with Arafat, told him to take from Egypt, '. . . all the arms you want, and take whatever the fighters need from our production'.[24] This was translated into the provision of increasing amounts of ammunition, arms, medical help and finances (particularly for the payment of salaries) as well as stepping up the provision of specialist military training. But all this must be seen as limited in relation to the overall aid provided by Egypt.

Perhaps the most important aspects of the assistance given by Egypt to the Palestinian terrorists prior to 1978 were political and moral. In 1971, the Egyptian Foreign Minister Mohammed Riad publicly stated on a visit to France that the Palestinian organisations had his complete support, particularly in view of their programme for 'wiping out the Jewish state'.[25] Similarly, Mohammed Heikal, editor of the Cairo newspaper *Al Ahram* wrote of the Lod airport massacre:

If there had been three Palestinians there instead of three Japanese, I should have been enthusiastic about it—in spite of the fact that at the bottom of my heart I'm for the Japanese.[26]

The Egyptian government was always kept well-informed about actual or proposed operations, so much so that a leading government-sponsored daily newspaper occasionally gave information about future Black September and other terrorist operations. The authorities also had the Diplomatic Corps put Fatah in contact with independent Western arms dealers. An

38

example of Egypt's assistance in spying on Fatah's behalf occurred in April 1972 when ten Egyptian diplomats and one Middle East News Agency reporter were expelled by the Jordanians, accused of political interference in Jordanian affairs.

Since 1978, Egypt has not in any known way supported the *fedayeen* terrorists. Significantly, following the Palestinian military débâcle in the Lebanon, Egypt made less than a token contribution to the costs of the PLO exodus—it actually waived canal toll charges for the five ships scheduled to carry the terrorists to Sudan and the People's Democratic Republic of Yemen. This was the very least which Egypt could do to still be seen to be contributing, and it falls in line with its consistent policy against extremism within its borders—a policy that, as much as anything else, has moulded its foreign policy. To this end, in an attempt to restrict the expansion of Islamic fundamental extremism, Egypt has been supplying arms to Iraq for some time.

The clearest indication of Egypt's current standpoint was given by President Mubarak at a meeting prior to the Delhi Non-Aligned Conference on 5 March 1983. At this meeting he held up the spectre of the possible expulsion of 40,000 Palestinians living in Egypt, if the PLO did not moderate its line concerning the Camp David Peace Treaty between Egypt and Israel. He also stated that many Arab leaders had privately approved of the treaty but had realised that to do so publicly would be to court disaster. President Mubarak further reiterated that he would not tolerate a 'state within a state' and had therefore not acceded to the request from President Reagan that Egypt should take 6,000 Palestinian terrorists evacuated from Beirut in 1982. Asserting that under no circumstances would he abrogate the Camp David agreements, he did little to mask his contempt for those Palestinian leaders who had neglected to visit either the West Bank or Gaza Strip for 15 or 20 years.[27]

Egypt, until 1980 and the Israeli hand-over of the Sinai oilfields, was a net oil importer as is Jordan today. However, it is significant that Egypt, always in need of financial assistance for development programmes, has sought to use its new-found oil revenues for the betterment of its people while other Arab states, cushioned from the hard facts of economic reality by the fantastic sums created by a surplus of oil-wealth, have preferred to finance regional terror. One of the largest recipients of oil-revenue aid is Syria—a country with few scruples about using the PLO terror machine.

III SYRIA

The Syrian government has, since 1948, fully co-operated in recruiting, fund-raising and providing aid to Palestinian guerrilla groups. Initially, this aid was provided by the Syrians alone and extended into allowing Damascus to be used as a Conference centre by the various *fedayeen* groups as well as the more obvious types of aid including training, information servicing, arms ammunition supplies, food and clothing. Similarly Syria was the first Arab state to encourage the establishment of Palestinian terrorist organisations, and support for them became a central tenet of the Syrian brand of revolutionary Ba'athism after 1966. Within the country, the government directly supports somewhere in the region of 9000 terrorists. Syria has always been proud that it is directly involved in the Palestinian terrorist struggle. As the Chairman of the Syrian Nationalist Party, Dr Abd Allah Sa'adah once remarked,

We are now working out new terrorist methods, so as to take part in the overall battle against the robber enemy.... We support [the] PLO ... without disparaging the fight of the other organisations.[28]

And President Assad has also noted that if it had not been for Syrian support, there would not have been *fedayeen* action.

Syria is the host nation to parts of the central command of terrorist groups such as Fatah, the PLA, PFLP and PDFLP, as well as the government-sponsored Sa'iqa, and allows the regional commands of these organisations to operate out of Damascus. The Syrian Government also bolsters the ranks of Sa'iqa by the use of its regular soldiers who serve as part of their normal military service. Other terrorist volunteers are individually screened by the Government before being permitted to operate on Syrian soil.

Prior to 1976 and the Syrian involvement in Lebanon against the PLO and other Palestinian terrorists, terrorist volunteers within Syria were allowed a limited but relatively unencumbered freedom of movement. After 1976, however, Palestinian terrorists in Syria were placed under much greater restriction and their freedom of movement was curtailed. Between 1966 and 1973, the Government encouraged the *fedayeen* terrorists to be particularly active on the Golan Heights, thus in many ways precipitating the conflicts of 1967 and 1973.

Syria, by directly providing the personnel for Sa'iqa as well as wholly financing it, is thus capable of exerting a measurable influence on the entire Palestinian terrorist movement. This is further enhanced by the fact that the PLA is a 3000 strong terrorist organisation wholly under Syrian command and largely financed by Syria. At the same time, the Government actively involves itself in the process of fund-raising for the *fedayeen* terrorist organisations, often demanding contributions to the various organisations' fighting funds. Following the Palestinian terrorists' expulsion from Jordan in 1970–1, the Syrian Government willingly gave permission for the PFLP and the PFLP–GC to establish bases of operation within her borders, alongside other terrorist groups who had previously obtained permission. The following table shows the various terrorist groups and the location of some of their major bases in Syria.

Base	Location	Function	Terrorist Group
El Hamma	6km south of Damascus	General and HQ	Fatah
Suwaida		rear base	
Burj Islam	north of Latakia	naval base	Fatah
Jeble	south of Latakia	naval base	Fatah
Montar	south of Tarsus	naval training base	Fatah
Massiaf		recruiting and training base for sabotage and explosives	Fatah
Donma		general training	Fatah
Sahm el-Julan	8km east of the cease-fire lines	Regional HQ	Fatah
Muzairib		general training	Sa'iqa
Harna	7km north of Damascus	general insurgency training	Sa'iqa
Ein-Saheh	12km north-west of Damascus	general training	PDFLP

Suwaida is thought to be a camp used by Black September—an

41

off-shoot of Fatah. Camps where no location is given are named after the town or village within, or outside of which they are situated. PLA bases are often attached to army camps where its members receive special training.[29]

In 1975, the Syrian Government began providing arms, equipment and technical-military advice to the PLO-inspired Leftist Moslem militants in Lebanon under the leadership of the late Kamal Jumblatt. This action that went a long way towards precipitating the murderous war against the Lebanese Christians which began in April 1975 and which necessitated Syrian military intervention in May 1976.

This was a hollow gesture, however, as when Syrian forces entered Lebanon the internecine war did not cease, but continued for a further four months. Had Syria displayed and deployed one third of its forces in Lebanon, it could have put a halt to the warfare between the Christian and the PLO-backed Moslem extremists in concert with Palestinian terrorists. As it was, Lebanese regions contiguous with Syria were placed under Syrian military domination while elsewhere they confined themselves to cutting communications between the PLO and Jumblatt, simultaneously channelling arms to Lebanese Christians and introducing Syrian-based Palestinians into the war. This last action exacerbated the disillusionment of the PLO terrorist faction with Syria and prompted heated exchanges between Syrian and Palestinian leaders. Open conflict was only avoided because the Arab League supported the Syrian presence in Lebanon—support which was quickly translated into finance to assist Syria with the additional expenditure incurred by fulfilling its rôle as 'peacemaker'—and because the Syrians did not concern themselves with Southern Lebanon which the PLO and other terrorists had turned into a fortress. Further disenchantment occurred between the Syrians and Palestinians following Israel's three-month occupation of Southern Lebanon as far as the Litani River as the Israelis attempted to clear Palestinian terrorists from operating within artillery-range of northern Israel. Syrian opposition was almost non-existent (apart from warnings to Israel not to extend its temporary occupation) and deaf ears were turned to Palestinian terrorists' pleas for assistance.

However, Syria and the PLO were reconciled and once again

became allies. Syrian troops evacuating certain areas of Lebanon, in accordance with cease-fire arrangements with Israel, actually handed over control to the PLO. From January 1981 onward Syria supplied the terrorists with dozens of tanks and, by April 1982, had entered into an agreement of cooperation with Fatah.

Both Syria and Libya had supplied the PLO with Soviet-made tanks and weaponry in 1982, as indeed it had done on previous occasions.[30] The PLO immediately began to create arms caches under office-buildings, schools, clinics, hospitals and mosques, while simultaneously using this weaponry to expand its area of dominance. This expansion encroached on the traditional Lebanese Christian heartland and was carried out with Syrian assistance as well as logistic and material support.

Since 1977, Syrian troops had given umbrella support to PLO terrorists in Lebanon to enable the latter to consolidate their gains, even though a decided coolness had occurred in relations between the two parties. The main thrust of Syrian involvement in Lebanon had been concerned with reducing the military capability of the Christian militias. To this end, from 1978 onwards Syrian troops indiscriminately bombarded Christian-held quarters in Beirut, resulting in the merciless slaughter of countless women and children. E. N. Barton, in a letter to the *Irish Times*, resolved that this was only allowed to occur because the Lebanese Christians had no 'vote-catching appeal in the Western democracies'.[31] This sort of action by Syrian troops continued almost unabated until the July 1982 invasion of Lebanon by Israel. So serious was the situation in 1981, that George Ediger was prompted to write:

Our fellow-Christians in the Lebanon are threatened with eradication ... And throughout the length and breadth of Christendom, there has not been a squeak of protest. Where once men flocked to the Crusades or prated of Lepanto, all that our forbears died to save is being cast away while fellow-Christians in the West have not seen fit to stir. Indeed, but for the Jews of Israel, there would be no Christian congregation left in all the lands through which St Paul preached to the Seven Churches of Asia. That Christians better than ourselves now only live because the Jews defended them, is a shame I never thought to suffer.[32]

However, Syria was not to have it all its own way. Opposition within Syria from the majority Sunni sect to the minority Alawite ruling sect, erupted in January 1982. President Assad, whose forces were seriously over-extended due to their participation in Lebanon, ordered sections of his remaining forces to surround, isolate and eradicate the Sunni rebels in their central town of Hama, on 2 and 3 February 1982.

Hama fell to Hafez al-Assad's troops and the rising was over. The bloody way in which the rebels were dispatched, served not only to indicate the extent of internal tension in Syria but also the magnitude with which the government viewed the problem. Within six weeks, Hafez-Assad had sent a total of six hit teams to Europe with orders to exterminate prominent exiled members of Syria's Moslem Brotherhood, particularly in Stuttgart and London. This would account for the reasons why Damascus was so unwilling to tie its fate to the PLO in Lebanon. Thus when the Israeli forces began to apply unremitting pressure on the PLO, the Syrian forces stood by. Consequently, the PLO were forced to send an SOS message to President Mubarak of Egypt pleading with him to intervene on their behalf, on the basis that 'the Syrians will wipe us out'.[33]

The bitterness of many Palestinian terrorists at what was seen as Syria's ineffective provision of aid during the Lebanese conflict, has turned into an unwelcomed open criticism of the régime. This has resulted in a weakening of its current status in the Arab world not only as a 'confrontation state' against Israel and the main Palestinian support and supply base, but also as a force for peace and as a representative of the remaining Arab League states in Lebanon. If this was to result in Damascus losing the PLO headquarters, it would not only lose prestige internationally but much of its legitimacy and internal prestige at home. This has also been exacerbated by its deepening enmity with Jordan and Iraq which again has weakened its position vis-à-vis the other Arab states.

Having expended so much of its own resources on the Palestinian terrorists, including a large portion of the aid granted to Syria by the Arab oil-producing countries, Syria also refused to accept *any* Palestinian terrorists from Lebanon unless it received a compensation payment of c.US$25b. That Syria did eventually accept a limited number of terrorists leads us to assume that money was paid by Saudi Arabia. Those Palestinian terrorists remaining in Syria, together with those accepted from Lebanon, have been placed under strict regulations concerning movement, speech and conditions and are housed in camps some distance from Damascus and are controlled by the army.

Lebanon is the fourth country that is contiguous with Israel. It is also the only Arab Middle Eastern country which does not have the 'Sharia' as the basis of its law. However, democratic government as it is known and understood in the West is impossible. As Professor Kelly remarked,

... Lebanon has paid the price for its singularity being ravaged by civil and confessional conflict, instigated and conducted by the Palestinian guerrilla forces to whom it has afforded sanctuary, while the guerrillas themselves have in turn been incited and supported by the more militant Islamic republics.[34]

Arab state support for the Palestinians continued because the general community had learnt to live with all the consequences of defeat except one—the plight of the Palestinians. Whereas this argument applies to many of the Arab states, in no way has it ever been applicable to Lebanon.

Since the 1948 war, in which Lebanese troops fought against the newly-created state of Israel, Lebanon has never engaged in any cross-border hostilities against Jerusalem—nor have any regular Lebanese soldiers been concerned or drafted into other hostile armies. In fact, the Israeli–Lebanese border has remained the most stable of Israel's borders until 1970–71. The Palestinian terrorists who had been ejected from Jordan then teemed into Lebanon, to overwhelm the small and confessionally unstable state.

Since 1949, Lebanon had granted 100,000 Palestinian refugees full citizenship, and allowed a further 160,000 to live within its borders in refugee camps despite the fact that the predominantly Moslem Palestinians would tip the fragile confessional balance. This fact was seized upon by some of the other Arab states, namely Syria, Iraq, Egypt and Libya, all of whom put pressure on Lebanon to sign the Cairo Agreement on 3 November 1969. This granted the PLO extra-territorial rights within Palestinian refugee camps in Lebanon, and a certain degree of freedom to conduct terrorist operations against Israel from Lebanese territory. The Agreement was signed between Yasser Arafat and the Lebanese Government and was guaranteed by the aforementioned states. Yet when the Lebanese tried to restrict the PLO's activities, the Syrian Government forced Lebanon into signing the Melkart Agreement of May 1973, which granted the PLO even more freedom of action. Two other agreements followed; Shtaura, in 1977 and the Arafat Agreement of 1978.

Persistently, the PLO broke all the promises to the Lebanese Government contained in each of these Agreements. The Palestinian terrorists had agreed not to use the refugee camps for military training, but habitually did so. The terrorists promised to curtail cross-border incursions into Israel from Lebanon but increased them. They also totally ignored promises to remove heavy weapons from the refugee camps. This, together with the Lebanese Government's inability to rectify the situation, resulted in Lebanon sacrificing its sovereignty to the Palestinian terrorists. But some of the Moslem institutions within Lebanon were anxious that this should occur, for they wanted Lebanon to become a wholly Moslem country. Thus the cross-border incursions into Israel increased and monetary incentives such as that offered by a leading Arab bank in Beirut would be paid per capita for every Israeli killed in a Palestinian raid on Israel itself.[35]

The Syrian and Jordanian Governments were able to prevent terrorist cross-border incursions into Israel from their own countries because of the overwhelming nature of Israel's counter-attacks and because they were strong enough to enforce their wishes. However, Lebanon was not strong enough to do likewise. Thus they received the brunt of the Israeli counter-offensive, being invaded as far as the Litani River in 1978 and then, in 1982, as far as Beirut. Prior to 1978 and between 1978 and 1982, Lebanon as a state was ravaged by the PLO and its constituent groups. The terror created, however, was one of 'allegiance terror' by which violence was used to create mass support. This support took the form of funds obtained through extortion by means of strikes, boycotts and civil disobedience, collusion which was obtained by threats of vengeance. The Lebanese Government, unable to control the situation, withdrew into its own impotence, shoring up its economy as best it could with financial grants to cushion the devastating effects of economic dislocation; this reached a point of no return with the war of 1976.

Prior to this dislocation the Lebanese government officials, and officials of the PLO and it constituent groups, met regularly, as indeed did Arafat and the Lebanese Moslem Prime Ministers, because Lebanon had granted diplomatic immunity to all PLO officials early in 1970. By the end of the decade the Palestinian–Syrian pressure on President Suleiman Franjieh was such that he felt compelled to issue a series of reforms which sought to end the fighting by expanding Moslem representation in government at the expense of the Christians. The PLO sensed victory and it rejected the proposals, instead opting to continue the fight. The Christians' plight became desperate and the Syrian army was forced to intervene on their behalf. Six years later, one commentator remarked, '... the President does not control his palace; the government does not even control its offices'.[36] Between 1976 and 1982, the PLO harassed the Lebanese in three ways. Firstly, by acting as a state within a state. Secondly, by guerrilla activities in and against Israel provoking counter attacks and thirdly, by engaging the Christians in a permanent civil war. The lack of Lebanese Government control ensured that real authority lay with the terrorists in collusion with the Syrians. Therefore Beirut and Sidon became terrorist 'free-ports' denying the Lebanese Government port duties, confiscating warehouses, preventing the use of the port's facilities to Lebanese businessmen, and creating further unemployment and additional dislocation to an already shattered economy.

Logistical support was provided by the Lebanese army which had, by 1972, cultivated excellent relations with terrorist leaders in the fields of co-ordination and planning of operations. With regard to the latter aspects, even *future* Black September operations became well known to many sections within the Lebanese government not to mention the press in Beirut. Lebanon also provided the terrorists with military bases—albeit unwillingly. Accordingly, the Lebanese Ambassador to the United Nations on several occasions had to deny the existence of terrorist bases, perhaps hoping to obtain a condemnation of Israel which might alleviate Arab pressure on Lebanon.

The PFLP, Fatah and Sa'iqa *all* had military bases in Lebanon, some of which were at Shoba Village, Beirut, Bariya, Rashiya al Fakher, Einata (Bint Jbeil) and the Arkub, Hasbeya, Dir el Ashir, Al Mazra'a, Al Suriya and in the refugee camps of Rushdiya, Sabra, Shatila and Ein el Hilwe. In all of these camps, the terrorists sited extensive arms caches often in UNRWA schools which the PLO had appropriated and turned into establishments for terror graduates. In addition, these locations functioned as training camps for women and children, with special Ashbal training camps for boys aged six years and upward. Large numbers of 13-year old and 14-year old children of both sexes were found at Rashidiye refugee camp near Tyre by the advancing Israelis in June 1982. All were carrying rocket-propelled grenade launchers (RPG). This followed a PLO policy of not conscripting children under 12-years old for front-line service[37] Such arbitrary actions were, however, only possible during a time of almost total anarchy, post-1976 in Lebanon.

The conflict which erupted in Lebanon in 1975, had its roots not only in the Arab League's abandonment of Lebanon to the Palestinians, but also in the close ties which the PLO engineered with leftist elements within that country during 1971. The following year saw the establishment of the Arab Assistance Front, headed by Kamal Jumblatt and, together with the PLO, an increased leftist influence in Lebanon further upset the delicate internal politico–confessional balance. Yet by the end of the civil war the Alliance itself was divided into innumerable factions in their bid for power, which, by the end of the decade, manifested itself in the indiscriminate shooting not only of each other, but also of innocent bystanders and civilians. By January 1982 the movement had splintered into more than 100 groups, and more than 50 of these groups were backed by their own militias. The catalyst which caused the eruption of open war between the Lebanese and Palestinians was provided by the terrorists themselves when one of their gang shot-up a Christian burial party. Naturally, the Lebanese tend to blame the PLO for beginning Lebanon's destruction and the Syrians for finishing it. One of the most prominent Phalangist leaders, Amin Gemayel, who was later to follow his assassinated brother as President of Lebanon, has referred to the internal conflict of 1975–6 not as a civil war, but as an attempt

48

by a failed Islamic civilisation to '... destroy a successful cultural experiment .... For the Lebanese the scale of destruction does not matter; what matters is the quality of reconstruction'.[38] On 14 October 1976, Edouard Ghorra, the Lebanese Ambassador to the UN, in a speech to the General Assembly, accused the Palestinians in Lebanon of thwarting Lebanese justice by hiding criminals in the refugee camps. He went on to blame them for the kidnapping of both Lebanese civilians and foreigners, for bank-rolling their operations by selling contraband goods in Lebanon's towns and villages and for acts of extortion, blackmail and bribery of not just individuals, but groups, institutions and even Government officials. That anarchy prevailed can be seen by the number of dead between April and October 1975—conservative estimates have put it as high as 70,000.[39]

The PLO's influence and status in the entire Middle East region is dependent on their possessing an independent territorial base—something which they had not enjoyed prior to their concentration in Lebanon. The PLO not only enjoyed both military and political power which enabled it to display the characteristics of a state but, in turn, it also allowed them to acquire some international standing. Having greater authority within certain parts of Lebanon than the government itself allowed the PLO to introduce its own law which included rape, murder, crucifixion, torture, castration and drowning. All these barbaric acts were committed on the old, on women and children and an example of this is Damour. Hence the PLO began to intimidate the press corps in Lebanon so to ensure that such acts were not reported and that they received a favourable press. (Like the Lebanese government the international press corps were successfully intimidated into impotence.)[40] Such tactics caused the deaths of 2,183 Lebanese and Palestinians in 1980 and a further 1,498 fatalities in 1981. Of the latter, only 15 per cent were killed in battles between the PLO and the IDF in July of that year. In 1982, the death-toll increased with 155 people killed in May alone. Many of these deaths and the fact that the PLO hid guns in hospitals, schools etc.,[41] remained unreported in the Western press thus enabling journalists and politicians to judge Israel's invasion on the basis of two yardsticks: earthly and eschatological. What was not taken into account was the fact that seriously wounded

49

Lebanese and Palestinian civilians were flown to Israel for treatment.

Israel's military activity together with US mediation over Lebanon, added up to a relatively coordinated strategy aimed at eliminating terrorist-controlled enclaves in the country. These enclaves were completely autonomous and were not subject to any kind of governmental control. It was thus a surprise to many Westerners to see how popular the IDF was when they were greeted by both Christians and Shiite Moslems upon invading Lebanon.

V SAUDI ARABIA

Since the 1920s, Saudi Arabian foreign policy has involved the use of money to promote inter-Arab compromise. For example, during the Iran–Iraq war, when the Saudis felt it necessary, they began to provide Iraq with substantial financial assistance while at the same time keeping open the possibility of serving as a mediator in the conflict. However, a further example of even greater direct intervention occurred in 1958. In that year Saudi Arabia involved itself in Syrian internal affairs by agreeing to pay £22m. if the Syrian–Egyptian merger into the United Arab Republic could be foiled and Gamal Abd el-Nasser liquidated.

Immediately prior to the outbreak of the Six-Day War in 1967 and with the prospect of British withdrawal from the Gulf area hanging over the region, King Feisal expressed his real concern about the consequences which he felt would occur following the withdrawal. His fear was, that if Britain pulled out of South Arabia altogether, the Gulf would be subverted in a matter of months. Thus subsequent payments to Palestinian terrorists must be viewed in this light; that in order to ensure the maintenance of the familial and hierarchical monarchy within Saudi Arabia, those who were ideologically opposed to such a system had to be kept where their subversive efforts would be minimised.

However, Saudi Arabia had some responsibility for the Palestinian problem, having been drawn into it by the British government in the 1930s. Thus this state had to appear wholly engaged in attempts to resolve the issue to avoid being vilified by the 'front-line' states of Egypt, Syria and Iraq. Prior to the

1967 War, however, the Gulf region as a whole was apathetic to the Palestinian question, an attitude which only changed with the Arab débâcle of that year. The consequences of the defeat were that the Gulf states became involved in an issue which, historically and geographically, was of little concern to them. Because of this, Saudi Arabia put up the bulk of the money which rescued Egypt financially and was to a lesser extent joined by Kuwait and Libya under King Idris. From 1967, Saudi Arabia contributed an average of £50m. to Egypt's recovery and war effort. This continued until December 1969, during the so-called War of Attrition, when Nasser demanded a further £40m. King Feisal refused. Kuwait, after some hesitation, offered to make a final payment of £10m. provided that the Kuwaiti National Assembly approved. The refusal of Saudi Arabia to agree to Nasser's request, must be viewed against its fear of subversion emanating from Egypt's self-appointed rôle as the Pan-Arab leader.

Although Saudi Arabia has refused various states aid on occasion, it has since 1964, contributed fluctuating annual sums to the Palestine National Fund. This aid, following the 1967 débâcle, was firmed up into direct financial contributions to the PLO which became exclusively channelled through Fatah after the latter gained dominance over the PLO in 1968. The most conscientious financiers of Fatah came from within the Saudi Arabian hierarchy.

Palestinians within Saudi Arabia were closely watched by the Government's internal security services and all political activity within the Palestinian community was suppressed in sharp contrast to the Saudi attitude towards financing the PLO. From 1968, public fund-raising on Fatah's behalf was freely permitted and the Saudi press were instructed to support it.

In 1968, Saudi contributions to the PLO totalled about US$100,000 per month and, beginning in 1969, 'the Saudi government and private individuals continued to give considerable help to the Palestinian guerrilla organisation al-Fatah'.[42] King Feisal preferred to fund Fatah rather than the PFLP, simply because the latter openly favoured overthrowing the feudal and traditional monarchy. By 1973, Saudi Arabia was financing Fatah to the tune of US$1.2m. per annum, as well as continuing to make its regular contributions to the other

Palestinian groups. Hence, Saudi Arabia was being sucked into the vicious cycle of paying 'protection money': a cycle that was perpetuated and increased by its own momentum.[43]

The almost constant worry of the Saudis regarding the possibility of insurrection was not exclusively theirs. The traditional and feudal-based Gulf Sheikhdoms were also partially paralysed by the same fear. At the beginning of May 1970, Sheikh Zayid ibn Sultan, ruler of Abu Dhabi, visited Riyadh. He expressed to King Feisal the apprehensions of all the Gulf Sheikhs about the growing menace of subversion in the region coming not only from the direction of the Palestinian and Islamic militant groups, but also from other Arab states. By the end of the decade one of the principal threats came from Colonel Gadhafi's Libya. Many Libyans fled Gadhafi's régime and settled in Saudi Arabia where several were recruited to run the Saudi-financed Sawt Libya group (Voice of Libya). Members of this group had, since its inception in 1969, been involved in helping the Saudi authorities to identify Libyans involved in subversion within Saudi Arabia. The Saudi princes understandably, preferred to minimise the threat. If the Palestinians could be bought off, then there was every reason to do so. Following the 1973 War, Saudi Arabia became Arafat's—and Fatah's—principal financial banker. Between 1973 and 1981, it is conservatively estimated that it gave the PLO, through Fatah, currency reserves of more than US$1000m.

The paranoia of the Saudi régime concerning the political subversion of the Gulf by Palestinian terrorist groups and their allies was to some extent justified by the hostage-taking at the Vienna OPEC meeting in 1975. The terrorist group led by Carlos was paid a large but undisclosed ransom by Saudi Arabia for the release of the Saudi oil minister, Sheikh Yamani; estimates vary between US$5 to US$50m. Large amounts of the payment went into the personal bank accounts of Carlos, Wadi Haddad and George Habash. More worrying for the Saudis, however, was that according to one of the participants, Gabriele Kröcher–Tiedemann, Iraq was the source behind the operation in an effort to destabilise the Saudi monarchy.[44]

From 1973, Saudi Arabia granted the PLO US$25m. annually in addition to *ad hoc* gifts, most of which amounted to much greater sums. In 1978, however, Yasser Arafat acknowledged that he, personally, had received US$67m. from the

Saudi King. This again was an *ad hoc* gift and undoubtably had strings attached to it[45]. But the most blatant gift to the PLO was in 1980 when Saudi Arabia contributed US$40m. because both the PFLP and the PDFLP had formulated plans to overthrow the Saudi monarchy. Following the announcement of Prince Fahd's peace plan at Fez towards the end of 1981, Abu Iyad, one of Arafat's deputies, remarked that from that moment, Saudi Arabia's role in the Arab world was seen by the PLO—and Fatah in particular—as purely financial. Since the rejection of the Fahd plans by the more revolutionary Marxist factions amongst the Palestinian terrorists, Saudi Arabia's attempt to put the Palestinian problem on a negotiated footing seemed to have done little more than raise the spectre of subversion once again. To try to prevent this, the Saudis began to draw much closer to the new Egyptian president, Hosni Mubarak. In January 1982, King Feisal agreed to finance a US$1b. purchase by Egypt of Mirage jet fighters from France. This move alarmed US officials who became concerned that King Feisal might begin to use his economic leverage to prevent President Mubarak from signing an agreement with Israel on Palestinian autonomy. At the same time, however, the Saudis were placed under continuing pressure from the Palestinian terrorists, particularly Arafat, for further financial grants to purchase weapons ordered from Warsaw Pact countries. For these purposes, just prior to June 1982 a PLO delegation to Riyadh was granted US$250m. by King Feisal.[46]

Although the Saudis have granted millions of dollars to Arafat and to the PLO, they were not prepared to enter into another oil embargo simply because there was an oil glut, and such action could do more harm to the Arab oil countries than to the West. This decision was in direct contradiction to the requests of the beleaguered Palestinian commanders in Lebanon.

Once the Palestinians had become entrenched in Lebanon, Saudi Arabia emerged as the terrorists' chief source of finance. Similarly, during the Israeli invasion of June 1982, it was reported that in Saudi Arabia,

... placards are up on all the counters in banks giving details of the Fateh (*sic*) account for contributions to the families of fighters, and enormous amounts of money have been collected.[47]

But this may well have been only applicable to Palestinian expatriates resident in Saudi Arabia. Following the Israeli invasion of Lebanon and the embarkation of the Palestinian fighters, Saudi Arabia continued to show its determination not to become embroiled once more in the Palestine issue.

The willingness on the part of the Saudis to offer vast sums of money to other states to accommodate the Palestinian terrorists (and offer Syria hundreds of millions of dollars to allow PLO guerrillas a haven there instead) contrasts significantly with Saudi unwillingness to succumb to US persuasion to pour billions of its surplus oil dollars into re-establishing Beirut as the Arab world's business centre. In fact, the only actual aid on record from Saudi Arabia to Lebanon concerns a contract, privately entered into, between King Fahd and an expatriate Lebanese construction millionaire domiciled in Saudi Arabia called Harir. This contract, worth a few million dollars, is for the repair of Beirut's streetlighting. By late 1982, Harir had donated some millions of dollars of his personal fortune to help clean up Beirut as quickly as possible following the Palestinian withdrawal.

The significant cooling off of relations between the PLO and Saudi Arabia can be attributed to two basic causes. Firstly, the failure of the Fahd Peace Plan to be accepted and adopted by the Arab world was a blow to the Saudis' prestige. Secondly, and perhaps more important, was the general tone of PLO comments following the plan's failure. That same November, Farook Khaddoumi, head of the PLO's political department, held up the spectral horror of Russian entanglement in the region, by stating that the PLO was particularly interested in, '... the development of good relations between our friends, the Soviet Union and the Kingdom of Saudi Arabia.'[48] This will only have added to Saudi fears of instability which had already been exacerbated by bouts of internal insurrection and now by a balance of payments deficit due to a world oil-glut. Yet whatever happens to the monarchy Saudi Arabia has lavished more money on the Palestinian terrorists since 1970 than some small countries generate in a year and so must be held responsible for enabling terrorism to be exported into the West by unscrupulous and dangerous men and women in order to keep those same men and women from destabilising Saudi Arabia.

VI   SOUTH YEMEN

From its inception, the People's Republic of South Yemen had
dedicated itself to extending the socialist revolution to Saudi
Arabia, Oman and the Gulf Sheikhdoms. For this purpose, it
provides terrorists of both the PFLOAG and its Omani counter-
part NDFLOAG with guerrilla training facilities. It has also
allied itself with the general Palestinian resistance movement
and with George Habash, Naif Hawatima and other 'rejection
front' groups in particular, providing considerable financial assistance, training facilities, refuge and military support. However, South Yemen is much more concerned with the export of
international and intercontinental terrorism under Soviet
auspices than with the question of Palestine and the general
Middle-Eastern farrago.

VII   IRAQ

The ruling Ba'ath party has ensured the export of revolution; it
has helped to promote subversion and genuinely encourage terrorism. All this has been done in the name of the Ba'athist
socialist ideals and Pan-Arabism. Baghdad has housed the
most ruthless of the Palestinian terrorist groups as well as
other revolutionary groups. Iraq has made every possible effort
to destabilise the Gulf region and thus has been the patron of
those groups, the activities of which have resulted in the fomen-
tation of sedition. With the Libyan military government, Iraq
has always given strong vocal support for the Marxist dictator-
ship of the PDRY. Iraq has also lent surreptitious support to
groups within Saudi Arabia in the hope that the monarchy will
be unhinged.

Iraq contributes regular sums to the PFLP and the PDFLP
particularly, while wholly organising and sponsoring its own
ALF. As far back as 1969, the government-controlled press
were expounding Ba'athist policy regarding its standpoint as
follows:

Seizing Israeli planes and their destruction, kidnapping Israelis and
people serving the Israelis, bombing Israeli institutions and paralys-

55

ing Israel's information media ... (are) no less effective than ... military operations.[49]

These aims coincided with those espoused by Habash and Hawatima; hence, the government opened up a training centre at a camp just outside Basra called Al Awda. Financing terrorist groups was an expensive venture and, realising this, Iraq attacked certain policy stipulations. This was no problem for the ALF, led by Abdul Wahab al-Kayyali an officer in the Iraqi secret services which financed the ALF as a wholly-owned subsidiary. The ALF operated in the Middle East, much as Iraqi Ba'athist agents operated in the Gulf. Both were concerned with destabilising régimes hostile to Iraq, and functioned by supporting clandestine opposition groups within those states by gun-running and offering other types of support.

Internationally Iraq appeared to be extremely influential in obtaining public support for the Palestinian cause from the USSR. It was during President Bakr's visit to that country in 1972, that the Soviet government on 19 September openly and publicly pledged both material and political support for the Palestinian terrorists. This was a *coup de maître* for Bakr and for the Palestinian terrorist groups, for it brought the USSR back into the Middle East *imbroglio* as a seeming ally of terrorism.[50]

As well as training camps, finance and the offer of safe havens for the PFLP, Iraq has also provided weapons. Furthermore, Iraq was gaining an international reputation as these facilities were not solely for the extremist Palestinians, but were also being made available to the PFLP's European, Latin American and Japanese links since both the IRA and the Japanese Red Army have been funded from and by Iraq.

Support for the Palestinians has been general Ba'athist policy since the coup which brought General Bakr to power in 1968. In that year, Iraq passed laws requiring all Palestinians in Iraq to pay the 'liberation tax' to the PLO. Following this direct public involvement, Iraq also equipped its own Palestinian terrorist group, the ALF, in order to off-set the influence Syria might gain within the Palestinian movement through Sa'iqa. Iraq, however, preferred to support the more extremist groups to the general exclusion of Fatah, particularly after 1970 when Iraqi–Fatah relations were at their lowest point. Relations continued to decline and dipped even further when Iraq gave sanctuary to one of Arafat's sternest critics, Abu Nidal.

Hassan Sabri al-Banna, alias Abu Nidal, was one of the founding members of Fatah and was sent to Baghdad as the PLO's representative in 1973. Whilst there, he tried to arrange for Arafat's assassination, for which, in 1974, he was condemned to death by Fatah. During the year-long Iraqi–Syrian rift in 1976 when Syria intervened in Lebanon, Iraq financed him to create, together with his small but fanatical number of supporters, a terrorist group to attack Syrian targets. Black June was formed by Abu Nidal (after the month in which Syrian intervention in Lebanon began), in order to prevent a Syrian-backed left-wing takeover of the country by large sections of the Palestinian movement. Carlos advised on, and was instrumental in, the formation of Black June. Within 18 months, Abu Nidal, on orders from Iraq and with its financial support, began a vicious round of assassinations against the Palestinian moderates. These moderates were men who advocated some sort of negotiation with Israel and, by doing so, were regarded in Baghdad as having betrayed the true Arab cause. The PLO representatives in London, Paris and Kuwait were killed and the PLO retaliated by attacking Iraqi diplomats and embassies as far afield as London, Beirut, Karachi and Ottowa. As November 1978 drew nearer, the carnage began to abate. Iraq, which was to host the Baghdad Arab League Summit that month, began to see Abu Nidal as somewhat of an embarrassment, so he was moved from Baghdad to Damascus. The Iraqi government still paid him an annual retainer and this was now supplemented by Syrian money. His removal allowed for an uneasy truce between the PLO and the Iraqi government. Abu Nidal was not heard of again until 1980, when Black June reemerged, this time concentrating its attention on Israeli and Jewish targets. Dr Issam Sartawi, a moderate PLO executive member until his resignation at the Palestine National Congress Meeting in Algiers in March 1983, and one of Arafat's closest advisers, remarked of Abu Nidal and Black June in a speech given in Paris, that they were paid agents of Israel, but this is a preposterous charge. It is much more likely that he was under orders from Syria which acts as a conduit for Arab state support—both financial and material—for the Palestinian terrorists in Lebanon.[51]

The extent of the financial support received by Abu Nidal for Black June (which also acts under the name Al-Asifa) from both Iraq and Syria is extensive for its small size. Iraq pays Nidal about US$10m. per annum while the yearly sum from Syria amounts to about US$1m. This, does not take into account living expenses, weaponry, clothing and other types of material support provided freely by Iraq and Syria. This money is further supplemented by blackmail money extorted from the smaller Gulf states, in particular from Kuwait and the United Arab Emirates. Among his other services, Nidal is also open to contractual offers for assassination. In 1976 Nidal attempted to assassinate the then Syrian Foreign Minister Abdel-Halim Khaddam, in return for a payment of around US$1m. from Rifa'at Assad, the brother of the current President of Syria. Even after his reported death in Baghdad in 1984, the strong family ties inherent within this renegade group allowed it to continue to function on behalf of the Syrians, while achieving some sort of rapprochement with Iraq.

Thus, the Iraqi administration has consistently aligned itself with the more extreme elements of the Palestinian terrorists. From 1972, Iraq increased its financial contributions to these groups, bringing the Palestinian terrorists closer to the USSR and opening its airports to receive large arms shipments on the terrorists' behalf. Even when the Arafat factions within the PLO sided with Iran following the outbreak of the Iran–Iraq war in 1980, Iraq still maintained its strong links with the extremists from all continents.

VIII   LIBYA

Since Colonel Gadhafi came to power on 1 September 1969, Libya has become the most important of the financial backers of the Palestinian terrorists and agreed to pay them £1m. per month. Although this support went mainly to Fatah, other groups received some portion of it. This heralded the establishment of new and close links between Libya and the terrorists which comprised financial aid, recruiting and training facilities and arms supplies. Libya also provides sanctuary and shelter as well as diplomatic assistance to the terrorists.

Currently, the Libyan government finances the rejectionist Palestinian terrorists to the near exclusion of Arafat and

Fatah, and provides them with training bases as well as recruiting offices in its embassies abroad. These embassies act as collection points for arms smuggled in by Libyan diplomats for use by the terrorists. These functions, however, are secondary to the provision of finance and weaponry.

Libya deducts a six per cent 'liberation tax' from the gross salaries of Palestinians working in Libya. In the early 1970s, the money received formed part of Libya's annual contribution to the terrorist groups and all the money was paid into the Palestine National Fund for distribution by Arafat and Fatah. Of the US$20m. annual contribution, US$11.5m. was derived from this tax, together with a three per cent 'Jihad tax' which was levied on the gross salaries of all Libyans. During this time, collections for the terrorists were also organised and even government ministers had to put a proportion of their salary into the Palestine Fund. Humble peasants did not escape either, for they each had to contribute the cost of a sheep. Seven months after ousting King Idris, Colonel Gadhafi stated, 'We are giving assistance to Fatah which we consider to represent the true *fedayeen* action.'[52] However, on 25 January 1973, angered by the PLO's drift to the left, Gadhafi suspended its annual allowances to the organisation which by then totalled US$40 million, but six months later, following a week of hard negotiations, the allowance was restored. It was at that point that Gadhafi decided to support the hard–line terrorists, the PFLP, PFLP–GC and PDFLP, by moving into European terrorism. This started with the financing of Carlo's Paris operation.

Since Gadhafi ascribes to fundamentalist Islamic ideals, when the conflict between the Christian Phalangists and Moslem Palestinians in Lebanon increased he took this opportunity to send his deputy, Major Jalloud, to Damascus in the summer of 1975. Jalloud's brief was to offer the Syrian government significant financial inducements to actively assist in turning Lebanon into a Moslem state. This motivated Gadhafi to spend more than US$100m. to provide the bulk of the arms needed by the Palestinian terrorists during the two-year Lebanese civil war. During the same period, Omar el-Maheshi, a former Libyan Minister of Planning, has estimated that Gadhafi managed to establish a reserve fund of US$580m. for his terrorist activities, including attempts to unseat conservative Arab rulers and to create subversion in the Gulf region.[53] By

1978, Libya was contributing US$75m. per annum on a regular basis, outside the amounts donated *via* the Arab League. That year, during the Baghdad Summit, Libya pledged a further US$39.3m. per annum to the PLO irrespective of the other contractual arrangements entered into and, within six months, had entirely paid this sum. The money was broken down into smaller amounts each of which was allocated to an individual terrorist group. By 18 June 1979, all the terrorist groups adumbrated within the PLO—including Fatah—had received their entitlement, as agreed at the Baghdad summit. It is a fact that there has never been a terrorist group in the Middle East, formed by Palestinians, which did not receive Libyan backing. Nor do further territories' boundaries stop Gadhafi's Libya from giving succour. The IRA and other European terrorist groups obtain financial aid, training and assistance in every possible way.

Following further meetings between the Libyan government and various terrorist organisations, Fatah was granted an *ad hoc* payment of US$10m. from Libya in June 1981. Two months later at a tripartite meeting held in Tripoli, additional funds and material support requested by the PLO and Jumblatt's Lebanese National Movement were granted by Gadhafi's government.[54]

All Gadhafi's support for terrorism hinges upon what he regards as acceptable terms on which to base a political solution to the Palestinian problem. He has expounded such terms and they make interesting reading. To begin with, he would require **the immediate cessation of all Jewish immigration into Israel together with the return of all Israelis to their country of origin.** These two points would be reinforced by the immediate cessation of all arms shipments to the Middle East region and the establishment of an independent democratic Palestinian republic for all Palestinian Jewish and Arab citizens. To this end, from the early 1970s, frequent meetings have taken place between Colonel Gadhafi and his Revolutionary Command Council and the leaders of Fatah, the PFLP, PDFLP, PFLP–GC as well as PLO principals. In one period of six months over 30 meetings took place between Libyan and Palestinian leaders. Between 6 April 1981 and 22 October 1981, Libyan leaders met Arafat at least ten times, Ahmed Jibril and other PFLP–GC principals five times, PFLP leaders

60

including Habash six times, PDFLP commanders three times and other Fatah officials five times.

Gadhafi has consistently armed the Palestinian terrorists with the latest weaponry. In late 1981, however, the world oil glut began to make severe in-roads into Libya's profits, so much so, that by early 1982, the Libyan leader was arguing that the West had engineered the oil glut in order to prevent Libya and other progressive Arab régimes from arming the Palestinians and, in turn, preventing them from continuing their legitimate armed struggle against Israel.[55] Libya, to quote Ahmed Jibril of the PFLP–GC, has provided '... full material support to the Palestinian revolution since 1969'. As early as 1972, Libya was providing bases and training facilities for the Palestinian terrorists with Russian assistance. This facility encouraged the government to begin financing its own terrorist organisation, the National Arab Youth for the Liberation of Palestine (NAYLP) headed by Marvan Hadad in late 1972. In June 1981, a new terrorist organisation was created, AONL, to operate on behalf of the Palestinians.

After the death of Wadi Haddad, Ahmed Jibril became Colonel Gadhafi's favourite Palestinian terrorist, enjoying full influence and receiving the latest Soviet weaponry—heavy long-range missiles capable of striking deep into the Israeli heartland. As far back as 1970, the PFLP–GC was receiving Libyan military assistance, which began only some months after Gadhafi's successful revolution. Jibril, himself, estimates the value of Libyan supplies of weapons and equipment at hundred of millions of dollars. This excludes financial grants and other additional assistance.[56]

Once a PLO–Syrian–Israeli cease-fire had been effected in July 1981, Libya announced its willingness to pay all the military and material costs of damage sustained by the 'Palestinian Revolution' and the Lebanese people as a result of Israeli attacks. What Libya actually contributed, was a 500-man SAM-9 anti-aircraft missile unit to the Palestinian terrorists in Lebanon, together with two 37-metre gunboats which were anchored in Syrian ports for use in launching sea-borne assault missions against Israel. As well as predictable supplies of small arms, ammunition and medium-range weaponry to the terrorists, the only offer of payment made to the Lebanese government by Libya was a US$2b. anti-aircraft missile defence system. Since the mid-1981 cease-fire, Libya renewed its assistance to Fatah. Prior to this, the Palestinian terrorist organisations which received almost exclusive Libyan aid were Habash's PFLP, Jibril's PFLP–GC, and Hawatima's PDFLP. During November 1979 to April 1981 there was a decided rift between Libya and the Fatah-dominated PLO. When support was resumed it included long-range 310mm artillery, tanks, mobile BM-21 rocket-launchers able to fire rapid salvos of 40 Katyusha rockets at targets 20km away and SAM-9 anti-aircraft missiles. All of this equipment was manufactured in the USSR and Eastern Europe. Libya freely admits that as well as arms and finances, it has also supplied volunteers to the PLO cause. The Libyan Foreign Affairs Liaison Secretary, Ali Treiki at a press conference in Kuwait acknowledged that his government had contributed many volunteers to the Palestinian terrorist-troops in Lebanon. During his speech to mark the 13th anniversary of the 1 September Al Fatah Revolution, Gadhafi proudly boasted,

Libyan volunteers were the first to arrive in Lebanon .... They were the first to fight side by side with the Palestinian forces and the Lebanese Patriotic Movement .... We gave money, we gave arms, and we provided the men.[57]

These 'volunteers' were sent to the terrorist groups in Lebanon via Syria. By 1973, 1,000 Libyan volunteers had seen service with the terrorists. They had been sent at regular intervals during the following years and their ranks included children aged only 13 and 14-years old. Further assistance was given by organising regional general mobilisations of expatriate Palestinians living in Libya. In September 1981, *Radio Libya* broadcast a call to all Palestinians aged over 18-years of age and living in the areas of Tobruk, Datha, Albizia, Almorg, Benghazi, Tripoli and Alzaviah, to register with their local PLO representatives for a general mobilisation.

Fadel Shrur, a member of the General Command of the PFLP–GC, stated in an interview with the Lebanese newspaper *Al-Kijak al-Arabi*, that about 50 per cent of all the fighters in Palestinian terrorist groups were from other Arab countries. Three months later, Colonel Gadhafi openly admitted that **hundreds of Libyans had recently volunteered to help the Lebanese National Movement and the Palestin-**

ians against Israel at Damour, Nabatiye, Tyre and Sidon.[58]

Kuwait has vacillated and displayed an ambiguous attitude towards both Arab terrorists and any others who have sought refuge there. On the one hand, Kuwait has desperately sought to project an image as an enlightened but at the same time radical Arab sympathiser, whilst on the other it has dealt harshly with Palestinians living within its borders. In 1965 Kuwait expelled nearly 10,000 Palestinians accusing them of intimate subversive links with Iraq, which has always coveted this tiny oil-rich state.

Kuwait has always been a place where disaffection and revolution has fomented as there are large numbers of Palestinians working there in government positions as well as in education and the oil industry, and because the Kuwaiti Palestinians were generally better educated than the indigenous population they became politically critical of the conservative régime. Therefore, in the mid-1960s it was not surprising that the PLO and Fatah terrorist Abu Iyad was able to address a 37,000-strong Palestinian audience who were given only two hours' notice of his intention to speak.

Kuwait has massively contributed to the Palestinian terrorist organisations and as with other states, the Kuwaiti government and its agencies have actively participated in recruiting terrorists for these organisations. As for the Palestinians who are Kuwaiti-domiciled, many of them are reluctant to jeopardise their homes and livelihoods. However, there are others who not only support the terrorist organisations but are active agents of them. The Kuwaiti authorities are reluctant to root-out terrorists, conspirators and other undesirables thoroughly, in case Kuwait's reputation for radicalism in Pan-Arab affairs is compromised. Kuwait surreptitiously encourages Palestinian terrorism, offering sanctuary to radical groups who promote sedition and insurrection elsewhere in the Arab world, while shrilly denouncing the West at every opportunity.

Palestinians in Kuwait give money to the PLO, and this transfer of funds is facilitated by the authorities. Again, like the other Arab states, the Kuwaiti government deducted at source from Palestinian salaries, a three per cent tax. In May

1968, this was supplemented by a general two per cent tax on petrol sales and movie tickets to support the PLO. By March of the following year, Kuwait accepted Arafat's demand that four million Kuwaiti dinars, ear-marked for the PLO, be released at once. At the same time, the Palestinian tax was raised to fifteen per cent. This money was supplemented by private donations from Kuwaitis such as Sheikh Sabah al-Salem al-Sabah who gave 100,000 Kuwaiti dinars to the families of those terrorists killed in action. The authorities also encouraged fund-raising at Palestinian rallies and, during 1970–1 Kuwait allocated five million Kuwaiti dinars from the national budget for the PLO and withheld a US$40m. subsidy to Jordan from September 1970 until September 1973 because the Palestinians were ejected from Jordan.[59]

The extent of the Kuwaitis' fear of the Palestinians can be seen quite clearly by the following account. In March 1973, Black September murdered the US Ambassador and other diplomats in Khartoum. Sheikh Sabah ibn Salim al-Sabah, the then ruler of Kuwait, publicly announced that in spite of the atrocity, Kuwait would not only continue financing the Palestinian terrorists, but they would also have unlimited financial support. This announcement is consistent with Kuwait's policy of trying to neutralise insurrection at home by buying-off the potential perpetrators while using the state as a clearing house for the distribution of radical propaganda, funds and arms in the Gulf. (Kuwait is the transit point for the movement of revolutionaries both into and out of the Gulf region.)

Kuwait indirectly supports Palestinian terrorists by ensuring them of constantly updated armaments. The sums of money disbursed by Kuwait in purchasing arms have been absolutely astronomical for a country with a defence force of about 10,000 men: for example, the April 1974 arms deal concluded with the USSR. This was followed by a second arms deal in January 1976. The total cost of the agreed programme is estimated at US$2.8b. The larger weaponry went to stock Egypt's depleted armouries while the smaller weapons (through circuitous routes) eventually found their way to the terrorists.

The Palestinian terrorist groups also survive by becoming the recipients of loans and grants from the Arab confrontation states. But Kuwait has also used this method to gain some token of immunity from insurrection and subversion. Kuwait gives grants and loans to Palestinian terrorists, and also to states like South Yemen which visibly and volubly support terrorism. Funding the Palestinian cause has, together with Kuwait's appeasement of political extremists, ensured its exemption as a revolutionary target of the ANM and its offspring, the PFLP and PDFLP.

Links between the Palestinian cause and Kuwait have been and are both long and complex. The ANM's Politburo for the entire Gulf region was its Kuwait branch. However, more personal links exist. Wadi Haddad and George Habash, while at the American University of Beirut Medical School, had a friend from Kuwait by the name of Ahmed Muhammed al-Khatib, who is a member of the Central Committee of the ANM's Kuwait branch as well as the Politburo of the PFLP. By 1970, Sheikh Ahmed Khatib as he was now known, was able to do a great service for the Palestinian terrorists. Prior to 1970, Kuwait annually subsidised Jordan to the tune of US$40m., and due to the Palestinian expulsion did not renew the subsidy until 1973. This suspension of funds was due to Khatib, who was by now a prominent Kuwaiti businessman and go-between for the KGB and the Palestinians. He also made sure that several million US dollars went quietly to the Palestinians to prevent insurrection being fomented by the terrorists amongst the Palestinian field workers in Kuwait. Interestingly enough, Khatib was driven to assist the Palestinian terrorists more out of a pathological hatred for the Kuwaiti royal family than out of socialist–Marxist convictions. He continued his machinations by exerting influence on the Palestinians who surround the Foreign Minister of Kuwait, Sheikh Jaber el-Ahmad, in an advisory capacity. He is apparently unafraid of retribution as should he die in any sort of mysterious circumstances, his death would ensure a visitation of Palestinian wrath on Kuwait by the Palestinian extremist terrorists.[60]

X   IRAN

While Mohammed Reza Pahlavi sat securely on the Peacock throne, Iran was more an ally of Israel than of Palestinian Arab terrorists. With his fall from grace in 1979, however, much changed. There have always been links between the Iranian Moslem fundamentalist activists and the Palestinian terrorists

65

since the Ayatollah Khomeini's enforced exile from Iran in the late 1960s. This point has been underlined by Ahmed Jibril of the PFLP–GC, who has been reported as saying,

... that we have been in touch with Iranian activists since 1970. We have trained tens of their leaders, giving them arms and experience.[61]

In return, the Iranian government under Khomeini has given assistance to the Palestinian terrorist organisations. The closeness between the Palestinian terrorists and the ideological standpoint of the Imam, has been made more clear by the PLO representative in Iran who, in November 1979, stated that, 'God willing, Yasser Arafat and the Imam will enter Jerusalem side by side and defeat the imperialists and the Zionists.'[62] **Having assumed power, Khomeini hired PLO assassins to kill his opponents overseas,** and in return, Iran paid the PLO a US$2 royalty on every barrel of oil produced. Again, the Mullahs turned to the Palestinian terrorists to assist them against the Americans. **Dr George Habash of the PFLP directly instructed, master-minded and participated in the US Embassy seizure in Teheran for which he was paid millions of dollars.** Although the total payment is unknown, one source has maintained that late in 1979, the sum of US$10m. was transferred from the Central Bank in Teheran to the PLO in Beirut.

Latterly, however, in an effort to launch even more successful attacks against Western targets, Khomeini urged the forming of an Iranian terror network of *ensan entehari*—suicide bombers—in Europe. The two men with the responsibility for this network are the former Iranian Prosecutor-General, Ayatollah Azari Qomi who began operations in London during August 1983 with a £4m. Jersey bank account, and Ayatollah Hadi Khosrow-Shahi, Iranian Ambassador to the Vatican, whose responsibilities extended to France, Spain and Italy. Both organisers recruited Moslems of varying nationalities for instruction at Mazariah camp north of Teheran and at Saleh-Abad camp just to the north of Qom. The responsibility for the success of the whole operation rests with Ayatollah Fazollah Mahalati who operates out of an office in central Teheran. Most of the volunteers are men between 16- and 30-years old. But **in 1984 up to 36 British girls (30 from Ulster) aged between 18 and 25 were undergoing training at two Universities in**

Iran; Melli National University, north-west of Teheran and at Shiraz University. **Many of the Ulster girls have IRA connexions** while other students are from Sa'iqa and ASALA, the Armenian terrorist group.

The Iranian authorities have supported subversion in neighbouring Arab countries particularly among Shiite Moslem communities living there. One example of direct support was the sending of Ayatollah Muhammed Montazari and a group of Iranian volunteers to Lebanon in January 1980—with the tacit agreement of the Israelis. Another more pertinent example of Iranian involvement in Lebanon, is the links between Iranian authorities and the various Lebanese Shiite groups.

In Lebanon, Shiites constitute 40 per cent of the population, but have long been regarded as second-class citizens. However, in 1969, Moussa Sadr, a highly educated Shiite cleric from Qom who had lived in Tyre for a number of years, founded the Higher Shiite Council to represent Shiite interests in the Beirut government. Six years later, having been granted the title of Imam, Sadr founded Amal (Hope). He had continuously supported the exiled Khomeini, thus firming up the links which would prove to be so useful to both Amal and Iran in later years. The year before the Iranian Revolution, however, Sadr disappeared on a visit to Libya and many Shiites believe that he remains captive, held by Gadhafi. Between 1978 and 1982, Amal's history becomes a chequered one of forged and abandoned alliances with Walid Jumblatt's Druze forces and during other periods when it acted as Syria's agent. It also began to receive direct support from Teheran, initially *via* the PLO which Iran wanted to use as the conduit for such aid, relying almost exclusively on Fatah.

After Sadr's disappearance, the leadership fell to a 40-year old Beirut lawyer, Nabih Berri, the son of a Lebanese merchant who lived in the former British colony of Sierra Leone.

The most important of the extremist Shiite groups in Lebanon which are funded and supported from Teheran are Islamic Jihad (Holy War) and the Hezbollah group. Both are under the combined leadership of Sheikh Ragheb Harb and Sheikh Mohammed Hussein Fadlallah. The latter is the more magnetic leader and is described as 'Khomeini's spiritual man in Lebanon'. **It was Fadlallah who orchestrated the 1983 attacks on the US Embassy in Beirut and on the US**

Marine barracks, killing 258 US marines. Similarly, these organisations have been responsible for a multitude of random acts of violence, kidnappings, bombings, shootings and, Fadlallah himself, has spoken openly of the efficiency of Khomeini-trained suicide attackers, and these have recently become the hallmark of Shia extremism. The headquarters of these two groups lies in the slum Shiite suburb of Burj-el-Barajnieh.

Palestinian terrorists and extreme Moslem fundamentalists make strange bed-fellows. Iran has traditionally had designs on Arab territory—namely the control of the Gulf region. Similarly, Iranians do not traditionally regard themselves as part of the Arab world and are fundamentally opposed to Marxism and Communism. Hence, it is no real surprise that **the Khomeini government has continued to support Israel.**

Since 2 August 1982, Iran has been supplying Israel with oil at US$22 per barrel against a spot price of US$31 and US$29. Commission was paid at US$5 per barrel to a Lebanese Shiite company based in Switzerland, which acted as intermediaries. The importance of this arrangement was that, effectively, it prevented the implementation of an Arab oil boycott during the Israeli Peace for Galilee operation. It has also been argued that the two countries orchestrated military action against the Arabs: Iran, in its June 1982 invasion of Iraq, which coincided with the Israeli operation. The Iranian attack on Iraq was launched, according to one Arab source, in order to neutralise 'at least one diplomatic, if not military, factor.' It is this factor which Jerusalem considers poses the more serious threat, and so is quite prepared to secretly assist Iran in its endeavours.

XI ALGERIA

Little is known specifically of Algeria's contribution to the Palestinian terrorists. However, it actively participates in the recruitment of terrorists and is the most important training centre outside Lebanon, Syria and Libya. Algeria also supplies arms and in addition acts as an entrepôt for Russian and Chinese equipment and weapons en route to the Palestinians. It also actively assisted these terrorists in hijacking operations and boasts of camps set up with Libyan money, staffed by Cubans, East Germans and North Koreans.

68

After the 1967 war, Algeria provided the Palestinian terrorist groups with both material and financial support from both private and government sources. During the 1973 war and immediately afterwards, Algerian aid was concentrated on a consignment of US$200m. worth of weapons to Egypt. However, during the Israeli invasion of Lebanon in June 1982, Algerian aid was directed at the Palestinian terrorists.

On an official visit to Sweden, the Algerian Foreign Minister, Dr Ahmed Taleb Ibrahimi, stated that in early June 1982 Arafat appealed for help to an Algerian delegation in Damascus. He presented them with a detailed list of small arms which the terrorists urgently required. When the news reached Algiers, President Chadli called an emergency cabinet meeting that night at 11 o'clock and by 4 o'clock the following morning the Soviet Ambassador was contacted and a cheque for US$20m. was handed over together with the list of weapons requirements. The weapons were airlifted from the USSR to Damascus within a few days and were used against the Israeli invasion forces in the fighting south of Beirut. At the same time, Algeria flew in plane-loads of weapons from its own arsenals to the terrorists and in Ibrahimi's words, 'gave the Palestinians everything they asked for'.

XII TUNISIA

Tunisia under President Bourghiba has never really entered into the Palestinian question. As far as can be ascertained, no actual financial support has been granted to the PLO under the government auspices, although some material help has been provided. This material aid has been given out of a need to ensure that Tunisia is not isolated from the Arab world as it is reluctant to be drawn into the Palestinian imbroglio. Such material assistance was provided between 1981 and 1982 almost exclusively, with Tunisia providing the Palestinians with four Bell-206 helicopters and passage for some volunteers—mostly Palestinian expatriate terrorist sympathisers—so that they would swiftly arrive in Lebanon.

Following the Palestinian débâcle in Lebanon, Tunisia provided a camp at Oued Juarga, 70km from Tunis. The camp was to house about 1,000 Palestinian terrorist fighters. On top of this, President Bourghiba emptied the Salwa Hotel (20km from the capital Tunis) for Yasser Arafat and 300 of his aides. However, conscious of the threat to his power, Bourghiba placed troops near Oued Juarga and installed 'protection' for Arafat. Yet this protection was not granted *carte blanche*. The Tunisian government did not create either an international or a diplomatic incident when the Israelis mounted their airborne bombing raid on Arafat's Headquarters. This followed the murder of three Israeli holidaymakers in Cyprus in September 1985. The raid, which took place the following month was wholly supported by President Reagan. Less than three weeks afterwards, another four Palestinian terrorists hijacked the Italian cruise ship the *Achille Lauro*. Units of the US Navy forced the plane carrying the terrorists back to Tunisia to divert to a NATO base in Italy. But this was only possible because President Bourghiba of Tunisia had ordered that the plane was not to be given landing permission anywhere in his country. It is not Bourghiba's intention to allow Tunisia to go the way of Lebanon.

XIII   MOROCCO

Morocco's attention is taken up with matters affecting the Spanish enclaves of Ceuta and Melilla and in the more recent years, the status of Western Sahara. Morocco managed to stay almost completely out of the Palestinian imbroglio until after the 1967 war. Morocco is a relatively stable monarchy, under the rule of King Hassan, and has been more concerned with trying to resolve the conflict with Israel rather than perpetuate it. This attitude culminated in the King hosting clandestine meetings between Israeli officials and representatives of the late President Sadat of Egypt, prior to his historic visit to Jerusalem.

At the same time, Morocco has always regarded itself as an integral member of the Arab fold and thus has keenly participated in Arab League Summits as well as hosting high-level Arab initiatives. In general, this is as far as Moroccan support has gone, except for two notable instances. On 22 January 1970, King Hassan pledged monetary aid of just over £1 million to the PLO and, a little over a year later, sent 20 US manufactured jeeps as a token offering to the Palestinian terrorists in Lebanon. Apart from these actions, no direct, or as far as can be ascertained indirect, assistance has been given to the Palestinian terrorists by Morocco—which, in terms of the acerbic and volatile nature of Middle-Eastern politics and inter-state relations, is no mean feat.

XIV SUDAN

Until 1969 when Colonel Numeiri seized power on a platform of radical socialism, Sudan had escaped involvement in the problems of Palestine. By 1972, however, the country was actively participating in terrorist recruitment and giving support to various Palestinian terrorist factions.

Sudan had taken the road of revolutionary radicalism on the promise of a sweeping transformation of the country's resources, aimed at a greater redistribution of wealth through nationalisation. This change blended in well with the radical Marxist ideologies of Palestinians like Habash and Hawatima and once this common goal was ascertained, Sudan's involvement with the radical Palestinian terrorist actions began.

Prior to the 1973 October War, President Numeiri had decided that the leftward drift of his country had gone far enough and that the progressives from within his government had to be purged. Supported by President Sadat of Egypt, he began to remove from government all the radical and progressive elements. The radicals replied by launching a rebellion in August 1973 with both Libyan and PFLP assistance. And although Numeiri successfully put down this attempt, the National Front attempted armed insurrections again, in September 1975 and July 1976.

By 1978, President Numeiri had once again consolidated his hold on the country and cemented his relations with Egypt by allying Sudan with President Sadat's participation in the Camp David Peace negotiations with Israel. This effectively made him a target for assassination by both Libyan and Palestinian terrorist gunmen. It also nullified the PLO's attempts to gain the support of black non-Moslem Africans for their cause.

XV THE PALESTINE LIBERATION ORGANISATION

The PLO, despite being the recipient of millions of dollars from the various Arab states, makes further attempts to generate its own cash flow. Arab estimates of the PLO's budget have centred on US$100m. per annum, but senior Fatah members regard such figures as 'mere peanuts'. Other analysts have estimated the organisation's **income** as **nearer US$1000m.** which most informed sources regard as nearer the mark. Much of this money has been funnelled through Beirut, particularly after the various PLO groups were ejected from Jordan in 1970.

By 1975 in Beirut, terrorism had reached the proportions of an 'industry'. Office blocks appeared, housing the PLO; the PLO Research Centre; the Institute for Palestine Studies; the headquarters of the PFLP, PDFLP and many other organisations including SAMED (the Sons of Palestinian Martyrs Society) and the Palestine Red Crescent Society. Each of these offices employed staff who worked normal office hours, took coffee breaks, and holidays. They each received salaries supplemented by annual increments and the security of a pension fund. This situation was supplemented in 1981 by a vast proliferation of newspapers, research publications and propaganda.[63]

Leading Palestinian terrorist officials have many numbered accounts with substantial sums in certain Beirut banks. In the vaults of over 100 Lebanese banks, in 1981, the total deposits were equivalent to £4.6b. The banks also serviced expatriate Lebanese money totalling between £68 and £86m. Similarly, the banks serviced this money, equivalent to £11.5m. per month from Arab embassies, for distribution to the various accounts of private militias within the Palestinian terrorist group in Beirut. As early as 1976, between L£1.5 and £2m. had been transferred via the banking conduit into the private accounts of several PLO leaders.[64] The banks also paid salaries regularly to the Arab terrorists on the PLO's payroll and the amounts were well above the average Arab earnings in the richest oil-fields. In order to justify such large regular payments, and the facilities maintained in the training bases, the Palestinian terrorists continued to dispense indiscriminate murder and destruction.

In 1972, the PLO's Operations Network, the Rasd, was estimated as possessing liquid resources of more than US$100m. Within three years the Rasd, together with Black September, had established extensive networks throughout Europe for the carrying out of political assassinations and underworld contracts. Through the Rasd, the terrorists' income is further supplemented by the smuggling of regular quantities of hashish into Europe.

Drug-smuggling has been consistently used by the PLO to raise money. In June 1977, the *Guardian* reported that Interpol had uncovered a PLO drug-smuggling ring in Europe, with accumulated profits of more than US$2m. which were ultimately used for arms purchases. More recently, the PLO have established connexions with the Mafia, regarding drug-smuggling into Europe from Syria *via* Lebanon to Sicily. Just after the Israeli invasion of Lebanon in 1982, in late July and August, the Palestinian terrorists harvested a huge crop of Lebanese 'Gold' (the highest quality cannabis) in the Beka'a valley. The 500 ton crop, worth about US$550m. at current black market prices, was smuggled out *via* fishing ports south of Beirut to Crete and then on to Greece. Syrian container lorries, changing number plates at each border, then ferried its consignment through Communist satellite countries into West Germany. It was then distributed by an Amsterdam drugs pedlar, who, in turn, passed the proceeds back to the PLO's Lebanese 'banker' operating out of Copenhagen.[65]

Hijacking was another lucrative source of income for the PLO. The PFLP ransomed a Lufthansa aircraft in February 1972 for US$5m. The ransom was paid by the West German government so that the 172 passengers on board could be released. In December 1975, a ransom of US$25m. was demanded and paid, for the release of OPEC hostages taken in Vienna.

A proportion of PLO money is spent on providing hospitals, education facilities and pensions—although not for the ordinary Palestinians, only for those families actually associated with the terrorists. Even the Palestine Red Crescent Society makes minimum charges for treating anyone—charges which generally have to be paid before treatment is given. SAMED is an arm of the Palestine terrorist organisation and is directly financed by the PLO. SAMED runs a network of highly efficient businesses manufacturing and produces a wide range of finished consumer goods. It also runs a cinema production company which makes propaganda films. It utilises a mixture of capitalist financing and populist work organisation and was re-established in Lebanon in 1970. By 1978 it employed 2,400 workers in 27 workshops and is largely self-financing with an annual turnover of US$29m. Both SAMED and the Red Crescent Society run profitable business ventures within the refugee camps ensuring that the profits all go to Fatah and the PLO.

What few people recognise, however, is that **the PLO and its constituent groups, receive a steady source of income from their vast investments in the West.** The PLO runs an ever-increasing network of manufacturing facilities and plantations abroad. The reasons for this investment of large amounts of their reserve funds, are two-fold: as an insurance policy, in case the Arab states renege on their agreed annual payments of US$250m. per annum; to bolster the resistance to the Israeli administration of the West Bank and Gaza Palestinians. The reserve fund is thus invested in development projects throughout and beyond the Mediterranean, giving its finances a momentum of their own. The PLO operates an investment portfolio in Wall Street, owns a management consultancy and a contracting company and has investments lodged in Switzerland, France, West Germany, Japan and the United Kingdom. It has investments in high-rise ventures and in real estate, it owns plantations which grow a variety of crops including opiates. The PLO funds businesses throughout the world and has its own incorporated oil company in Western Europe. Within the PLO, Fatah has assumed the main responsibility for the organisation's financial affairs and has its own 'Istithmarat' or investment bureau.[66]

The Palestinian terrorists, 'rely heavily for financial support on donations and dues from Palestinians working in oil countries'. Although many PLO supporters exaggerate the extent and importance of these contributions, such cash does ensure a minimum of funds which can be used for operational expenses; in reality it is little more than petty cash. However, its purpose is threefold: to add to profits, to ensure a constant cash-flow and, more important, to give a semblance of respectability to an organisation which declares that it speaks for Palestinians everywhere. Many of the donations are exacted at

74

the point of a gun or a knife and Palestinians living in the US, UK, France and West Germany are also regularly called upon for contributions. Such contributions also enable the terrorists to keep a register of Palestinians abroad. This register also monitors the response to calls to return for periodic bouts of three-month military training exercises; regularly large numbers of Palestinian students have been recalled from the US, Europe and the Eastern Bloc.

Following the June 1967 War, the terrorists began to collect their own taxes from Palestinians in the southern Lebanon refugee camps until, by 1982, all people whether Palestinian or Lebanese, in terrorist-dominated areas in Lebanon, were paying taxes to the Palestinian terrorists.

The Shiite community of Lebanon were first moved to support the Palestinian terrorists because of the latter's avowed claim to represent the oppressed masses and accordingly were supplied with weapons and equipment. The terrorists replied by bringing with them unmerciful destruction and taking over the predominantly Shiite cities of Tyre and Sidon, using the Palestinian refugee camps as jumping-off points. However, the Shiite–Palestinian alliance did not break down until the terrorists supplanted the local authorities and began to employ extortion and racketeering against the local population. On 16 May 1981, 57 shops were destroyed and 30 others damaged in Sidon costing an estimated US$20m. By 18 May 1982 more than 50 people had died during an overnight battle between the Shiite militia Amal and the terrorists in Beirut. Palestinian terrorist treatment of the Shiite community had been so bad that not only did the Shiite leaders repudiate both the 1969 Cairo Agreement and the Palestinian terrorists, they also made contact with Major Sa'ad Haddad in the south. Following the Israeli invasion in 1982, the Amal leadership publicly welcomed the expulsion of both the terrorists and Syrian forces and stated that they would not only prevent their return, but would hand over any captured terrorist to the IDF. By May 1985, the Shiite ascendancy was powerful enough to take on the Palestinian remnants by initiating a full-frontal attack. They did this on the pretext that too many of the Palestinian gunmen, put to flight in 1982, were returning. The trained Palestinian street-fighters now had to fight for their very existence—they had nowhere to go. Yet within three weeks Amal had subdued

Sabra refugee camp and within four weeks, Shatilla. Casualties were high on both sides and the Bourj-el-Barajnieh camp remained an invincible Palestinian stronghold. It was only the June 1985 hijacking of the TWA jetliner with the US hostages on board that broke the stalemate and allowed an uneasy truce. But the Shiites have served notice on the Palestinians that any thoughts they may have about returning to Lebanon and assuming their pre-1982 position will cost them dearly.[67]

The reason for such a *volte-face* was the total disrespect that the PLO has for life, law and property. The ordinary terrorist was expected to supplement his income by blackmail, ransom and extortion in order to suppress the local Lebanese Moslem population's opposition to the PLO state. Thus, money was extorted through threats, physical violence and theft on a scale never before seen. Between September 1980 and July 1982, the PLO in Lebanon made 40 attacks on foreign diplomats and diplomatic missions, employing kidnap, murder, missile attacks, assassination, grenade attacks, car-bombs, robbery and theft; 30 embassies were attacked and more than 100 diplomatic cars stolen. All these attacks took place in that half of Beirut under Palestinian–Syrian control. In Tyre, Sidon and other coastal townships nearly every family had, at one time or another, been the victim of Palestinian terrorist attacks, including robbery, the confiscation of property, murder and kidnap. Whatever they wanted, they simply took. They showed their 'caring' ways by intimidating and robbing even those people trying to bring supplies of food and water in to sealed-off areas. By the same token, the Palestinian terrorists indiscriminately shelled civilian homes, and committed further atrocities by torturing the local people, many of whom they later murdered. Not satisfied, the Palestinian terrorists smuggled goods and demanded protection money and abducted young children to supplement their ranks.[68]

Thus the PLO and its members within the Palestinian terrorist groups wherever they operate dispense lucrative rewards and horrific punishments; they operate as common violent thugs by controlling instruments of coercion such as banks, law enforcement and judiciary, as well as material resources. Because it appropriates and reallocates those resources to others, it actually becomes a powerful vehicle of upward social mobility for the political aspirants. Similarly, because of the

UN, which together with the Arab world affords the PLO recognition, few are now courageous enough to contest its rôle. This further enhances the status of those who identify and are identified with it, thus projecting them forward as a political élite. What must not be forgotten, however, is that whatever control is achieved over local resources will determine how much of the local resources can be diverted to satisfy the needs of the terrorists. The more that can be diverted in this way, *gratis*, the more money remains available for the purchase of weapons and sophisticated equipment.

*

The result of all this financial and logistical assistance given to the Palestinian terrorists was their dispersal from Beirut to Algeria, Iraq, Jordan, North Yemen, the PDRY, Sudan, Syria and Tunisia which will never allow them the same degree of autonomy they enjoyed in Lebanon. It is notable that with the exception of Iraq, not one Arab oil-producing state admitted the evacuated terrorists to its territory. The PLO and its constituent groups have now become weak and fragmented, unable to place any pressure upon their host governments, and cross-border raids from existing Palestinian bases into Israel will continue to undergo severe curtailment. In such an atmosphere, it is difficult to perceive how the terrorists will be able to maintain their political thrust and status. The terrorist predicament has been neatly summed up: 'There is no way that the PLO can find through its own resources a renewed political life after a military death.'[69]

In internationalising the conflict to include Jews and Israelis everywhere the Palestinian terrorists have been greatly assisted by European terrorist groupings anxious to enjoy the freely available wealth given by the Arab oil-producing governments. Previously, this wealth was available 'on demand' to assist the Palestinian terrorists. Since the Israeli invasion of Lebanon in 1982, the taps have been turned off, leaving the PLO to survive on its investments and any hoarded cash. This in turn, reduces the PLO's prestige, as such collateral is further eaten away in an attempt to preserve its pre-1982 standing. With a reduction in the terrorists' political clout in the region, the Palestinian issue with assume a lesser importance, leaving individual states to manoeuvre in an attempt to find a peaceful accommodation with Israel. In recognition of this the Arafat-dominated PLO factions have become more active in 1985 in a dual attempt to rekindle the flagging spirits of the Palestinians and to bolster Arafat's own waning stature on the international political scene.

PART THREE

Palestinian support for the international terror network

'TERRORISM' IS EMPLOYED with the strategic intent of alienating the masses from the legitimate government until its isolation is both total and irreversible. At the same time, however, terrorism includes a revolutionary strategy that aims to direct unacceptable violence at a representative selection of victims with the single intention of changing both their political behaviour and attitudes. Such 'revolutionary' terrorism seeks to effect a complete and total change within the political system by employing extraordinary forms of violence. The deed therefore becomes more important than the word, and the terrorists view their collective image as that of 'the chosen few'. Their claims to be either liberation movements or guerrilla groups engaged in a war of liberation, are their attempts to purely inject a previously withheld legitimacy. Thus the primary aim of terrorists is to induce terror into entire populations, specific societal sectors or individuals—but always to choose innocent people as their victims, those who are unable to fight back, thus adding to the terror value of the act. The exaltation of violence over all other forms of public democratic activities leads to a moral justification of murder for its own sake their code becomes 'the end justifies the means'. Violence is then substituted by terrorists for the entire democratic political process in an attempt to make a country unworkable and assist the spread of the totalitarian state. To this end, terrorism attempts to destabilise and destroy democracy but in turn poses no threat to totalitarian states who deliberately employ terrorism as a means of foreign policy.

Some apologists for the terrorist movement claim that acts of terrorism are aimed at the redress of specific grievances and that terrorism itself is simply 'a weapon of the weak used to fight wars by peoples without armies'. However, Paul Johnson, the English writer and historian noted,

Terrorism and its condonation, even encouragement, by legal governments is the greatest evil of our age, a more serious threat to our culture and survival than the possibility of thermonuclear war or the
rapid depletion of the planet's natural resources.... Civilisation not
only has a right but a positive and imperative duty to defend itself. We
are the beneficiaries of the past, and, more importantly, the trustees of
the future.[1]

This being so, it is important to recognise that terrorism often
saps the will of a civilised society to defend itself, and this in
turn leads to governments entering into negotiations with terrorists usually in the form of ransoms and the release of convicted criminals. Such actions not only accord the terrorists the
rights, advantages, status and legitimacy of negotiating partners, but in all cases, the inevitable result is to concede some of
the terrorists' demands.

Terrorism is not a new phenomenon but what is new is the international nature of terrorism—a development aided by
modern technology. Accordingly, many terrorist groups have
international links, so that violence is employed for political
purposes with the intention of influencing attitudes and behaviour of a pre-selected group in a wider range than the immediate victims—the ramifications of which transcend national
boundaries.

**The central perpetrator of international terrorism is
the Palestine Liberation Organisation** and its constituent
groups. The PLO is not only the one major destabilising factor
in the Middle East (due to its declared desire for statehood); it is
the single most important factor in the attempts by international terrorists to destabilise the Western democracies.
Such attempts, although both preposterous and illegal, have
their defenders who refer, for the purposes of comparison, to
Jewish terrorism in pre-Israeli Palestine. Such a comparison is
ill-considered, and untenable. Jewish terrorist groups, not only
had the support of the population, but also in the main confined
their attacks to military establishments and personnel. In contrast international terrorism today preordains its targets as
innocent civilians, which include women and children and the
old. The vast majority of terrorist acts carried out by the
Palestinians have *not* been against Israeli military or even

government personnel, but against tourists, children and other civilians. Similarly, **the phenomenon of international terrorism occurred simultaneously with the PLO's declared aim of embracing global terrorism.**

The chief recipients of Arab assistance are Fatah and the PFLP. It takes the form of finance, arms, safe havens for wanted terrorists, training camps and diplomatic support. The PLO acts as agent for both government and private arms dealers simply because it has the organisational and administrative structures to do so. Thus its offices serve as clearing houses for arms transfers between the suppliers and other terrorists, as well as organising training and tactics for terrorist groups on a global basis. However, not all the weapons used are provided as the result of commercial transactions. Terrorists often obtain weapons by theft. Automatic rifles stolen from US army bases in Europe have appeared in the hands of Venezuelan and Palestinian terrorists as well as the IRA. Between 1971 and 1974, the number of weapons stolen was enough to arm and equip ten battalions totalling approximately 8,000 men. There are now more rifles being produced throughout the world than there are soldiers to fire them.[2]

Weapons used for terrorist operations must be compact and easily concealed, simple to use and man-portable. Favourites with the international terrorist community are the Sten gun and other light, compact sub-machine guns (SMG) such as the US produced M10 which fires 1,090 deadly rounds per minute. Heavier weapons like the M60 GPMG and anti-tank rockets such as the Soviet made RPG-7 together with the SAM-7 and other anti-aircraft missiles are favourites of the Red Brigades and are supplied *via* Lebanon. Many of these weapons, sold by private dealers to legitimate states, eventually find their way into the black markets of Paris, Beirut, Lisbon, Brussels, Amsterdam and Rome.

While the extent of assistance given to the PLO by Arab states has already been noted, what is not so well known is **the tremendous logistical support given to the Palestinians by the USSR** and other Communist countries throughout the world. **The USSR uses the Palestinians not only to ensure the continued instability of the Middle East region, but also as a conduit for supplies to Marxist-oriented terrorist groups throughout the world.** Expediency ensures strange bedfellows—but none stranger than the heads of Arab states, whom the Soviets would like to see ousted, and the world's pre-eminent Communist state espousing doctrines which devout Moslems regard as anathema. The answer to this dichotomy lies in the fact that **Soviet and Arab support for international terrorism is founded on a shared attitude of common antagonism towards liberal and democratic states and institutions.** So antagonistic are some Arab states towards Western democracies, that direct aid is given to terrorist groups like the IRA, the South Moluccans, the Japanese Red Army, the Italian Red Brigades, the German Baader–Meinhof Gang and the Dutch Red Help Organisation.[3] All terrorists, whether from left or right persuasions, share a hatred of democracy, a love of street confrontation together with violence for its own sake, and a propensity for terrorism. All extremist groups have strong traditions of assassination and they are indiscriminate in this aim. What is terrifying, however, is that terrorists are now displaying a marked tendency to step beyond individual assassination into the realms of mass slaughter as seen at Lod Airport and during the Munich Olympics in 1972. Contract killers—the best known being Carlos—are increasingly employed by terrorist groups throughout the world. These sub-human assassins, both men and women, are paid by such groups—as well as governments—as enforcers of policies.

Since 1968, there has been a twenty-fold increase in attacks using small arms, while bombing represents more than 56 per cent of reported terrorist attacks. Kidnapping and hostage-taking has also dramatically increased in incidence since 1968. Between 1968 and 1981 the US Government estimated that there were 94 incidents of US businessmen being taken hostage—the 1981 figure alone was 22 per cent of the total. The second-highest group at risk prove to be UK citizens.[4] The consequence of global terrorist incidents reveal that in over 3,000 cases more than 2,000 people were killed and 5,000 wounded: 1,750 of the killed and wounded were US nationals.[5]

I SOCIO-ECONOMIC DEPRIVATION—A LINK
WITH TERRORISM

The growth of international terrorism has gone hand in hand with the Western European economic situation. It is a fact that societies which undergo severe socio-economic strains look to minorities as scapegoats for the failures of the system. Italy is a prime example of a country which has been suffering such a plight since 1945, and since 1971 Western Europe began to face much the same problems. Unemployment, recession and inflation, severely strained the resources of cities which found it increasingly difficult to cope with large influxes of workers who had turned their backs on the countryside. From 1973 onwards, these socio-economic conditions have been exacerbated and intensified because of the Arab-created oil 'crisis'. Indeed, a parallel may be drawn with the 1981 and 1985 urban riots in the UK.

European crime-rates have peaked as more and more individuals have begun to disregard the law in an attempt to maintain their living standards. Simultaneously, recruits to terrorism have increased in direct proportion to the deepening socio-economic crisis. Prior to the last decade, terrorists generally drifted into such activities out of a sense of commitment and idealism, whereas from 1971 onwards, terrorism saw an increase in recruits from the criminal fraternity. Thus, close links were forged between both terrorists and criminals which resulted in many terrorist groups being seduced from their ideological goals, lured by quick and virtually effortless material gain from criminal activities. The continuance of their public espousal of the original ideological goals is at worst a seeking to legitimise their crimes and at best, purely empty justification.

The PLO spearheaded the drive towards global terrorism and its main driving force is propaganda used as an essential weapon. Issam Sartawi, one of the PLO's representatives in Europe, remarked that the main thrust of PLO propaganda was to stress the economic and political strategic difficulties between the USA and Europe in an attempt to alienate European states from the US. In fact, the PLO and its allied groups saw America as the major obstacle to obtaining its aims in the Middle East and was therefore quite prepared to employ the terror-tactic in Europe, hoping that the less resilient European states would capitulate to Palestinian demands and put considerable diplomatic pressure on the USA. To this end, in 1981 after President Reagan condemned both terrorists and guerrillas, Yasser Arafat in a vitriolic rejoinder threatened retaliation against US bases. He stated:

We are a great revolution that can never be intimidated. We have connections with all revolutionary movements around the world, in Salvador, in Nicaragua—and I reiterate Salvador—and elsewhere in the world.[6]

This was a continuation of Arafat's attempts, begun in the early 1970s, to focus attention on the USA as the major enemy of world 'revolution'. In 1979 and 1980 Arafat threatened to employ terrorism against US interests on a world scale. He continued his threat that should the US attempt to control Arab petroleum resources militarily in the event of the Gulf states collapsing in revolution, he, Arafat, would set them ablaze. Always implicit in his threats was that other terrorist groups throughout the world would be used in a co-operative and combined effort to force the US into an isolationist stand.[7] Throughout the world, there is only one country totally committed and prepared to face the PLO and refusing steadfastly to give it any semblance of legitimacy by negotiating with it. That country is Israel, and the full force of international terrorism is used against her.

II THE PLO'S GLOBAL ASPIRATIONS

Initially, the PLO was a small organisation which operated solely against Israel. However, by the mid-1970s, it had grown into the 'principal co-ordinating, logistic and supply centre' for both anarchistic and terrorist groups on a global basis. The phenomenal growth was not only because of the substantial financial backing but also due to the extra-territorial status and assistance given to the PLO by Jordan until 1970 and afterwards by Lebanon and other Arab states. In return for co-operation and aid, the PLO helped to finance the activities of radical underground groups throughout the world. In the Middle East alone, the PLO has disbursed more than US$300m. to various subversive movements. Thus any small terrorist cell could rely on finance from Fatah—or, indeed, from any one of the other major terrorist groups. During its expansion, **the PLO attained a pivotal role in international terrorism** simply because no other single group has trained and equipped so many other terrorists and no other group has been so effective in achieving the amount of media coverage. Similarly no other group has been so successful in intimidating both governments and institutions and therefore **the PLO became the organisational centre for several diverse Western terrorist groups.**

PLO unity at the Palestine National Council meeting in March 1983, was only possible because of its ejection from Beirut. This meant that the prime short-term objective of the PLO was simply to hold their organisation together. The perennial problems of political and ideological disunity within the PLO is exacerbated by religious divisions. The PFLP, for example, is headed by Christians and has an overwhelming Christian membership. It also carries on a Christian political tradition, borrowing heavily from like movements outside the Middle East. Thus both Christians and heretical Moslems—outside the mainstream of Middle Eastern societal forces—are normally drawn to radical, extreme and secular ideologies in an attempt to transcend sectarianism in the Islamic Middle East.[8] The PFLP has the strongest ties to other international terrorists. **George Habash,** the group's leader, firmly **believes that moderate Arab régimes should be overthrown and that terrorism should extend to Israel's allies—particularly the US.** To this end, the PFLP has strong links with the Japanese Red Army (JRA), the Baader–Meinhof gang (BMG) including the Red Army Faction (RAF), the Tupamaros guerrillas in Uruguay and also with Cuba. In mid-1978, Charles Russell, then chief of the Acquisitions and Analysis division within the USAF Directorate of Counter-intelligence, linked 14 countries with the international operations of the PFLP. He disclosed that in PFLP international operations, more West German nationals had been involved than Palestinians.[9] The PFLP is largely financed by Iraq, owing to the links of one of its founders, Wadi Haddad. He forged the links that the PFLP has with the Provisional Wing of the Irish Republican Army (PIRA), the JRA, the Junta de Coordinacion Revolucionara (an umbrella organisation of South American revolutionaries) and with the Baader–Meinhof Gang. Haddad was also a good friend of the former President of Uganda, Field Marshall Idi Amin Dada. **The PFLP** under Haddad and other Palestinian groups, had **actively participated in Amin's atrocities.** Documents found in 1979 prove that the **PFLP also trained Amin's**

murder squads. Other strong links include Algeria and Libya where the PFLP are fêted in preference to other Palestinian groups.[10]

After the 1973 Yom Kippur War, the Palestinians were in a position to firmly and finally believe that substantial strides towards statehood could be gained through diplomacy. As preparations began for the Geneva negotiations, the Rejection Front was born. In order to succeed in diplomatic circles, the PLO decided that it had to change its tactics: its public image needed to acquire an aura of statesmanship. This public image was amply aided by the Western media.

But plans to export Palestinian terrorism began to appear dubious to those in the upper echelons of the PLO. Accordingly, Arafat's Fatah group pulled out of Europe, leaving it exclusively to Habash, Haddad and the PFLP. Whereas Arafat was publicly—if not privately—prepared to imply eventual acceptance of some sort of Zionist entity in the region, Habash was not. He was also unconcerned as to whether or not the actions of the PFLP would act as the catalyst for the Third World War. Naturally, however, as time went by and no tangible steps towards the goal of statehood were achieved, Arafat reintroduced **the exportation of Palestinian terrorism into Europe** which reached a height prior to Israel's invasion of Lebanon. Between 24 July 1981 and 6 June 1982, Palestinian terrorists attempted more than 150 terrorist acts within Israel and the southern Lebanese enclave of Major Sa'ad Haddad, and against Jewish or Israeli targets in Rome, Vienna, Paris, London, Athens, Antwerp, West Berlin, Istanbul and Limassol in Cyprus. In all, 35 people were killed and 432 wounded by artillery shells, land mines, explosive devices, hand-grenades, guns and knives. There were also 90 incidents of kidnapping, shooting or beatings against UNIFIL personnel in southern Lebanon.

Following the expulsion of the Palestinians from Jordan Black September was formed. This vicious organisation was headed by Salah Khalaf (code-named Abu Iyad) and determined to hit *any* Israeli targets. It also came under the aegis of Fatah and all its missions and targets were approved by Arafat. But in order to export terrorism, Black September needed a European director; Hassan Salameh (code-named Abu Hassan) was chosen and directed to Switzerland from where he commanded hand-picked teams of super-secret death squads from both Fatah and the PFLP. Salameh collaborated closely with Wadi Haddad's lieutenant, Mohammed Boudia. Boudia was a long-time Communist and PFLP European coordinator. It was Salameh who travelled to Sofia to meet with Black September leaders in order to finalise the plans for the Munich Olympic massacre. Abu Daoud, the leader of the Black September team was also in Bulgaria purchasing weapons. In May 1980, the leader of Black September was ousted from the PNC because of his alliance with anti-Arafat forces in Syria and Libya. Immediately after the expulsion, Salameh began a five-month tour of Eastern Europe, the Gulf Emirates, Kuwait, Tunisia and Libya. He managed to collect US$40m. to finance independent actions and began by backing the Lebanese Shiite Amal group. Following several successful terrorist actions, Salah Khalaf was financed by Libya and to this end, in 1981, he allied himself with the Al-Thawra group (The Revolution) led by Taysir Hassan, Abdul Karim and Hawdi Abdul Said. This group had developed **links** with the **neo-Nazis** in both West Germany and France.[11] Thus, the network built up by Black September underwent a split, increasing the effectiveness of the more extreme Al-Thawra whilst reducing that of Black September.

In September 1967, George Habash formed the PFLP. Shortly afterwards, the wealthy Italian publisher Giangiacomo Feltrinelli, began to urge him to **internationalise the conflict with Israel with the distinct aim of sowing panic not just in the Middle East but also in Europe and the rest of the free world.** Habash saw the advantages of such action, and accordingly, began his preparations on the grounds that killing one Jew far from the battlefield was much more effective than killing 100 Jews on the battlefield.

His first exploit was the sending of Palestinian terrorists to Rome in 1968, with the express instructions to hijack an El Al aeroplane. The mentor and organisational genius of this emerging international terrorist network was not Habash but Dr Wadi Haddad.

Habash was now preoccupied. His main targets were—and still are—the moderate Arab oil-producing states. The cutting of the oil supply to the West has always been regarded as a last-ditch defensive measure by Habash and his supporting Palestinians. In 1980, the PLO as a group threatened to take

89

concerted and co-ordinated action to cut oil supplies to the West by blowing up tankers in the Straits of Hormuz. In November of the following year, this strategy was taken a stage further. A plan was put into operation to blow up a North Sea oil platform. However, the Norwegian police at Stavanger received a tip-off to this effect and informed the UK. The 300-man SBS, Commachio Squad of the Royal Marines at Arbroath in Scotland was put on alert and in all likelihood, deterred the Palestinians from going ahead with the attack.

As the terrorists are now an important element in the struggle for control of the Middle East oil supplies, the possibility of subversion in Saudi Arabia and the more vulnerable targets of the smaller Gulf Sheikhdoms assumes a greater degree of importance. These Sheikhdoms and Saudi Arabia are aware of the possibilities and so contribute substantially to terrorist funds in buying an immunity which is never guaranteed. Some months after the fall of the Pahlavi dynasty in Iran, Saudi Arabia was threatened by PLO emissaries with a similar fate if it did not take action against US interests within its borders. The PLO in April 1979 had already made an unsuccessful attempt to blow up a fuel storage depôt in West Berlin and had to rethink its policy regarding attacks on Western oil supplies. In fact **they came to the decision that the most effective method of reducing—or indeed cutting off—supplies to the West was to concentrate its activities against the Arab oil-states.**

III   FORGING LINKS WITH EUROPEAN TERRORIST GROUPS

Once the decision to export terrorism from the Middle East to Europe had been made, **the Palestinians were sought out by both extreme left and right wing European terrorist groups.** Feltrinelli provided Habash and the PFLP with arms by the ship-load **in the hope that a Communist revolution would be hastened.** Likewise, **neo-Fascist groups on Colonel Gadhafi's payroll did the same because of the common bond that existed, anti-Semitism.** Once contacts and agreements had been made, the very best of the Red International's terrorist fighters went into the Palestinian's Middle East camps for training, while Palestinians went into Black International training camps in the Spanish Pyrenees and nor-

90

thern Italy. The latter were sent to a special camp set up in Malga Croun in the Trento region by the Avanguardia Nazionale group with the specific intention 'to forge young Palestinians'.[12] The initial result of this cooperation was an horrific escalation of terrorist activities, with oil pipelines and tankers being blown up in the Middle East, assassinations in Egypt, airport massacres in Israel and the Olympic massacre in West Germany. The JRA, the Red Brigades (RB), BMG and RAF, PIRA, several Latin American groups as well as the Iranian fedayeen all began to assist Fatah and the PFLP and each other in the carrying out of operations, training, the sharing of weapons and in organisational support. In return, **all the Palestinian groups passed on their knowledge and expertise to nearly the whole of the international terrorist network.** At the same time, the Rejection Front, spearheaded by Libya and Syria, began to mount its own multinational terrorist hits out of South Yemen.

The *mélange* of international terrorist contacts between the various European groups and in turn, between them and the various Palestinian groups was formalised at a secret terrorist summit meeting at Baddawi Refugee Camp, just outside Tripoli, in 1972. Present at this meeting were representatives from the Red Brigade, ETA, PIRA, JRA, BMG, RAF, Tupamaros and other Latin American groups. It was here that Habash unequivocally stated that, **'Palestine has joined the European Revolution; we have forged organic links with the revolution of the whole world.'**[13] The network of international terrorism was further consolidated at a series of clandestine meetings in Dublin, between December 1973 and January 1974. The meeting's function was to organise intergroup courier routes, methods of weapons procurement, the establishment of safe-houses, inter-group exchanges and frontier escape routes amongst other items. During these meetings, at which they were strongly represented, the PFLP offered training facilities in Lebanon and proposed to donate US$1m. worth of modern weaponry for distribution throughout the European terror network. Needless to say, the PFLP offer was quickly taken up, much to Habash's pleasure. (**Habash's men,** together with Fatah's members **received advanced training in the USSR.**) By 1976, the PFLP, PDFLP and PFLP-GC were the main co-ordinators of international terror within the

Palestinian movement. One of the devices employed by these groups was to 'create' hitherto unheard of groups who would accept responsibility for certain terrorist acts, thus confusing the Western security forces. One such group, 'The Sons of South Lebanon' (SOSL) was specifically created so that Arafat and other Palestinian leaders could justifiably claim that it did not form part of the PLO. The SOSL accepted responsibility for a planned operation to massacre passengers at Orly Airport in Paris, which had been foiled by the French Deuxième Bureau. It is now known that SOSL was linked to the PFLP and financed by Iraq. Significantly, it has not been heard of since!

In order to extend and firm-up his international links, Habash attended two meetings in October 1978. The first was held in Yugoslavia and comprised representatives from both Central and South American terrorist groups together with the Red Brigades and PIRA. The second meeting took place in Portugal and included representatives from PIRA, the Red Brigades and ETA. All these groups held radical left-wing ideologies and were in total accord with Habash's views. Eventually, on 14 April 1981, **Arafat** while in Damascus, **declared that all Palestinians were obliged to support all revolutionary movements anywhere in the world which were aimed against the USA.** This statement clearly revealed the connexion between the USSR and radical Arab states on the one hand while on the other, the USSR and Cuba. Both Cuba and the USSR strongly back Latin American liberation organisations, whereas both the USSR and the radical Arab states back the Palestinians. These links explain other connexions: the relationship between the Palestinians and the Revolutionary Co-ordination Group of Latin American terrorists; Carlos' activities as a hitman not only for Gadhafi but for Naif Hawatima's group.[14]

Despite Arafat's posturing, he was never free to pursue peace through diplomatic means beyond what was acceptable to both the USSR and Marxist-oriented groups within the PLO. One classic example of this diathesis took place on the eve of the European Economic Community's Conference at Venice. The nine member countries were, as a result of Arafat's lobbying, preparing to recognise the PLO. Members of Fatah kidnapped him and then proceeded to hold its first conference since 1971. At this conference, Fatah called unanimously for physical annihilation of Israel and the total liquidation of the 'Zionist entity'. Although Arafat later declared that the resolution had not been adopted by a majority of the Congress, the result was that 'the nine' were unable now to recognise the PLO and put forward what amounted to a diluted statement which was of no help to anyone.[15]

IV   THE TRAINING CAMPS OF INTERNATIONAL TERROR

The escalation of international terrorism and the increasing incidence of international 'hit' groups, is directly related to the number of European terrorists undergoing training in Palestinian camps. In 1969, about 200 such terrorists were being trained in both Fatah and PFLP camps. Within three years, they were to be found in Palestinian training camps as far afield as Baghdad and Algiers. In order to increase their profits and off-set the training costs, the PFLP began to charge high prices for training. The PLO on the other hand charged much lower prices for training as the bulk of oil-state money went directly to the mainstream groups of the PLO. However, despite the level of charges, both the PFLP and its allied groups including Fatah, expected to be repaid in armed propaganda. Thus, a terrorist having undergone training in a Palestinian camp would, on returning to his group, ensure that a terrorist act was perpetrated which would not only draw attention to his own cause, but also to that of the Palestinians. For example, a Nicaraguan was killed on 6 September 1970 while assisting Leila Khaled to hijack an El Al aeroplane at London's Heathrow airport. Other examples followed and were the birth-pangs of the first multi-national terrorist group.

Towards the end of the 1970s, however, the Palestinians' importance to the international terrorist movement had become much more specialised. In 1979, the Fatah camps began to instruct selected terrorists in bacteriological and chemical warfare techniques and in 1980 began to put on courses in assassination, demolition and computer fraud. These courses were all held at camps in the PLO's southern Lebanon enclave. At the same time, the PDFLP was looking for fresh terrorist links and began training Corsican Separatists; the results of which were to be heard and seen in 1982 and 1983 as a wave of explosions shook France and Corsica. In 1981, the PLO representative in

London, Nabil Ramlawi, created firm links with the New Communist Party in Britain, while **PLO camps began to provide training—particularly for PIRA terrorists**—for attacks on offshore oil rigs and nuclear power plants.[16]

Apart from increasing its destabilising potential in the Middle East, **by the mid 1970s the PLO was the pivot of international terrorism, being totally involved in it.** It had plotted assassinations, *coup d'état* and subversion in many countries including Turkey and Lebanon; and was also responsible for assassinations in most of the European capitals. Many of these terrorist acts were carried out by local terrorists acting on behalf or together with, the Palestinians in a multinational operation. In the mid-1970s, members of the Dutch Red Help (DRH) terrorist group began training at the PFLP camp in South Yemen, together with Norwegian, Swiss and Belgian volunteers. **By 1979 the number of foreign nationals who had received training at nine Palestinian camps, numbered nearly 2,000.** The nine training camps were those of Hamouriyah and the 'September 17th' group base both near Damascus in Syria; the four Lebanese camps of Burj el-Barajnieh, Shatilla, Katirmaya and Damour; the Ras Hilal camp in Libya; the Sani-San camp near Baghdad in Iraq; and at Socotra, the PFLP training base in South Yemen. Of the nearly 2,000 foreign nationals, **580 were Iranians—followers of Ayatollah Khomeini;** more than 300 trained in Syria, near Beirut in Lebanon and in Libya were Turks; 44 PIRA terrorists were trained at Burj el-Barajnie and Damour and in Socotra; also trained were 32 Red Brigades members and 21 members of the JRA together with 113 Spanish terrorists (mainly from ETA) the latter of which were trained in Syria. **In November 1980,** Western Intelligence sources had received evidence that **more than 2,000 non-Arab terrorists were undergoing training at PLO camps.** In June 1980, of the 519 non-Palestinians undergoing training at the Syrian PLO (Fatah) Hamouriyah camp, nearly 400 were non-Arabs. The exact figures were as follows: 4 West Germans, 6 Italians, 4 JRA members, 3 ETA members, 28 Argentinian Montoneros, 12 Brazilians, 130 Armenian Turks, 130 Africans, 32 Asians (mainly Filipinos) and 170 Iranians. Hamouriyah is a relatively small camp and nowhere near the size of the PFLP Socotra camp. Thus there must have been more than 5,000 non-

94

Arabs undergoing training—more than twice the official figure. By August 1982, there were **more than 1,000 foreigners serving with the Palestinian terrorists in Lebanon, including IRA** and JRA members, and Black terrorists as well as several hundred Pakistanis and Bangladeshis. Carlos and ten ETA terrorists, were in fact trapped in Beirut by the Israeli advance.[17] They were saved only by the intervention of President Bourghiba of Tunisia who offered Arafat and his Force 17 supporters a haven south of Tunis.

V   TERROR AND CRIME

The Palestinians have been heavily involved in the Lebanese cannabis trade, particularly prior to the Israeli invasion, and because of the high profit margin and the low risk factor. It proved to be a natural development employing as part of the distribution network, the Italian Red Brigades, ETA, PIRA and the anti-Castro organisation Omega-7 in the US. They were aided in their distribution of the drugs by the close criminal links of some of the groups. The Red Brigade had positive links with both the Neapolitan Camorra and the Mafia which handled most of the Southern European distribution side. This was further enhanced by the Brigades' firming up their links with the Calabrian Ndragheta. Through the Red Brigades, the PLO entered into a positive understanding with the Mafia. This understanding grew into maturity once **PIRA firmed-up its own Mafia links in Boston.** Thus the US and Italian and Sicilian Mafia were linked together with the RB, so that the **PLO and PIRA developed the largest drug-smuggling network in the world.** The operation was simple: the PLO shipped cannabis to the Red Brigades who, in turn, handed it over to the three criminal organisations and the distribution was handled by them in Europe. As far as the US was concerned the PLO shipped the cannabis to Ulster where PIRA and OIRA (Official Wing of the Irish Republican Army) took over. Their responsibility was to ship the cannabis to the USA where the Boston Mafia took over its distribution.[18]

VI   NEO-NAZISM/PALESTINIAN CONNEXION

The World Conference of neo-Nazi organisations was held in

Barcelona on 2 April 1969. It attracted 100 delegates from both Europe and Latin America, together with two Fatah recruiters. The Conference adopted a resolution to assist the PLO in every possible way. **Two former SS officers were dispatched to Palestinian camps** on the Conference's authority. They were Erich Altern (code-named Ali Bella), a former regional leader of the Gestapo's Jewish Affairs Section in Galicia, and Willi Berner (code-named Ali ben Keshir), **a former SS officer at Mauthausen Concentration Camp.** Berner had also commanded the Brandenburg Waffen-SS Division and he was now recruited by the PFLP to command their training camp at Basra in Southern Iraq; Altern went to a Fatah camp in Lebanon.

VII COMMUNIST/PALESTINIAN LINK

The Palestinians have always been happier about their connexions with the extreme left becoming public as there is no discordance between ideologies. Perhaps the strongest links have existed between the Palestinians and the Italian Red Brigades and particularly between George Habash of the PFLP and Giangiacomo Feltrinelli. In late 1968, Feltrinelli borrowed US$1m. from the Italian financier Guiseppe Pasquale in order to purchase a shipload of weapons for Habash in Beirut. He told Pasquale that the money was required to finance the production of some films. Later he told Pasquale that the money could not be paid back, and the latter went bankrupt. As it happened, the Israeli navy intercepted the ship.

Feltrinelli had always wanted to internationalise terrorist activities and had approached Habash just after the PFLP had been formed. In order to firm up the links between the PFLP and the Red Brigades contacts, Feltrinelli organised one of the first ever international terrorist summits in a Florentine Jesuit college in early October 1971. Sixteen underground terrorist groups were represented there including the IRA, ETA, the Argentine Trotskyist ERP, and the other Palestinian factions. At the Jesuit Stensen Institute Summit, Negri, one of the left's leading lights, gave a report on the Palestinian resistance and called for other summits to be held. Further summits were indeed held in Beirut, Tripoli, Dublin and Belgrade.[19]

Feltrinelli's links with other Marxist-oriented terror groups

throughout the world were institutionalised into 'The Organisation'. Headquartered in Zurich, it offered links, safe-houses,
papers, documents and the other paraphernalia essential for
terrorists. Following the 1971 Summit, it was agreed to set up a
new continental headquarters at the Eco-Libro Bookshop,
Engelstrasse 42, also in Zurich. The following year the bookshop superseded the Red Brigade's own Operaio Zurich International Office. It tied together operations carried out in Italy,
Greece, West Germany, France, Spain and Ireland, both North
and South, and also in Lebanon, Iraq, Syria, South Yemen and
Egypt. The leaders of the new 'Organisation' were all bookshop
workers and included Carlo Fiorini, Giangiacomo Feltrinelli
and Antonio Negri. Its links with the Middle East were only
discovered when 28 terrorists of assorted nationality were
arrested in Cairo, trying to disrupt the initial Egyptian–Israeli
Peace talks.

In December 1971, Feltrinelli felt the need to brush up his
own self-taught terrorist skills and accordingly boarded an
aeroplane in Milan *en route* for Cairo. Once there, he flew
onward to the Jordanian capital, Amman, and then made his
way to a PFLP terrorist training camp. On his return, he was so
enamoured with his experience that he made contact with left-
wing terrorist groups in both Italy and France, in an attempt to
recruit young potential terrorists for George Habash's PFLP
training camps. The French authorities did not relish such activities openly taking place on their soil and so promptly threw
him out of the country.

The linkage between the Palestinians and Feltrinelli's 'Organisation' was not just of benefit to the Palestinians. Instructors from Habash's PFLP training camps were brought into
their Swiss and Northern Italian training camps, while Antonio Negri successfully negotiated terms with Habash to have his
terrorists trained in the Lebanon. Thus, **by 1972,** there were
**more than 100 Italian terrorists who had been trained at
camps all over the Middle East. In 1975, more than 1,000
Red Brigades terrorists fought** with the PFLP at the battle
of Tel-al-Zatar **in Lebanon.**[20]

There were links, however, with other Arab Palestinian
groups and the Red Brigades; these included Abu Nidal and
Fatah. The Red Brigades, however, preferred to enter into joint
operations only with the PFLP, while using other Palestinian

groups to provide back-up assistance. In November 1979, several Red Brigades and PFLP terrorists were arrested in Rome on their way to blow up an El Al aeroplane with Russian hand-held Strella missiles. In Verona, in March 1982, it was finally established that the weaponry used by the Red Brigade's group who kidnapped US Brigadier-General James Dozier, had been smuggled to the terrorists by Fatah *via* the diplomatic pouch of an Arab embassy. In late 1979, the PFLP managed to smuggle into Italy, on board a Lebanese ship, a Soviet-made SAM-7 surface-to-air missile, to be used by the Red Brigade terrorists to attack Israeli aeroplanes. Similarly, the kidnap and murder of Aldo Moro highlighted several other aspects of the international terrorist linkage, including Libyan support both materially and financially as well as that supplied by the PFLP, Fatah and Abu Nidal's group.

The extent of Palestinian help for the Red Brigades was uncovered in 1980 with the arrest of Patrizio Peci, the Turin commander of the Red Brigades, towards the end of 1979. In his testimony, he stated that all the arms reaching Italian terrorists, whether from the left or the right persuasion, with the exception of those taken from policemen and Caribinieri, originated from a single Palestinian distribution centre in Lebanon. Large caches of arms were organised in 1977 and again in 1979, and the Red Brigades acted as arms distributors to other terrorist groups affiliated to the 'Organisation' including ETA, PIRA, the Baader–Meinhof Gang and the RAF. The arms came from the PFLP and were often shipped on the cargo ship *Sidon*, transhipment being organised by the PFLP's Italian agent Saleh Abu Anseh. Anseh was a Jordanian, travelling on a South Yemen passport. Following the arrival of the second cache of arms, Saleh was captured and imprisoned by the Italian authorities on 8 November 1979. Some of the heavy machine guns and explosives were being kept exclusively for the use of Palestinian terrorists in Italy.

VIII   CARLOS, CURIEL AND THE PHILBY CONNEXION

The other Organisation link-man in Europe was Carlos. His name first entered into CIA files in 1969 when Orlando Castro Hidalgo, a Cuban diplomat and former member of Cuba's intelligence service the DGI, defected to the US. He gave the CIA information concerning Cuba's guerrilla training camps and this included the obscure name of Illyich Ramirez Sanchez, a graduate of Camp Matanza just outside Havana. **Sanchez's chief instructor was a KGB official** who used a fake Ecuadorian passport and the alias, Antonio Dages Bouvier. Sanchez's first introduction to members of the PFLP happened while at the Patrice Lumumba University in Moscow where he met Mohammed Boudia. A close aide of Habash, Boudia warmly recommended Sanchez. Boudia went to Moscow on his appointment as the PFLP's chief organiser in Europe, and, following Habash's acceptance of his recommendation, Boudia sent Sanchez to meet Habash and Wadi Haddad. On his way to the meeting, Sanchez toured East Germany, inspecting the newly set up rapid-transit system for both terrorists and weapons. Sanchez, now known as **Carlos,** was in Jordan during Black September, after which he **was assigned by Habash and Haddad to work alongside, his former KGB instructor,** Bouvier, in London. Their assignment was the compilation of lists of Jews to be assassinated in the name of Palestine Resistance. He was then diverted to Paris. On Boudia's death, Carlos met with Haddad in Aden and returned to Paris with the efficient Michel Moukharbal as his second-in-command.[21]

In 1968, Michel Moukharbal, a Lebanese, approached Petra Krause, informing her that he was working for the PFLP and that he needed to secure a supply of weapons for some of his connexions in Europe. He did not mention that he was Carlos' chief aide in Paris. Krause was, at the time, acting as the quartermaster of the 'Organisation'. The weapons were provided and a useful link established, *via* Feltrinelli and Carlos, to the Palestinians during their European terrorist jaunts.

Paris, however, was the nucleus of the PFLP's European network. The suburban villa provided for Carlos at Villiers-sur-Marne with PFLP funds, housed an arsenal of weapons and explosives, many of which came by way of Bulgaria. It also housed a forgery factory and was the nerve-centre of PFLP plans. Also available close-by for back-up service, was **Henri Curiel—a link-man for the international terrorists** who became the top Soviet NKVD agent in Europe and the Middle East. He knew intimately many of the Palestinian leaders including Habash, and needed only to ask and help would be provided.

Henri Curiel was an Egyptian Communist of long-standing. On 5 November 1951, he organised a meeting in Algiers, attended by several North African Communist leaders as well as by representatives of the KGB with whom he was also familiar. In 1954, he became the Algerian FLN's key man in Paris while his **younger first cousin, George Bihar, went on to devastate Britain's Secret Intelligence Service, M.I.6, as the Russian double-agent George Blake.** Bihar had moved into the Curiel family household after his father's death so that he could complete his studies at Cairo University. During and following this period, **Curiel was working for Britain's M.I.6** providing information on pro-Nazi elements in Egypt and, for the French DST, vetting prospective recruits for the Free French. It is thus that one of the NKVD moles in British Intelligence, namely Philby, was able to positively vet Bihar (who was also Curiel's assistant) and permit his entry into M.I.6 in 1944. Curiel's direct personal links with the NKVD—the forerunner to the KGB—did not surface until 1952 in Casablanca. There would have been no concern within M.I.6 about recruiting someone with such an apparently pro-Western and anti-Nazi pedigree. In 1966, having been imprisoned in Wormwood Scrubs prison in London, Blake was spirited away with the help of Sean Bourke of the IRA who died in 1982. **Bourke was under orders from Moscow through Blake's cousin Curiel, Moscow's top terrorist co-ordinator.**[22] In 1962 Curiel resigned from the FLN in order to start up his own terrorist group Aide et Amitié which was in full swing when Carlos arrived in Paris to take over the Palestinian end from the deceased Boudia.

It was Carlos who used all the international connexions at his disposal in order to create a valid terrorist network of international proportions. Each group had its own rôle to play and its actions were closely coordinated with other groups. French, Dutch and Belgians were used to plant bombs and to survey international airline routes and airports, while South American female-terrorists were used to plant and carry booby-trapped devices onto aeroplanes. The Baader–Meinhof Gang, the RAF and German neo-Nazi groups together with the Swiss Anarchists in Zurich were used to acquire specific weaponry, generally adding to the Villiers-sur-Marne arsenal and supplying explosives and explosive devices to ETA and PIRA. Henri

Curiel's group Aide et Amitié was increasingly employed in the creation of forged passports for the JRA, South American terrorists and South Korean 'freedom fighters'. Carlos' transportation was organised by West German and Italian terrorists especially for his international and multinational hit teams, while the Red Brigades supplied a constant stream of stolen passports. Whereas Turkish terrorists smuggled weapons to Carlos from Eastern Europe, the Baader–Meinhof Gang and the RAF relayed cratefuls of weapons brought in by Libyan diplomatic pouches, to and from a variety of European destinations.

Such close liaison gradually developed into the creation of selected multi-national hit teams with members taken from Aide et Amitié, the JRA, PFLP, Fatah and Black September, Nidal's Black June, the Baader–Meinhof Gang and the RAF. An example of this co-operation occurred in July 1974. On 26 July, Furuya Yukata, an active member of the JRA, was arrested by the French police and charged with terrorist activities. Immediately Carlos arranged for three fellow JRA terrorists to be shipped out of Aden to Baghdad and to arrive in Europe *via* Geneva Airport. The Dutch Red Help organisation assisted the three JRA terrorists to occupy the French Embassy at The Hague with weapons supplied by the Zurich Anarchist group and the RAF. Simultaneously, Carlos arranged for the bombing of a left-bank coffee bar and several business establishments in Paris. Once Yukata was freed by the French government, and put on a plane for Damascus with US$300,000 ransom, the Baader–Meinhof Gang whisked the JRA terrorists from The Hague.[23]

Following a brief return to Patrice Lumumba University for some advanced terrorist training, **Carlos** and Moukharbal returned to Paris *via* Libya. There they **received Colonel Gadhafi's promise to pay whatever was necessary to establish** Wadi Haddad with **a centralised command—not just for the Palestinian but also for** the BMG, Revolutionary Cells and the June 2 Movement and all other constituent groups of **the International Terrorist Network.** Wadi Haddad was paying US$3000 per month to revolutionary groups in order to secure co-ordinated action; therefore, he was the controller of the international terrorist network while Carlos supervised the operations.

Carlos, in the meantime, was participating in other active terrorist operations. One notable failure of his occurred during this period in December 1973 when **he personally made an unsuccessful attempt to murder Lord Sieff,** one of the leaders of the Jewish community in London. The contract had been issued by the PFLP. But perhaps his most notorious terrorist act took place two years later on 21 December 1975. On that day, a multi-national hit team supervised by Carlos, held the OPEC Vienna Convention to ransom. The terrorist team comprised members from the PFLP, the JRA and the Baader–Meinhof Gang. Carlos chose his team personally, including within it, Gabriele Kröcher-Tiedemann. She won warm praise from both Carlos and Wadi Haddad as a killer. Only Hans-Joachim Klein—another BMG member of the Team—dissented from this view. He regarded her killing of the elderly Austrian policeman (whom she shot in the back of the neck with her Makarov firearm) as he was making his escape towards the elevator, as nothing more than a gangster killing which had nothing to do with revolution.[24]

With regard to Carlos' brief reign in Paris, one PFLP spokesman referred to him as 'one of our most brilliant agents' and as **the leader of a 'guerrilla network reaching from Europe to the Middle East, South America and the Orient'.** In the only interview Carlos ever gave, he tended to dwell on his own expertise and skirted around the reasons for his being in Paris—probably because to admit to simply being there to carry out Wadi Haddad's orders as they emanated from Aden, is less than glamorous.

IX THE WIDENING OF THE TERRORIST NETWORK

Although the PFLP's links with European terrorist groups did constitute something of a monopoly in the Palestinian movement, Fatah also enjoyed extensive intimate relations with a number of small European terrorist cells. In Cyprus, the leftist EDEK political party in the Greek zone has been involved for many years in the training of both Palestinian and Greek terrorist groups in bases on the island. In the winter of 1976, one of the EDEK luminaries, Vassos Lyssarides, met with Arafat several times in Beirut to discuss the transformation of Cyprus into a jumping-off point for Fatah's operations into both Europe and Israel.

The links between the Turkish People's Liberation Army (TPLA) and the PFLP were firmed-up considerably in May 1971, when the latter sent in instructors to TPLA camps to train young Turks in the art of urban guerrilla warfare, as well as hijackings and other related techniques. The TPLA also undertook the kidnapping of NATO servicemen and the occasional Israeli diplomat as 'partial payment' to the Palestinians for training them. One such example was the kidnap and subsequent assassination of the Israeli Consul together with that of three NATO technicians holidaying on the Black Sea coast. Links became even stronger during Carlos' sojourn in Paris, when the TPLA sent a large contingent to work directly under him. In return the TPLA were given representation in the PFLP's inner circle.

A few days after the fall of the Shah, Hani al-Hassan, a PLO (Fatah) leader stated that Turkey would be the next to explode. To reinforce the authority of this statement, Palestinian terrorists seized the Egyptian Embassy in Ankara, an act which established their ascendancy in Turkey. The government of Prime Minister Bulent Eçevit surrendered at once and recognised the PLO, and his interior minister publicly embraced the Palestinian terrorists on their emergence from the Embassy. Despite being on cordial terms with the Palestinians, Eçevit turned to Colonel Gadhafi of Libya to rescue him from a multi-million dollar trading deficit. However, during this period the various **Palestinian groups were planning a heavy assault on Turkey with large numbers of armed Palestinians infiltrating into the country** in order to link up with TPLA guerrillas. Having achieved the terrorist link-up, they fanned out eastwards towards the Iranian border in the hope that they would be able to foment religious and ethnic warfare and urban violence. 'Military operations' against the Turkish régime were formally announced at a PFLP-organised press conference (held deep in the Sidon Casbah in Lebanon) by hooded male and female Armenian and Kurdish terrorists from Turkey. Throughout the conference they were ringed by supportive Palestinian gunmen. The terrorists praised the Soviet Union and berated the USA for provoking the USSR into invading Afghanistan. The situation in Turkey was only saved by the military taking power, under the leadership of General Evren.

Palestinian links with Armenian terrorists had begun as long ago as 1973 when the first ASALA operations were financed by Fatah. Shortly afterwards, the PFLP gained ascendancy in Turko–Palestinian terrorist circles and firmed up existing loose connexions with left-wing Kurdish and Turkish organisations. As the years went by, so the financial, logistic and material support increased, flowing from Palestinian sources *via* Fatah and the PFLP, and being repaid in kind by ASALA terrorists who have become Palestinian proxies. Hence, the number of ASALA actions mounted, increased proportionately with the support given by the Palestinians. Between 1973 and 1981 ASALA mounted nearly 60 terrorist operations of which only three took place in Turkey. The remainder of ASALA actions took place in the United States (4), Australia (1), the Middle East (6) and Europe (44). Of the European countries, Italy and the Vatican experienced ASALA terrorism 12 times; France 13; Switzerland 6; Spain 3; the UK, the Netherlands and Denmark twice each; and Austria, West Germany, Belgium and Greece once each.[25]

Perhaps one of the most successful of the Palestinian links was with the fanatical Iranian Moslem *fedayeen*. The bonds between the Iranian *fedayeen* and the Palestinians began shortly after the 1967 Six-Day War when Palestinian disillusionment with Arab governments reached a new low—matched only by that of the *fedayeen* for the Shah. By 1971, 45 *fedayeen* terrorists were operating together with the PFLP in the Middle East in a specially constituted 'Palestinian Brigade'. Over the next few years, the PFLP sent several *fedayeen* terrorists to the USSR for specialist training and introduced them to the international terrorist network. However, it was not until 1979, **after the *fedayeen*'s success in Iran, that the PFLP openly acknowledged the help it had given.** In January of that year, Bassam Abu Sharif, the PFLP's chief spokesman, confirmed that **the Iranian terrorists had been given training 'in everything from propaganda to the use of weapons' by the PFLP.** A month later, Fatah spokesman Farook Kaddoumi, confirmed that hundreds of Iranian terrorists had fought alongside the Palestinians since 1969.

One of the most important European links for the Palestinians to cultivate, proved to be that with the Irish Republican Army. This organisation has two 'wings': the more politically

104

oriented 'Official' wing (OIRA) and its more extreme and radical partner, the 'Provisional' wing (PIRA). The latter over the years, has become almost completely independent and divorced from OIRA and is basically a para-military terrorist outfit with its own command structure, paying lip-service to Marxist ideology. It is not only opposed to anything British in Northern Ireland, but also towards the government of Eire and its constitution. Overtly, its aim is to reunite Ireland using whatever means possible and to this end it runs protection rackets, drug-smuggling operations, bank robberies and has, in the past, implemented its own 'liberation' tax. It employs assassination, bombing, arson and murder, together with its notorious 'knee-capping' and 'tar-and-feathering' methods.

Initial contact between Fatah and the IRA took place *via* the PLO staff agent in London who worked out of the PLO office. His job was to work actively against British interests in a myriad of ways while, at the same time, liaising with both neo-fascist and 'red' terrorists and groups. Liaison between the PLO and the IRA was relatively easy considering that many of their methods were identical and that both waged a 'liberation' struggle of sorts. **The IRA's Marxist ideology, however, attracted it more to Habash's PFLP which held similar views.** As links were formed and firmed-up, so mutual assistance began to develop. The PFLP first invited both OIRA and PIRA personnel to the Middle East in 1968 and, on arrival they went into training camps in Jordan. Similarly, the PFLP have also
donated armaments to PIRA terrorists.

At the Baddawi Terrorist Summit in Lebanon, in May 1972, Habash and Haddad allowed PIRA observer status and representation at their inner council meetings. Apart from this, a bilateral pact of mutual assistance was negotiated between PIRA and the PFLP, which was signed at a further international summit held later the same month in Dublin. Two months later saw the PFLP issue a formal 'Declaration of Support' for PIRA and twelve other national terrorist groups. From that time onwards, **PIRA personnel were selected for advanced training in Lebanon and South Yemen at PFLP camps where they were to be instructed by Cubans and East Germans.** In December 1973, as added evidence of the mutuality of relations, not only was further specialised train-

105

ing made available to PIRA personnel in Lebanon, but £1m. worth of modern weapons was donated by Habash to his new-found European ally.

PIRA terrorists continued to receive Palestinian support and training in Lebanon even after the UNIFIL entry into Lebanon. When PIRA began to employ vehicle bombs, two Fatah experts were sent to advise their operatives on the most effective use of this method. In fact, **Thomas McMahon, the PIRA terrorist found guilty of the murder of Lord Mountbatten of Burma in 1979 was taught remote control and bomb-making techniques at the PFLP camp at Sebha,** 180 km south of the Libyan Tripoli.[26]

PIRA and its relatively recent off-shoot, the Irish National Liberation Army have regularly been supplied with arms by Fatah and the PFLP. As far back as December 1972, a ship carrying arms from Fatah's Lebanese repository to PIRA was intercepted by the Belgian authorities in Antwerp. In the August of 1982, members of PIRA and INLA came to Beirut to purchase weapons to replace those discovered by the security forces and to build up stocks for a proposed winter 'offensive'. In 1978, Fatah and the PFLP sent a further ship-load of 5 tons of explosives, arms and ammunition *via* Antwerp which, once again, was apprehended. However, Belgian officials estimated that about US$500,000 worth had already been passed along the pipeline. It has recently been established that weapons sent to certain Arab countries since 1980 by British manufacturers have, in fact, within a year ended up in the hands of PIRA and INLA terrorists in Northern Ireland.

Following the Israeli Peace for Galilee Operation in the summer of 1982, the PIRA weapons began to dry up. The Palestinians now needed every weapon they could lay their hands on. Arab countries which could be counted on to supplement their weaponry now exclusively supplied the Palestinians. But the greatest blow came when the New York-based organisation, NORAID, came under close Federal scrutiny and five members, including the founder, 80-year-old Michael Flannery were charged with conspiracy. **During the trial the defendants openly admitted that they had been actively involved in smuggling guns from the US to Eire for over 25 years.** In desperation, PIRA negotiators tried without success to buy large numbers of Soviet-made weapons including

Kalashnikovs which had been discarded by guerrillas at the end of the Rhodesian civil war in 1980. The following August a PIRA terrorist and a French journalist were arrested at Le Havre trying to smuggle 28 handguns, 12,000 cartridges, 23 lbs of explosives, 2 grenades and 200 detonators to Eire. Despite the setbacks, NORAID money to PIRA was used to purchase weapons which were added to those successfully smuggled into Eire from the United States and elsewhere. At the same time, PIRA's purchasing officers were negotiating for the purchase of surface-to-air 'Red Eye' missiles in the US. In early 1984 the US authorities continued to apply the pressure by arresting individuals attempting to purchase weapons for use by PIRA, by making false declarations on federal weapons forms.[27]

X   FURTHER LINKS BETWEEN TERRORIST GROUPS

The Palestinians, however, did not simply initiate links with existing terrorist groups but also with disaffected and dissatisfied individuals, whom they hoped could be forged into terrorist groups. One country where they felt relatively hopeful of success was Sweden. As early as 12 August 1969, Fatah sent its first batch of 300 disaffected Swedes to its guerrilla training camp in Algeria. The PFLP, meanwhile, entered into a standing agreement with a small group of Swedish Maoists to hide Palestinians between missions. At the same time, PFLP recruitment of individuals continued apace and these recruits were dispatched to PFLP camps to be welded into groups in Jordan and Syria. By 1975, one dissident Irishman, had been contracted to set up a 'rump' Refugee Council in Stockholm which initiated and maintained close relations and support between PFLP terrorists, Iranian *fedayeen* and Chilean terrorist expatriates. These connexions proved extremely useful to Carlos when, on 13 September 1974, the whole JRA hit-team who had occupied the French Embassy in The Hague, were packed off to Sweden to lie low until the chase had died down.

The most successful bonding initiated by the PFLP was with the JRA. So close had the links become that by 1972, Soraya Antonius, wife of the Palestinian historian and secretary of the Fifth of June Society, became an important Beirut conduit through which JRA terrorists could get to see many Palestinian leaders, including Habash. These links, begun in 1968,

107

were initiated by the PFLP and right from the start included the participation of JRA personnel in training exercises at their camps in Jordan. By 1970, JRA members were participating with PFLP terrorists on various international operations—the most horrific of which was the Lod Airport massacre on 30 May 1972. Nearly two years later, the JRA and PFLP jointly attacked a Japan Air Lines plane, hijacking and blowing it up. They also attacked the Japanese Embassy in Kuwait and a Singapore oil refinery, doing considerable damage to the latter. On joint-operations, the PFLP undertook to secure refuge for JRA terrorists and provide specific operational training. At the same time, a Command Centre was created in the Middle East, organised by the PFLP and including representatives from the Baader–Meinhof Gang and the JRA, and solely concerned with supervising and co-ordinating international skyjacking. When the Lebanese civil war broke out in 1975, about 100 JRA terrorists, undergoing training at PFLP camps in Syria and Lebanon, fought alongside the PFLP against both the Lebanese Phalangists and the Syrians.

Another major connexion forged by the Palestinians was with the various terrorist groups in West Germany. The Baader–Meinhof Gang and the Red Army Faction began joint operations mainly with the PFLP in late 1969 when on 12 December, the El Al office in West Berlin and various US Army installations in West Germany were attacked in a co-ordinated joint bombing operation. These groups were led by **Ulrike Meinhof, Andreas Baader and Gudrun Ensslin who, together with other leaders of the BMG, had received training in PFLP camps** in late 1969. At the same time, links were established between the RAF and the PFLP camps when Horst Mahler, the RAF founder, was encouraged to go to PFLP camps in the Middle East for specialist training. However, one of the RAF splinter groups paid an estimated DM10,000 (about US$4000) to the PFLP for training Gabriele Kröcher-Tiedemann.

Similarly, the other services offered by the Palestinians were also costly, the cash going into the coffers of the Palestinian terrorists. In the early 1970s, West German terrorists seeking refuge from international authorities paid DM3,000 to secure refuge of a temporary nature in either Lebanon or Iraq. Ulrich Schmucker paid DM15,000 for explosives and the same amount for small arms, while the Palestinians were charging DM5,000 each for hand grenades and machine pistols.[28]

Clients of the Palestinian terrorists, however, had the added bonus of introductions into the large international terrorist network, and this ensured international co-operation. The BMG and the RAF were particularly indebted to the Red Brigades which at various times provided sanctuary for hunted terrorists in the form of safe houses.

The West German connexion was extremely important for the Palestinians, particularly when Black September were considering assassinating and kidnapping the Israeli athletes at the Munich Olympics. **The forward preparations for this outrage were negotiated by Hassan Salameh, Yasser Arafat's cousin.** It was Salameh who arranged for the ultra-left BMG and RAF to make all the necessary arrangements in Munich and to provide essential back-up services. A preliminary BMG–Black September action was planned as a trial run—the target, also in Munich, was a Jewish old people's home. Following the Olympic massacre, the links were reinforced with Andreas Baader's visit to the Middle East for more consultations on collaboration prospects. And, it was this outrage which introduced the BMG to the Palestinian's Stockholm connexion. The Refugee Council housed the Black September Munich hit-team in Stockholm's Gangsgaten area, both before and after the massacre.[29]

The need for accurate information and impeccable forward planning for the Olympic massacre was great. West German authorities had taken special precautions and had conducted international security consultations with other European governments and security forces; there was extensive security force deployment. Seven thousand six hundred Federal Border Guards were also deployed and severe restrictions were placed on Arabs living in West Germany. Hence the Palestinians needed reliable, accurate sources of information, together with assistance on the ground in order to carry out this atrocity. The massacre itself highlighted two very important considerations for both terrorists and governments: the fact that the West German authorities were caught off-guard and were totally unprepared for such a large-scale public terrorist operation was exacerbated and emphasised; it showed how restricted governments were in the realms of flexibility owing to their dependence on international co-ordination.

In April 1975, the June 2 Movement organised a joint action with the remnants of the Baader–Meinhof Gang. Not having the resources to expedite such an international terrorist action, Wadi Haddad was approached in South Yemen. He not only assisted in working out the plan of attack, but also instructed Carlos to use his Paris organisation to give what assistance he could. Norbert Kröcher, Gabriele's husband, had set up a branch of the June 2 Movement in Stockholm, Sweden, and had decided to lay siege to the West German Embassy there in the hope that some of the terrorists imprisoned in West Germany would be released. The Baader–Meinhof remnants were led by the Heidelberg lawyer Siegfried Haag, who, following the abortive attack on 24 April, fled to Socotra Island.

The height of this Palestinian–West German collaboration came in 1976 with the hi-jacking of an Air France aeroplane which was subsequently flown to Uganda, by way of Benghazi in Libya. In January of that year, Wadi Haddad, Brigitte Schulz and Thomas Reuter made an unsuccessful attempt to hit an El Al airliner at Nairobi Airport with Soviet ground-to-air Strella missiles. In June, it was decided that El Al security was too tight and that one of the other carriers from Jerusalem should be hit. Accordingly, Haddad made arrangements with President Idi Amin Dada to allow the plane to land in Uganda unmolested. These matters were negotiated *via* the **PFLP terrorists already in Kampala who were acting in a dual capacity of Presidential bodyguard cum murder squad.** Athens was chosen as the terrorists' boarding-point because security arrangements were particularly lax. Wadi Haddad and his lieutenant Bouvier (KGB), were both on hand, with the latter taking command of the entire operation. The terrorist force comprised five PFLP and two West German terrorists including Wilfred Böse, leader of the Revolutionary Cells group (a specialist group of Baader–Meinhof veterans). Böse was one of those West German terrorists who had been connected with Black September's Munich massacre four years earlier.

Once in Entebbe, the 78 Jews were separated from the other 168 passengers. This 'selection' and isolation process was accomplished in a similar manner to that used in the Buchen-wald extermination camp. Unfortunately many of the Jews on the flight were camp survivors. This process was further enhanced when the release of the other 90 passengers was nego-tiated. It is to the eternal credit and courage of the Air France pilot that he refused the release of himself and his crew until the 78 Jews were liberated. However, his concern and bravery were not matched by the governments which were negotiating the release of their nationals. Israel stood alone. Haddad and Bouvier escaped but Böse and the remainder of the terrorist squad were liquidated when the Israeli Defence Force rescued the passengers and crew. The importance of the Entebbe rescue was that it was the first dramatic rescue to show a positive governmental response in the war against terrorism, and Israel must take the credit alone. Not only the world, but the terror-ists were also stunned. Fifteen months later this new attitude was confirmed.

The Entebbe set-back, however, did not slow Palestinian and West German terrorists' negotiations on closer collaboration. In early 1977 at a summit meeting in Munich, the Baader–Meinhof remnants, the RAF and the other clusters of terrorists ratified their negotiations and agreed on closer collaboration with the Palestinians, even inviting a Fatah representative to act as 'adviser'. The outcome of this terrorist summit meeting was yet another hijack attempt. On 15 October 1977 a Luf-thansa jet *en route* from Palma to Frankfurt was hijacked and flown to Mogadishu in Somalia. The terrorists demanded the release of eleven Baader–Meinhof and two Black September personnel imprisoned in West Germany. The government response was to send a troop of GSG9 soldiers with two SAS advisers from the UK. The successful attack on the plane ended hijacking as a lucrative pastime for the terrorists.[30]

XII THE NEW EUROPEAN/PALESTINIAN TERRORIST AGREEMENTS

These two instances coincided with other factors to change the nature of the existing collaboration and co-operation agree-ments between German terrorists and Palestinians. Emphasis began to be placed on kidnapping, ransom, and bank robberies and on furthering the links between themselves and other

European terrorist groups. However, the Palestinians, already caught up in the Lebanese civil war, were unable to offer the same assistance in the supplying of munitions and weaponry that they had previously given and had to substantially increase their charges for services rendered. Thus, the cost of terrorism rose sharply and nowhere more so than in West Germany. The West German change of attitude had generated a police offensive which meant that the terrorists were forced to keep on the move. Hence, the terrorists had to increase their money-making activities while at the same time trying to keep the authorities off-balance. They hoped that the general private negotiations between kidnappers and their victims' families would create a quiet but secure source of income, but in order to effect this new emphasis the German terrorists had to ask for operational help from the Italian Red Brigades. Plans to kidnap and murder the West German businessman Hans-Martin Schleyer in 1977 were identical with those involving the Italian statesman Aldo Moro. The Palestinians helped in the Schleyer incident by considerably complicating matters for the authorities when the Padua to Frankfurt jetliner was hijacked in a co-ordinated operation.[31]

Co-operation in 1980 resulted in one West German terrorist trying to place a bomb-laden suitcase on an El Al flight at Zurich airport. Mainly, however, the terrorists planned small multinational raids with hit-teams concentrating on a commonly identified target or simply playing hosts to the roaming Palestinian murder squads that began to appear in Europe and elsewhere in the early 1980s. But this multinational co-operation raised the level of proficiency of the West German terrorists. Weakened by the constant police and security pressure, they had been forced to tighten up on security and had adopted a 'tight-cell' structure. In 1981 a new bombing campaign, spearheaded by the RAF took off, directed at NATO officials and at establishment figures. In November, however, the West German security forces captured three of the terrorist leaders: Brigitte Mohnhaupt Adelheid Schulz, and Christian Klar. This effectively threw the remnants of the BMG and the RAF into disarray. However, over Christmas 1984, a renewed series of attacks began against NATO targets in support of the hunger strike by 39 imprisoned members of the group. In the first month of 1985, more than 25 serious bombing and shooting

112

outrages were perpetrated. It was a reflection of the post-1982 demise of the Palestinians, and the USSR and its surrogates had stepped into the breach.[32]

One other means of co-operation, was for the European terrorists to send personnel to help revive the flagging fortunes of the Palestinians in Lebanon. In 1982, eleven Baader–Meinhof and RAF terrorists were arrested by the Lebanese army. (This was in just one small operation.) However, it has been estimated that **several hundred West Germans actually fought alongside the Palestinians** in their hour of need. Since 1978, Israel has increasingly become the target of the terrorists because, by pressuring the Palestinians, the latter are forced to use all their resources to defend themselves. Hence there is little left for the nihilist terrorists of Europe. The incidence of terrorism has dropped considerably but the use of Israeli targets has increased considerably.

The Argov shooting in London in June 1982 revealed the long-term planning and strategy of Palestinian terrorism. The perpetrators were all members of Abu Nidal's renegade Black June group, who operate out of Iraq. Abu Nidal, their leader, resides at his headquarters at Ramadi, 3 miles west of Baghdad. Following a training programme in Iraq in 1980, Nidal began to organise the planting of 'sleepers' (agents) in various western European capitals. On their arrival in England, the group compiled a hit-list which included among others Sir Immanuel Jacobowitz, the Chief Rabbi; Mr Grenville Janner MP; and Mr Walter Goldsmith. Significantly the name of Nabil Ramlawi, at that time the PLO representative in London, was also on the assassination list. The group also possessed an internal plan of the Israeli Embassy and obtained prior intelligence of Ambassador Argov's acceptance of the Dorchester Hotel's invitation. At their trial, they were all found guilty of attempting to murder Argov and received lengthy prison sentences. Needless to say, links became apparent between this group and ultra right-wing groups in London as well as with PIRA.[33]

XIII   THE LATIN AMERICAN THEATRE

Outside the European theatre, only Latin America proves to be as fertile a ground for Palestinian terrorist co-operation. This is made possible for two basic reasons: firstly, a politico-military advance spearheaded by the oil-rich Arab countries on the Palestinians' behalf and, secondly, a radical leftist subversive military movement exists which allies the groups struggling for 'liberation' in central and southern America with the international terrorist network. It is further fuelled by indigenous Catholic priests espousing 'liberationist theology' to enhance their appeal to the faithful—frowned upon by Paul VI and John Paul II but understood by John Paul I. Since the oil-crisis of 1973/4, the more radical oil-rich Arab countries have put pressure on Latin American countries who are heavily dependent on Arab aid and investment. Their aim is to increase and make more vocal the pro-Palestinian international voices and, to permit the establishment of PLO bureaux within their borders to secure further politico-diplomatic bases for the Palestinians and harness more thoroughly, Nazi, neo-Nazi and Palestinian links. The success of this policy can be seen in the Latin American UN voting patterns since the oil-crisis. Prior to 1973, as a bloc these countries were pro-Israel; now, at most there are only six pro-Israeli (and thus anti-Palestinian) votes. As a counter to this, the US Government sanctioned an interest in borrowing facilities available to this region as a whole.

Political pressure has, however, not always worked. Colombia is anti-Palestinian in its voting despite the fact that, or perhaps because, Colombian M19 terrorists have undergone training in Palestinian camps and have fought with the Palestinian terrorists in Lebanon. By the same token, Brazil has resisted the extreme and constant pressure from radical and reactionary Arab oil states only by permitting the PLO representative to act in a covert form as a member of the local Arab League Bureau Staff. As the PLO and other Palestinian groups are strongly suspected of encouraging and financing local terrorist groups in Brazil, in September 1980 the Brazilian Government refused to sell the Palestinians their missiles. The government was well aware that weapons previously purchased from Brazil by Libya ended up in the hands of Ahmed Jibril's PFLP–GC group.

In Uruguay, the Palestinians still have strong links with the Tupamaros terrorists, while in Chile, active support is given to the Movimiento de la Izuierda Revolucionaria (MIR) terrorists. In early 1982, a group of MIR terrorists underwent training in

Lebanon and then stayed on to fight alongside the Palestinians. This is a similar situation to the one which exists in Argentina where close bonds exist between the Palestinians and the Montonero terrorists. In 1980, two Palestinian-trained Montonero groups infiltrated Argentina with the sole intent of assassinating government officials while in early 1982 several Montoneros were identified fighting against the Israelis in southern Lebanon.

The two countries in which the Palestinians have been most successful have been Nicaragua and El Salvador. **Nicaragua is today the most important Latin American base for Palestinians.** The Frente Sandinista de Liberacion Nacional (FSLN) was first contacted by the Palestinians in 1969 and this resulted in one of the important Sandanista figureheads and leaders, Tomas Borge Martinez (now the Nicaraguan Interior Minister) visiting Arafat some months later in the guise of Fidel Castro's personal emissary to the Middle East. Throughout the decade, visits and financial deals criss-crossed over the Atlantic, culminating in a joint FSLN–PLO treaty pledging mutual assistance, signed in July 1979. The immediate outcome of this treaty was that the PLO sent a plane-load of weapons to the FSLN while the FSLN sent a military delegation to meet Abu Jihad, the PLO and Fatah military chief. The following July, at the conclusion of Arafat's visit to Managua, open diplomatic relations at ambassadorial level were jointly announced by the PLO and Nicaragua; the former opening an Embassy staffed by more than 70 people, nearly ten times more than the number which staffed the former US Embassy! Four months later, Arafat organised a US$10m. grant from the PLO to the Nicaraguan government and in return, three training camps were set up in order to train Salvadoran, Guatemalan and Honduran terrorists, all under Palestinian control.

The Palestinians forged links with terrorists in El Salvador in August 1979, when representatives of the LP-28 organisation asked George Habash for help. The following May, a LP-28 delegation in Beirut was promised arms deliveries and in the July of that year, all the major Salvadoran terrorist groups were represented in Managua during Arafat's 'state' visit when he offered help *via* Shafik Handal. Handal, a Salvadoran of Arab descent, was now the major conduit for the dispersal of

Palestinian aid to the Salvadoran terrorists organised *via* the Salvadoran Communist Party which he led. Much of the Palestinians' general support for the Salvadoran terrorists came in the form of heavy-duty helicopters, transport aircraft and Palestinian pilots, which were used to drop arms and equipment into the bush. Some Palestinians were also infiltrated into El Salvador in order to 'beef-up' the terrorists' resolve as well as their fighting capability.

*

Thus, **by the mid 1970s, a plethora of terrorist groups from four continents had been welded together in a Terror International—a network which was created by the Palestinians, financed by them, and logistically supported by them.** The aim of the network was two-fold: to increase terrorist pressure on Israel directly and, secondly, to increase pressure on Israel's Western allies in the hope that they would become not only more supportive towards the Palestinians' cause, but also more antagonistic towards Israel. To these ends, Arab governments gave both diplomatic and financial support to the Palestinians. However, **a more covert aim resulted in aid from Communist countries flowing in the direction of the Palestinians; the intention of which was to overthrow and replace Western-oriented governments with Marxist ones through a process of destabilising Western societies.** Habash has always intended **to overthrow the Middle-Eastern monarchies, which was in accord with Moscow's desires. It was a bonus for the Soviet Union that the Palestinians were prepared to organise an international terrorist network, financed by Arab oil money.** Without logistical and material support, however, such an organisation would be doomed to failure. It is now necessary, to determine what other support—apart from that freely given by radical and other Arab governments—the Palestinians received (and still receive). We can then gauge the extent of Palestinian-inspired terrorism and see **the degree of support the Palestinians have given to other groups within the international terrorist network in order to hasten the collapse of the West.**

116

PART FOUR

Arab state support for the international terror network

THE ONSLAUGHT ON democracy has been methodically and systematically prepared by all European terrorist groups who employ the same elements of international arms procurement and the acquisition of arms by theft from military depôts. In the former instance, assistance is given by other terrorist groups with established links.

I   RED TERRORISTS

Red terrorists are closer to the Palestinians in their political philosophy and outlook, and they gained financial assistance from Feltrinelli in the establishment of some form of organisation. Thus by 1968, a weapons service was in full operation in Zurich to assist members of the PIRA, BMG, Carlos and Palestinian terrorists who were loose in Europe. It was run by Petra Krause, known as 'Annababi', who by that time was the lynchpin of Feltrinelli's whole organisation. Gradually, however, the weapons service was supplanted by more copious flows of arms and ammunition from Soviet-bloc countries, Libya and other Arab countries.[1]

The system of links and the advantages continued and were fully manifested in 1979 when the Dutch Red Help Movement gave active assistance to members of PIRA in their successful attempt to assassinate a British diplomat in the Netherlands. In the same year, the Italian Red Brigades divided up a large cache of Palestinian arms and ammunition with PIRA and ETA. But Western European Intelligence authorities discovered connexions between the Italian Red Brigades and the West German RAF. Links also existed in training techniques between ETA and both wings of the IRA and between ETA and Tupamaros representatives in West Germany. Similarly both Basque and Breton Separatists and Portuguese left-wing ter-

119

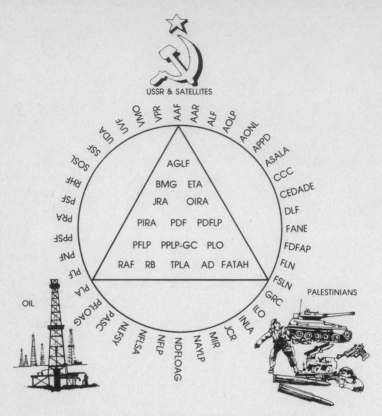

THE INTERNATIONAL TERRORIST MOVEMENT: THE TRIANGLE
showing how the central groups (within the Triangle) receive direct aid from the USSR and satellites, the Palestinians and Arab oil revenues, and disburse aid to the groups around the circle which are totally dependent on the Triangle.

For list of abbreviations and the full title of each movement see Appendix (pages 257–58).

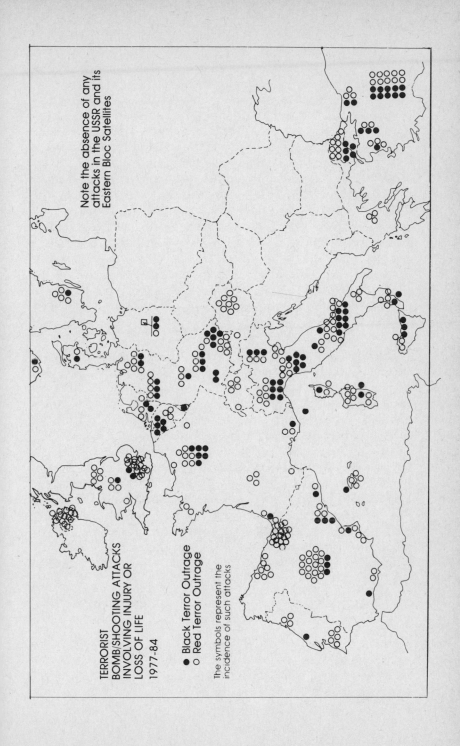

TERRORIST
BOMB/SHOOTING ATTACKS
INVOLVING INJURY OR
LOSS OF LIFE
1977–84

● Black Terror Outrage
○ Red Terror Outrage

The symbols represent the
incidence of such attacks

Note the absence of any
attacks in the USSR and its
Eastern Bloc Satellites

rorists had contacts with the PIRA, while the Dutch South Moluccan terrorists had links not only with certain African countries but also with a variety of subnational groups.[2]

The Israeli Mossad were instrumental in processing information to the West German authorities and this led to the rounding up of the entire BMG leadership. The information came from an Israeli agent within the ranks of the BMG and as it began to crumble as a cohesive group, so other European terrorist groups followed. This information also unearthed **links between the BMG, PIRA and the Angry Brigade in the UK,** and the Japanese Red Army and the Red Brigades. **All these groups,** in turn, **have strong links with the PFLP.** Significantly, all the groups have a strong nihilistic doctrine in common. To this end, PIRA bomb teams had frequent rendezvous with other terrorist groups in Europe and in the spring of 1978, two members of the RAF travelled to Belfast in Northern Ireland for consultations with PIRA leaders. These meetings set up better communications between both wings of the IRA and terrorist groups elsewhere.

The United States did not escape the linking of world-wide terrorism. Having undertaken a major investigation into a number of radical groups in the United States, the FBI discovered strong links between a series of bank robberies and a number of underground groups active in the early 1970s but thought to be defunct. Remnants of the Weathermen, the Black Liberation Army and the Puerto Rican FALN were all strongly interconnected. Similarly, in 1981, US treasury figures showed that from donations given by US citizens, **PIRA raised over US$500,000 through its support group NORAID.** However, this sum only represents the tip of the iceberg. In fact, just to meet its operational costs, PIRA has a current annual funding requirement in the region of US$1.5m; this sum is continually rising.

II ARAB COUNTRIES WHO SUPPORT TERRORISM
A. LIBYA

Terrorism as such, could not survive without continual nourishment. Without cash, the availability of weaponry and a refuge, terrorism in Western Europe would, within months, die a swift death.

More than any other Arab state and more than many East European states, Libya serves as a refuge for terrorists, and is actively involved in their recruitment. From early 1972 onwards, Libyan Embassies in Cairo and other Arab capitals became open recruiting offices for the Palestinian terrorist groups. Once signed-on, Palestinians receive 'head money' and the volunteers are then dispatched to a camp outside Benghazi in Libya for training. **In the first three years of Colonel Gadhafi's rule, it is conservatively estimated that Libya was responsible for the training of more than 8,000 terrorists, all of whom were also provided with weapons.**

Libyan involvement with the Palestinian terrorists was well known after the Munich Olympic Massacre. **This event had been financed by Libyan money, as was the attack on the OPEC oil ministers.** Yet, it is only recently that the extent of Libyan direct involvement with international terrorist groups has at last come to light.

In the latter half of the 1970s, Libya, having received large supplies of arms from the USSR and other Eastern bloc countries, has allowed the equipment to be used by international terrorist groups. This was simply a continuation of a policy begun when Colonel Gadhafi took power. Initially, Gadhafi supported Black Terrorist groups because the USSR was unsure about the political effect of exporting Arab terrorism into Europe. Thirteen days after the Olympic Massacre, however, the USSR began to supply weaponry *via* Libya, for Fatah's use in Europe: **Arab terrorism had proved to be a potent weapon against the Western democracies.**[3] From this point onwards, **Libya gave its full support to a variety of terrorist organisations.** During the summer of that year, Libyan Radio announced that, 'The Libyan Arab Republic has stood by the revolutionaries of Ireland .... There are arms and there is support for the revolutionaries of Ireland....'[4] **A close relationship was thus initiated between Libya and PIRA.**

In the summer of 1972, PIRA sent one of their members to Tripoli as Gadhafi's personal adviser, and he was still there at the end of the decade. The following year, the PIRA Belfast Brigade Commander, Joe Cahill, went personally to Tripoli in order to negotiate a shipment of 250 Kalashnikov rifles and other weaponry from the vast arsenal supplied to Libya by the USSR. This resulted in the commissioning of the SS *Claudia* to carry five tons of weaponry back to Ireland. Joe Cahill and the shipment of weapons were seized by the Irish Navy on 29 March 1973. At the same time, Gadhafi was considering giving weapons to the Protestant-orientated UDA. He invited the UDA leadership to Tripoli in April and May of 1973 on the basis that whatever their religious beliefs, they were essentially anti-imperialist. However, four years passed before Gadhafi attempted to infiltrate weapons directly into Ireland. In November 1977, the SS *Towerstream*, loaded in Lebanon, was seized off Antwerp, containing **US$500,000 worth of weaponry provided by Libya *via* the PLO for PIRA.**

Apart from these two occasions, arms and money were channelled into PIRA hands via European terrorist groups, from Libya. **Between 1972 and 1976, Colonel Gadhafi invested more than US$2.3m in cash alone, in PIRA's cause.** The Provisionals were so overwhelmed by this support that they paid homage to Gadhafi in their own publications, lauding not just him, but also his government. So flattered was he by such accolades, that **from 1976 onwards, he increased his contributions to PIRA, to about US$5m per annum.**[5] **At the same time, he opened up his training facilities to members of PIRA.** The three most important camps used by PIRA members were at Tokra, north-east of Benghazi which was run by Cuban instructors; Sebha, deep in the desert south of Tripoli; and at Az Zamiah which was known as the 'Europeans' Camp'. Members of PIRA were still there in 1980 and have, indeed, been there since. On 23 April 1984, following the return of the Libyans expelled from the UK after the murder of WPC Yvonne Fletcher, Gadhafi stated that:

The revolutionary forces will co-operate with the IRA for the liberation of Ireland.... If the British Government acts against the Libyans in Britain then the Libyan revolutionary forces will help the IRA do the same in Britain.

There is evidence to suggest that the Brighton Conservative Party Conference bomb in 1984, perpetrated by PIRA, but containing similar Eastern bloc explosive to that used in the Libyan 1984 Manchester bombings and similar detonating devices to the Austrian-made ones found in the Libyan London bombs of the same year (see pp. 140–1) **was the result of supplies made by Gadhafi.** Similarly, **the thwarted PIRA**

124

1985 summer bombing campaign of 12 English seaside resorts reflected bombing techniques used elsewhere by Libyan-trained terrorists.[6]

From 1972, Gadhafi had made public statements that Libya was sending not only arms and money, but also volunteers to help both wings of the IRA as well as Filipino Moslem groups. In 1973, he ordered an Egyptian submarine—temporarily under his command in Libyan waters—to torpedo the *Queen Elizabeth II* which was carrying hundreds of Jews from Southampton to Haifa to join the celebrations of Israel's twenty-fifth anniversary. The order was countermanded by President Sadat of Egypt when he discovered what was happening.[7]

Four months later, in September 1973, the Italian police, following a tip-off from the Israeli Mossad, discovered two top-secret SAM-7 missile launchers mounted on an Ostia balcony. These had been provided by Gadhafi, *via* a Greek courier Archimedes Doxi, on a request from Carlos. Three of the five Palestinian PFLP terrorists apprehended in Ostia, were 'repatriated' to Libya by the Italian Air Force. The following December, the PFLP attacked a Pan Am aeroplane at Fiumicino Airport near Rome. It was later ascertained by the Italian authorities that Colonel Gadhafi had not only armed and financed the operation but had also personally approved it. Thirty-one trapped passengers burnt to death.

In the December 1975 Vienna OPEC raid by Carlos, it has been strongly argued that most, if not all, of the inside information was supplied by Colonel Gadhafi. Six months prior to the raid, Carlos had spent time in Libya, where he perfected his tactics and began to orchestrate events. He was assisted by members of Libyan intelligence and by officers of the Libyan army, and received government assistance in shipping the required weaponry to Europe—*via* the Libyan diplomatic pouch. While in Libya, Carlos recruited his international hit-team for the operation, all of whom had graduated from the PFLP's Socotra camp in South Yemen. The team included Hans Joachim Klein and Gabriele Kröcher-Tiedemann, all of whom arrived in Vienna with Carlos just prior to Christmas. A back-up team of Revolutionary Cell members organised the translocation of the weaponry and then withdrew to a hamlet 40 miles away to await events. Meanwhile, the hit-team simply walked into the OPEC meeting, killing three security guards as 'an

125

exemplary precedent', and left after several hours with eleven hostages on a Boeing jet provided by the Austrian government. Carlos is reported to have taken on the assignment only on the understanding that Sheikh Yamani of Saudi Arabia and Amusegar of Iran would be killed. On reaching Algeria, however, Carlos called the whole operation off for a reported sum of US$5m. He resigned from Wadi Haddad's PFLP and urged the latter 'not to get any funny ideas'. This done, he then shot his aide, Moukarbal, between the eyes and disappeared to Russia. In this context, it has also been argued that he was recalled to Moscow, simply as a 'blown' agent. Sheikh Yamani commented that in his opinion, Carlos had begun by obeying Moscow's orders and had then exceeded them. He added that, 'Carlos doesn't really believe in the Palestinian cause, except as a way of spreading international revolution,'[8] thus reinforcing Carlos's less well-known KGB connections. After the OPEC raid, when Carlos surfaced once again in Libya, Colonel Gadhafi gave him a beachside villa and a US$10 million 'bonus'. Hans-Joachim Klein was also given a house. Other terrorists involved in the raid were housed in a block of flats in a fashionable Tripoli suburb. Wadi Haddad was waiting for the terrorists to return to Libya and had flown in for a scheduled conference with both Colonel Gadhafi and Lt. Colonel el-Kharubi.[9]

1976 was an important year which gave added impetus to the international terrorist network. **Gadhafi began to provide training facilities for PFLP, PDFLP and PFLP-GC terrorists on a grand scale. He hired Cubans as instructors** and opened up his training camps to other terrorist groups—his first invitation went to ETA, the Spanish Basque terrorist group. Simultaneously, he arranged for Cubans to train the Syrian army and to staff Syrian terrorist camps which were also opened up to non-Arab terrorists that year. Towards the end of that year and over the following two years, Cubans began arriving in Lebanon. They took up posts as instructors at camps mainly near Tyre and Beaufort Castle in South Lebanon and, after an eight months training stint, **Colonel Gadhafi directed the Cubans to send their newly-trained men into the Arab sheikhdoms of the Persian Gulf and Iran in order to link up with weapons stockpiles that Gadhafi had already transferred to those states. Cuban involve-**

ment in Libyan-inspired disaffection and terrorism grew steadily, until by 1980 there were about 150 Cuban instructors on guerrilla warfare resident in Libya alone, together with nearly 200 in Algeria training the Polisario guerrillas. It is no wonder therefore that the Shah of Iran was overthrown in 1979. Two years previously it was documented that Libya was giving both financial support and training to Iranian terrorists and was subsidising them indirectly through Habash's PFLP.[10]

It was *Al-Anwar* which first published documentary evidence on 22 May 1976 testifying to the network of support which existed between Libya, the PFLP and International Terrorists. Yet what was not fully realised was the extent of Gadhafi's interest in Africa. Two thousand Egyptians underwent training at the El-Beida camp near Tobruk under Soviet instructors; there were Sudanese and Chadians at the Maaten Biskara camp, training with both Soviet and Cuban instructors; and Tunisians at the Bab Aziza camp under instruction from Syrians and Palestinians. Gadhafi also formed his 7,000 strong 'Foreign Legion' which was made up of dissidents and disaffected elements from Mali, Nigeria, Mauritania, the Cameroons, Tunisia, Egypt, Sudan, Benin, Niger, Chad, Senegal and the Ivory Coast. His interests also lay in fomenting trouble in Indonesia and, to this end, he supplied Indonesian terrorists with both money and weapons through the Libyan Embassy in Kuala Lumpur. Meanwhile, in 1982, he promised to champion black rights in the USA and UK and threatened to support any measures that Africans might decide to take to better their lot—including revolt. He also called on black US soldiers to desert.[11]

Colonel Gadhafi finances international terrorist groups from a petro-dollar US$1000m. slush fund set aside for this very purpose. This money, given annually, is used to support 'national liberation movements' in about 45 countries *including the USA* where Chicago Black Moslem groups were directly financed *via* the Libyan Embassy. To cause instability in the West, Greek Orthodox and Maltese Roman Catholic groups are in receipt of significant amounts of financial aid. The funding of such groups contrasts sharply with the even more generous funding of the PLO and other Palestinian groups. The same aim of destabilising the Western democracies is further enhanced by Gadhafi's continuing arrangements for the delivery of Soviet-made arms to the BMG, JRA, Turkish insurgents and terrorists in Yemen, Chile, the Philippines and to Carlos' group. Such arrangements are usually supervised by the PFLP. Gadhafi is able to do this, since vast shipments of Soviet arms have been delivered to Libya—far above the absorptive capacity of the Libyan armed forces and, of these, anti-aircraft missiles and MIG trainers in particular, have been made available to terrorist groups. Yet it is not just Soviet-made weapons which are dispensed to terrorists. Libya arms terrorists with weapons from official shipments signed for by Libyan Army officials from a variety of countries. Two UK-made machine guns, dropped by local terrorists during attacks in Northern Ireland and West Germany, were both part of an official UK arms consignment to Libya.[12] Thus, under Colonel Gadhafi, Libya has become: 'The world's most unbashed governmental proponent of revolutionary violence.'[13] And, as David Newsom a former US Ambassador to Libya stated,

Apart from helping Palestinian groups, the Libyans have provided money, training and in some cases arms for virtually every group in the world with revolutionary credentials.[14]

Colonel Gadhafi has also tried repeatedly to give the international terrorist network some kind of organisational umbrella. In June 1977, he convened the ultra-left groups of Western Europe at a conference in Malta, together with the left-wing underground of Iran, Chile, Oman and Puerto Rico. Its success encouraged him to convene a further international conference eighteen months later at Benghazi. This conference, however, had very special aims, all concerned with the increase of international terrorism. Represented at the conference were Sandanistas from Nicaragua, Uruguayan Tupamaros, Argentine Monteneros, as well as Marxist terrorists from Chile, Costa Rica, Bolivia, Mexico and Brazil. Delegates representing various French left-wing groups, the Italian Red Brigades and the small Maoist factions in Stockholm, together with ETA, were also present. This conference dealt with the problem of how to increase the participation of exiled Latin American terrorists in the terrorism of Western Europe and the Middle East. Colonel Gadhafi strongly urged for the revival of Castro's sagging Latin American Junta for Revolutionary Coordination as well as for the re-establishment of its European Brigade. This was agreed and thus the links between European and South American terrorism were welded ever stronger. The PFLP, PDFLP and PFLP–GC all considered how such exiles could be usefully deployed in the cause of anti-Zionism and were unanimously in favour of their general recruitment. The conference also agreed to **step-up support for the Nicaraguan Sandanistas by increasing support** *via* **Cuba and by opening a new route for supplies** *via* **Panama, to be funded by Libyan petro-dollars.** Libya also undertook to put the Brazilian government under as much pressure as possible with the aim of getting the latter to agree to allow the PLO to open an officially recognised office in Brasilia.[15]

In November 1977, another international meeting was sponsored by Colonel Gadhafi. Between 2 and 6 November, the PLO and the KGB-influenced World Peace Council met in Portugal. Colonel Gadhafi paid more than US$1.5m. to bring 750 delegates—mostly from Soviet bloc-countries—together in Lisbon to express their solidarity with the Palestinian Rejection Front. Solidarity by all concerned, was also expressed with the socialist countries and the Soviet Union as well as with the people's struggle in Europe, the American continents and elsewhere. The Palestinian representatives came almost exclusively from the Marxist-oriented PFLP, PFLP–GC and the PDFLP, all of which held ideologies compatible with all the other delegates and, to some extent, with Gadhafi's own views.

Despite his links with socialist countries—particularly the Soviet Union—and with Marxist-orientated terrorist groups throughout Europe, **Colonel Gadhafi has never neglected his links with Black terrorist groups and was implicated in the Bologna railway station bombing when 84 people were killed** and more than 200 injured.

This once more underscored the fact that **Gadhafi's major aim was to destabilise the Western democracies in Europe by providing international terrorist groups with the means to create anarchy within those states.** As will be seen, this was employed as just one means of reducing the West's capacity to resist the pressures initiated by the Arab oil-producing states in a variety of spheres. **It was, and still is, an attempt to undermine the very fibre of Western society.**

Libya's aim in this respect was actively aided and abetted by several of the Western governments. **France, the United Kingdom, West Germany and Italy, all reached discreet understandings with both Colonel Gadhafi** and the radical Palestinian Rejection Front **in order to secure a degree of immunity against international terrorist operations,** skyjacking and other measures, including oil embargoes.

Meanwhile, Colonel Gadhafi continued his effort to take over the leadership of the radical Arab cause and become a personality to be reckoned with in the international political arena. To this end, on 27 August 1981, he convened a World Conference of Solidarity with the Libyan People at which he proposed that Libya become a new centre of 'international resistance against imperialism, colonialism, reaction and racism in all its forms'. By this means **he appointed Libya as a world leader of liberation movements.** To understand the sort of groups which would almost automatically win Libyan financial and material support for their causes, one need look no further than the organisations represented at the Conference. The variance was extreme, from the Moslem Lebanese Nationalist Movement to Fatah and the PDFLP from the Palestinian terrorist organisations; from the Sandanista coordinator, Commandant Daniel Ortega to 600 other delegates from 86 countries representing 260 organisations including political parties, national liberation movements, terrorist organisations, trades unions and a variety of international bodies (including some directly connected with UN agencies).

In 1981 the West discovered the means by which some Libyan aid was channelled to European terrorist groups. Members of the Red Brigades and 'Frontline' organisations arrested by the Italian police had confirmed that Libya made arrangements to direct frequent arms shipments to these groups and others (including the BMG and RAF in West Germany, PIRA in the UK and Eire and various French terrorist groups) **via the PFLP.** The PFLP's main liaison man was 27-year-old Moritio Polini who was trained and had lived in Libya. Since the discovery of his rôle he has lived in Eastern Europe, using travel documents supplied by the Palestinian Rejection Front.

Colonel Gadhafi's link-man with Italian Black terror between 1973 until his arrest for complicity in the Bologna railway station bombing of 2 August 1980, was Claudio Mutti. He had founded the Italy–Libyan Association in 1973 **following a visit to Libya and receipt of a large financial grant from Gadhafi. Regular payments to Mutti and his close associates from Gadhafi were made through the Libyan Embassy in Rome—as was Libyan financial and material aid eventually destined for Black terrorist groups in Italy.**[16]

This aid is not confined to simply weaponry and cash. Forged passports, documents of all descriptions including travel permits, identity cards and driving licences; contacts not simply *via* Libyan Embassies but also directly with international terrorists are also provided. Help is not just available within Libya but is also provided *via* the Libyan diplomatic pouch. As late as February 1982, several Red Brigades terrorists informed the Italian police on their capture that they had received six months training in Libya immediately prior to the kidnapping of General James Dozier. This evidence further suggests that **Libya's intentions are anti-American.**

1. *The US/Libyan Connexion*

Gadhafi has openly admitted to supporting guerrilla groups which exist within the United States while at the same time, forging links with US citizens who possess expertise in a variety of fields which are useful to him. **Various American citizens run terrorist training camps for Colonel Gadhafi in Libya,** acting as instructors for courses in night fighting, silent killing and the booby-trapping of alarm clocks and ash trays. Others illegally organise the exportation of arms and explosives while some act as hit-men against Libyan dissidents domiciled both in the USA and elsewhere.[17] One example of this latter point concerned the Colorado State University sociology student Faisal Abdulaze Zagalai, who survived two bullet wounds when he was shot at home at close quarters. His assailant, Eugene Tafoya was a former Green Beret and holder of the Bronze Star. When Tafoya was apprehended, he had in his possession a list of 100 other Libyans domiciled in North America, all of whom had been marked for assassination. One of the documents also found in his possession led the FBI to other US citizens also marked for assassination, and on another was the Libyan telex number of a former CIA agent, Edwin Wilson. It transpired after further investigations that the seven US citizens had, at one time or another, hampered Wilson's activities and, for doing so, were placed on an assassination list.

Edwin Wilson played a key rôle in the training and supplying of commandos for Colonel Gadhafi and was also involved with another former CIA operative, Frank Terpil, in illegal arms procurement for Libya. In 1980, together with Jerome Brower a Californian explosives manufacturer, both **Wilson and Terpil were involved with arrangements to supply Libya with 40,000lbs of explosives together with delayed-action timers** through one of Wilson's front companies, Intercontinenal. **Both the FBI and CIA knew about the operation but nothing was done to stop it until 1980.** Brower has since been federally indicted with running guns to Libya in 1976–7. According to documents found in files appropriated by the FBI, the purpose was to train Libyans in 'covert operations, employing the latest techniques of clandestine explosive ordnance'.

In 1976, Wilson was responsible for hiring the assassin who made an abortive attempt on the life of Libyan dissident Omar Abdullah Maheshi in Cairo. Following the successful murder of Muhammad Mustafa Ramadan, another opponent of Colonel Gadhafi living in London, a .38 revolver found near the scene of the assassination, was traced to one of Frank Terpil's associates. Again in 1976, Wilson and Terpil recruited two employees from California's China Lake Naval Weapons Center to their organisation and some months later, a Federal Grand Jury in Fresno, California, indicted six men on charges of pilfering night-vision scopes, a low-light television camera and a remote-control helicopter from the China Lake Center. All the items procured were destined for use in Libya. **Wilson's headquarters were in Tripoli, and staffed almost exclusively by US Vietnam veterans.**

Frank Terpil, Wilson's associate, had wide connexions within the CIA and Scotland Yard as well as with Colonel Gadhafi, Carlos, the Turkish Grey Wolves and with Idi Amin and the Emperor Bokassa. On 3 September 1980, Terpil, together with George 'Garry' Gregory Korkala, left the USA for the Middle East. On arrival, he took a penthouse suite in the Hamra district of Beirut with Ruth Boyd. On Saturday, 7 November 1981, Terpil left Boyd at the penthouse suite and accompanied three members of Syrian intelligence to an unknown destination. Although he has not been seen since, it is rumoured that he is living in seclusion and under constant guard in Damascus. It is interesting to note that at the time of his disappearance, he was in the midst of making arrangements to meet a US congressman, in an effort to trade highly sensitive information on the White House, the CIA, FBI and other government agencies and officials, in return for a full pardon.

Terpil had been active in the Middle East since 1974, conducting deals and operations throughout the area as well as in Nicaragua and in the Central African Republic, then ruled by the self-appointed Emperor, Bokassa. In that year, he set up a company called Intercontinental Import-Export Inc. which had three directors: Kevin Mulcahy, himself and Edwin Wilson.

Pat Loomis, an Intercontinental employee, was involved in the recruitment of Master-Sergeant Luke F. Thompson, an ex-Green Beret and Vietnam veteran to head a five-man team to Libya. **Thompson, concerned about national security's reaction to an acceptance of the offer, telephoned counter-intelligence. He was told, officially, that the relevant authorities regarded it as totally legal.** His anxieties assuaged, he therefore went ahead and recruited his team. On arrival in Libya, Thompson and his four associates were taken to a desert palace where US personnel were making up explosive devices. The whole manufacturing side at the palace was under the personal control of Frank Terpil who also controlled the US instructors. Those undergoing training at the palace included members of the Libyan military who were being instructed in bomb-making and booby-trapping techniques alongside members of terrorist organisations such as ETA, JRA and PIRA. On Thompson's return, the CIA tried to run a check on the entire operation, but could not go very far, since inquiries were being blocked at a variety of levels. It is patently obvious, therefore, that **both the CIA organisation together with CIA personnel had been used by Terpil** and thus implicated at a high level.

Heathrow airport in London was also a crucial factor in both Terpil and Wilson's activities. Its importance can best be illustrated by considering its function with regard to the 1976 Libyan shipment already described. **This shipment only escaped discovery by British customs and excise officials because a member of Britain's Secret Intelligence Service**

133

(sometimes known as MI6) smoothed the way for the shipment's passage through the airport. This person, code-
named 'The Babysitter' also procured supplies for Terpil,
on the basis of his belief that supplying Colonel Gadhafi
with such weaponry was for the 'betterment of the Western World'. The Babysitter also assisted in organising warehouses throughout England where Terpil could store weapons
and bombs in transit to the Middle East. The shipment of 1976
was provided with the compulsory End-User Certificate (destination the Philippines) through the efforts of a retired British
Marine, Colonel Warren. Terpil and Warren were connected by
a common friend who acted as an intermediary in the deal—
Robin Bray-Taylor. Bray-Taylor understood completely that he
was involved in an illegal operation and admitted that he was
in it solely for the money. Through The Babysitter, Frank
Terpil arranged with Hamilton Spence, manager of Interarms
Ltd, a Manchester-based company, to meet the shipment at
Manchester's Ringway airport. Spence knew that the weapons
were not going to the Philippines, but was satisfied that
Colonel Warren could simply 'walk the papers through'. As one
undercover New York detective, James Rodriguez put it,
'England is an easy port for obtaining weapons'.

By 1982, it was well-established that **Libyan terrorists and
other members of terrorist groups such as Red Brigades,
INLA, Fatah, the PFLP, PDFLP and PFLP-GC had all
been trained at Libyan camps by US personnel who were
also involved in the infiltration of Libyan terrorists into
Europe *via* Italy.** By this time, Edwin Wilson had become
Colonel Gadhafi's quartermaster, even providing support for
Colonel Gadhafi's Chad operation.

Both Wilson and Terpil had 'good' US connexions. In CIA
circles, Wilson was known as 'the Ice-man' and had been the
paymaster in the abortive Bay of Pigs fiasco. He was also
involved in later attempts to destabilise Castro's Cuba.
Wilson's associates included Terpil, Theodore Shackley, Kevin
Mulcahy and Rafael Villaverday, all of whom were ex-CIA
agents. Terpil, even while working for the CIA, had good
Libyan connexions—once, offering to take Villaverday to a
Libyan Consulate in order to obtain the weapons necessary to
complete a 'job'. Omar Maheshi, a former Libyan General,
offered Terpil US$1m. plus US$20,000 per month to go to Libya

to train terrorists together with Russian and Chinese instructors already there. Having accepted this appointment, Terpil then approached certain Special Forces personnel, who provided airline tickets to Libya *via* Zurich to **serving members of the Green Berets who were allocated leave from duty in order to implement the operation. Thus the Special Forces knew the full details of the operation and despite this, condoned it.** Each participating member of the initiative received a payment of US$6,500 per month. On their arrival in Libya, one of Colonel Gadhafi's aides, Abdul Senoussi, asked the Green Berets to train 'my commandos'—which they did. What is, perhaps, not readily realised, is that many of the Green Berets remained until President Reagan ended diplomatic relations with Libya in 1983 and, that those former Green Berets who were there in 1983, were still there in 1984, instructing terrorists in six bases, the three most important of which are those at Tripoli, Benghazi and Kufra.

Most of the equipment used by Terpil and Wilson in Libya, is procured directly from US companies by front companies established for that very purpose. One such company, Scientific Communications Inc. of Dallas, Texas, was hoodwinked into providing 100,000 delayed-action timers of the electronic, solid-state variety in 1980. The same year, Wilson paid US$1m. to GOEX Co. Inc. of Houston, Texas for 40 tons of plastic explosives. At Houston Airport it took 18 hours for the aeroplane to be loaded, yet customs officials did not investigate nor did either the CIA or FBI do anything to prevent the shipment from taking off.

All this was done under the guise of a minefield clearing operation for an oil company. Front companies which had been in existence for many years, set up by Wilson and Terpil, were used to throw a screen over the financial arrangements and to mask the real destination of the purchased goods. The companies used, were situated in such widespread places as London, Miami, Brussels, Geneva and Liberia. It was these same companies which, under Wilson and Terpil's guidance, also handled the illegal transportation and smuggling of computer- and telephone-tapping equipment from the US to Libya *via* London.

One of the other partners in this deception was Theodore Shackley who had been a Senior Case Officer with the CIA. He had known about the Libyan venture from the start and has constantly maintained that **top intelligence men have direct links with terrorist organisations.** **Terpil consistently received the help of British Intelligence in getting his illegal cargoes safely in and out of the UK.** Terpil and his associates were of help to governments other than Libya. Terpil is reputed to have manufactured the bomb which killed the only white man in the Kenyan Cabinet, MacKenzie, who had been instrumental in allowing the Israelis to refuel during the Entebbe operation. In 1978, MacKenzie's plane—a light aircraft—blew up on his return from Uganda. Terpil has been described as the sort of man the CIA need to recruit but such a man is capable of training current terrorists as well as participating directly in terrorism himself. As an interrogator he employs inhuman tactics; one of his favourite techniques is to tie a starving and tormented rat onto his bound and immobile victim's stomach and watch gleefully while his frantic, helpless victim screams as the rat escapes by slowly chewing through the victim's stomach and intestines and finally escapes through the by now dead victim's back.

Libya paid Terpil well. By the late 1970s Terpil could afford to pay cash for a £250,000 London town house and more than £600,000 for a country estate also in England. In return, tangible results were expected and, as Colonel Gadhafi began to concentrate on the destabilisation of the Middle East, so these were expected more quickly. **Many of those trained by US personnel in Libya were involved in Gadhafi's attempt to seize the Tunisian town of Gafsa in January 1980.**

The Gafsa adventure was an attempt by Colonel Gadhafi to overthrow President Habib Bourghiba of Tunisia. It was commanded by Ahmad Mergheni, a Tunisian, who had been in hiding in Libya for 15 years. In 1972, Colonel Gadhafi sent him back into Tunisia to blow up both the US embassy and the Tunis synagogue. However, he was caught and gaoled. On his return to Libya he was immediately sent to Tinduf guerrilla camp to undergo special training from US personnel there. On completion of his training, Mergheni and 60 raiders were sent across the Tunisian border at two o'clock on a Sunday morning, from Algeria. US$1m. worth of weaponry awaited them in Gafsa. The composition of the force is extremely interesting. Given US$5m. by Gadhafi, Merghani went immediately to

Lebanon to recruit disaffected Tunisians already undergoing training there at PFLP and PDFLP camps. From these, he chose 28 and together, they flew into Algiers *via* Rome in order to meet up with another 32 insurgents picked out from trainees at Libyan terrorist camps. Their rendezvous was at a point near the 'Gadhafi trail'. They had been told that **weapons had been stashed near every major Tunisian city and, were also advised that additional repositories existed and could be drawn from both Sicily and Corsica.** The Tunisian army made short shrift of the insurgents but, the important point is, that **together with Russian, Chinese and Cubans, US personnel were actively involved in training guerrillas and terrorists who would then be unleashed against countries friendly to the USA.** Libyan involvement could also be seen in the 1983 food riots in which Gafsa saw some of the earliest disturbances and, in January 1984, Libyan insurgents blew up an oil pipeline from the Algerian In Amenas oil field to the Tunisian coast at Gabes.

Both the CIA and the FBI, together with the Justice Department of the United States, have all along had the means through their legal and juridicial powers, to put both Edwin Wilson and Frank Terpil, together with their associates, out of business. That no action was taken against them until 1983, was due almost entirely to the CIA's 'old boy' network. It was FBI men who lured Wilson to the Dominican Republic in June 1982 where he was immediately put on a plane for New York. Similarly, **no action has yet been taken by the UK government against either 'the Babysitter' or the British pilots who, under Wilson's direction, flew planes for Gadhafi during his involvement in Chad.**

Concerned about Colonel Gadhafi's expansionist and destabilising ambitions, the US sixth fleet was ordered to the Gulf of Sirte, regarded by Libya as its own, by President Reagan. Fears of an escalating crisis grew, when two Libyan jets were shot down by US planes after repeated warnings to stay clear of the fleet which was undergoing manoeuvres. Of the loss of his two planes, Colonel Gadhafi stated,

Imperialism has now openly adopted a flagrant policy of aggression. Therefore we are now determined to confront it. Strengthening relations of our own people with the Socialist camp is an important step towards this aim.

The Egyptian Defence Minister, General Abdel-Halim Abu-Ghazala, however, thought that,

The Russians were behind Gaddafi [*sic*] pushing him to intercept the F-14s, to find an excuse to become more involved in Libya, to bring more advisers and more Cubans.[18]

Following the Gulf of Sirte incident, Colonel Gadhafi took matters into his own hands. From August 1981, when the incident occurred, both the FBI and the CIA were faced with an accumulation of growing evidence from a variety of sources that Gadhafi had ordered out a number of hit teams with a twin purpose: first to assassinate President Reagan, secondly to attack US embassies in Rome, Paris, Athens and Ankara. These assassination squads had been exclusively trained by Edwin Wilson, Frank Terpil and twelve other former US personnel of the CIA or the Green Berets. **Two hit teams were sent out to assassinate President Reagan: one, under the direction of Carlos** and another multi-national team including a West German, a Lebanese, two Iranians and a Palestinian. In September 1981, a Libyan plot was uncovered to kill Maxwell Rabb, the US Ambassador to Rome. He was immediately recalled to Washington and the following month Italian security forces despatched more than five Libyans to Tripoli. In October the French authorities received information about a proposed assassination in Paris and, simultaneously, Christian Chapman, the US Chargé d'Affaires, received threats over the telephone from Libya. In November, he and his chauffeur narrowly escaped an assassination attempt.[19] At the same time, Colonel Gadhafi offered the services of hired assassins to other terrorist groups. The PIRA asked Gadhafi to provide someone unconnected with them to fulfil a contract on a UK Irish Unionist MP. Gadhafi informed Terpil who arranged for one of his associates, another former Green Beret, to take up the contract. He, however, was arrested by the FBI before he could leave the United States. The mounting evidence was such that finally, in May 1982, the US expelled the entire Libyan diplomatic mission. By the turn of the year it had decided to block all oil imports from Libya and institute a series of economic sanctions. At the same time, the US led other Western governments in applying pressure on friendly African states to stay away from the forthcoming OAU summit in Tripoli.[20]

If there was ever any real doubt about Libyan involvement in international terrorism, it was dispelled by the end of the 1970s. In February 1979, Muhammed al-Zuwayy, the Libyan Secretary of Information stated categorically that,

We assert to the whole world that we provide material, moral and political support to every liberation revolution in the world.[21]

To this end, **Libya, South Yemen and the PLO all train disaffected terrorists and were heavily involved in overthrowing the Shah of Iran** while taking a keen interest in Western European terrorism. What, however, is particularly interesting, is that **all** Gadhafi's terrorist trainees have been from non-Communist countries in Western Europe, Africa and the Middle East and, in the case of the former, included Basques, Bretons, Corsicans, Italians, Greeks and Turks, all of whom underwent training.

To ensure that Libyan-trained terrorists and hijackers continued to be well-motivated and free from worry, Gadhafi extended his 'insurance scheme' which was already in operation for Palestinian and European volunteers. This method ensured that all terrorists and their families would be provided with substantial payments if the terrorist was either shot and wounded or killed 'in the line of duty'. As far as can be ascertained, such pledges were promptly adhered to. Similarly, continuous support was given to the terrorists by Libya, not simply just 'on the ground' aid but more importantly in international forums. Admittedly, the comprehensive ground and operative support which Libya provided was essential to the continuing survival of terrorism. As has been mentioned, this took the form of provision of arms, money, sanctuary and the free use of embassies, diplomatic pouches and false passports etc., all contributed to raise the standard of performance and the potential level of operative success. Most importantly, however, such support was and still is significantly enhanced by Libya's political backing in international arenas such as those supplied by the United Nations. What reinforces this evidence, is that no terrorism exists in any country that gives assistance to international terrorism—such existence is reserved almost exclus-

139

ively for the Western democracies.

It is therefore, abundantly clear that Colonel Gadhafi will employ any available personnel to further his own aims. Although he remains fairly secure within the borders of his own country, a vehement opposition exists amongst exiled Libyans now domiciled in Western democracies. The extremely vocal nature of this opposition has ensured that a more temperate view of the Libyan Jamahiriya has pertained in the Western world, much to Gadhafi's annoyance. So successful are some of these exiles in exposing the nature of Libya's involvement in destabilisation not only within the Middle East but elsewhere, that Gadhafi ordered that all outspoken exiled opponents of his should be sentenced to death, and he hired assassins to carry out the executions. However, having initially enrolled the PFLP, PDFLP, and PFLP-GC to man his murder squads, he found the Palestinians to be less than reliable. Having handsomely paid Black September to bring out from Italy a Libyan accused of crimes against the people during the reign of King Idris, the Palestinians tried to double-cross him. On finding the Libyan concerned, the Black September group offered him a deal: if they were paid a substantial sum, the man would be allowed to go into hiding and the Palestinians would inform Gadhafi that he could not be found. It was after experiences such as this that Gadhafi turned to Wilson and Terpil, not just to provide him with assassins who could be trusted, but to train some of his own supporters in the necessary techniques. So successful were they and so ardently did they perform their duties, that the West German authorities charged two Libyans with the torture and mutilation of two exiled Libyan students at the Libyan Peoples Bureau in Bonn. The torture had lasted for the two days, 13 and 14 November 1982. It emerged that both students suffered permanent physical damage and disablement of one sort of another.

2. *Libyan Involvement in the murder of WPC Fletcher*
The most vociferous group of anti-Gadhafi dissident opinion, however, resides in the UK and, in February 1984, Colonel Gadhafi determined to put an end to it. On 1 March, a communications 'intercept' was decoded revealing that a Libyan machine-gun squad had been made operational and was heading for the UK. A second 'intercept' in which Libyan Peoples'

Bureau personnel were ordered to fire on demonstrators was not decoded in time.

At the same time, the Jamahiriya News Agency in London was frantically trying to overcome industrial problems created by the non-payment of salary to one journalist. In desperation, they tried to settle the problem prior to the commencement of the action against anti-Gadhafi dissidents, and the Director of the Agency, Salim Najim, threatened to kill the disputing journalists.

On Saturday 11 March, seven bombs went off in London and Manchester. In London, L'Auberge, a club in Berkeley Street was blown up injuring 23 people, three seriously. The club was partly owned by Libyan dissidents and had a Middle East clientele. In Whalley Range, Manchester, a car bomb exploded followed by a bomb left on the windowledge of a house owned by Libyan dissidents, which injured three people. Four other bombs were found in London where they had been left at Newsagents or news stands selling Arab newspapers but only one exploded. Britain sent two strongly worded communications to Tripoli, but had taken no action when a group of students seized control of the Libyan Peoples' Bureau in St James's Square on 18 February and dismissed the accredited chargé d'affaires. Further bombs were uncovered on Monday, 13 March. Dr Omar Sodani, the Bureau's spokesman, denied any responsibility for the bombings but yet issued a statement from the External Liaison Bureau in Tripoli, that Britain harboured 'renegades guilty of fraud, corruption and of masterminding terrorist campaigns . . . .'

Within three days, four Libyan students had been charged with serious offences, another five had been served with deportation orders and more than ten others were being held by the police for questioning. The whole scenario had been orchestrated by Ali el-Giahour, a businessman who died six months later. Records of the bank accounts of those charged showed regular payments from Libyan government accounts and other large unexplained amounts. The explosive used was of Czechoslovak military design while the detonators were Austrian-made and all parts carried incriminating fingerprints. Three more Libyan bombers were arrested in Manchester, led by Khalid Mansour who was head of the Libyan Students Union and one of Gadhafi's most trusted agents.

On 16 April, two Libyans went to the Foreign Office to protest about the proposed demonstration by anti-Gadhafi dissidents due to take place the following day, stating that they would not be responsible for the consequences. The demonstration, arranged at short notice, was heightened by the news that the previous day, the Students Revolutionary Committee of Tripoli University announced that two students would be publicly hanged for treason. Thousands of vomiting frightened and shrieking students watched in horror as the sentence was carried out. It was the expected backlash which prompted the Peoples' Bureau in London to strongly urge that the demonstration be prevented. But it had already been cancelled once—on 7 April—for fear of violence from the Bureau, and the demonstrators were determined to express their feelings on 17 April in the wake of the Tripoli student hangings.

At about 8.00 a.m, police began erecting barriers to prevent the demonstrators from spilling onto the road. Dr Sodani, a personal friend of Colonel Gadhafi, and the organiser of the 1977 Benghazi student hangings, demanded that the police remove the barriers. Continuing to argue, he was arrested between 9.00 a.m. and 9.30 a.m. by a policeman unaware of his diplomatic status. Sodani was bundled into a van and remained in custody until released at 2.25 a.m. the following morning after being cautioned. Meanwhile, an atmosphere of near-hysteria developed within the Bureau and a group of revolutionaries determined to teach the dissidents a lesson. Just before 10.00 a.m. a group of pro-Gadhafi demonstrators emerged from the Bureau and walked to the corner of Duke of York Street—a safe distance from the Bureau. A few minutes after 10.00 a.m. the hooded anti-Gadhafi demonstrators arrived and began to chant. Suddenly, at 10.20 a.m., shots were fired from a first floor window in the Bureau, and 25-year-old WPC Yvonne Fletcher fell to the ground fatally wounded. Eleven anti-Gadhafi demonstrators were also wounded by the 9mm submachine gun fire. Police acted swiftly to contain the situation and the Libyan Peoples' Bureau siege had begun—**with Gadhafi's personally selected hit-team inside.** This team had entered the UK on false United Arab Emirates passports, and was one of two teams despatched by Gadhafi to Europe.

Early in 1984, Gadhafi's 35-year-old cousin, Sayed Gadafadem, travelled to Italy, supposedly for medical treatment. Soon after his arrival, however, he went to Switzerland where he met with a senior Syrian intelligence officer, Esaldin Suleiman. At the meeting it was agreed that if Gadhafi sent two hit-teams to Europe, the Syrians would unleash the Abu Nidal group and all three could be coordinated by an officer in Libya's Madrid Bureau. Despite this knowledge, the UK government found itself caught up in a web of legal niceties regarding the Bureau siege and the questions of diplomatic immunity, bringing into account the Vienna Convention to the eleven out of 30 Libyans in the Bureau whom the UK Home Secretary agreed did not have diplomatic status. Nevertheless, as the expelled Libyans arrived back in Tripoli, they were rapturously received and treated to a vitriolic attack on Britain by Colonel Gadhafi who ordered a search of the British Embassy in Tripoli in retaliation for the search of the Peoples' Bureau by UK security services after the Libyans' expulsion. Just prior to the end of the siege a 2lb bomb exploded in the baggage reclaim area of Terminal Two at Heathrow airport injuring 25 people. A Libyan link was strongly suspected as there were certain similarities to the way in which the other bombs were assembled.

Following the murder of the British policewoman, a large number of Libyans carrying diplomatic passports arrived in France—two of them with Tunisian diplomatic papers shortly after they had exited with Libyan documents. West German intelligence sources informed France that Carlos had been let loose by Gadhafi, and was now operating out of Prague, Bucharest, Budapest and East Berlin, with France as his main target because of the arrest in 1982 of his West German terrorist girlfriend, Magdalena Kopp. In response, **Carlos organised the destruction of the French Cultural Centre in West Berlin and the TGV rail-bombing on the line between Marseilles and Paris,** with his deputy, former BMG terrorist Johannes Weinrich.

Another example of Gadhafi's use of foreigners to carry out his dirty work occurred in November 1984. Having failed to get his hit squad released from UK prisons by holding Britons hostage in Libya, Gadhafi then turned his attention to Egypt. He deceived two UK businessmen Anthony Gill, aged 48, from Colchester, Essex, and Godfrey Shiner, aged 47, from Warwickshire, into becoming unwittingly involved in a plot to assassinate a former Libyan Prime Minister and Gadhafi-critic, Abdel

143

Hamid Bakoush in Cairo. They deny receiving US$400,000 to find the hit-team and carry out the assassination, but were captured by Egyptian Intelligence, which then faked Bakoush's death and released photographs of the supposed murder which found their way to Tripoli. Each of the two Britons received US$90,000 which was confiscated by the Egyptian authorities. They recruited two Maltese, whose names they were given by Libyan officials—Romeo Chakambari and Edgar Cacia. On 15 November, Radio Tripoli announced that Bakoush had been executed. Two days later, the Egyptian President Hosni Mubarak, revealed that his intelligence forces had uncovered a Libyan hit-list which included the names of Mrs Thatcher, Chancellor Kohl of West Germany and other world leaders including King Fahd of Saudi Arabia. The two Britons had allowed themselves to become involved hoping that they would thereby gain more business. Enmeshed in this scheme was a plan for the escape from Britain of Mohammed Shebli, a brother-in-law of Colonel Gadhafi who faced criminal charges concerned with cocaine smuggling, in January 1984.[22]

At a press conference during a state visit to Austria on 12 March 1982, Colonel Gadhafi denied all allegations that Libyan oil revenues funded international terrorism. Yet during the same month he addressed the preparatory committee of the International Forum for Resisting Imperialism, Zionism, Racism and Reaction, urging that members should send direct material and military aid to liberation movements. The Forum was a new body, set up to co-ordinate assistance to liberation movements including those operating in both El Salvador and Guatemala, together with the PLO.[23] Such statements are consonant with Gadhafi's actions: on the one hand denial and on the other, support. On 1 September 1983, Gadhafi held a Terror Summit in Tripoli at which all the major terrorist groups as well as the KGB, were represented. And following the killing of WPC Fletcher in London in April 1984, he was determined to kill Mrs Thatcher and bring down the Conservative government. In March 1985, a further summit was held with pride of place going to PIRA and INLA which have recently had their funding significantly upgraded. **The previous month saw an attempt by Gadhafi to blow up the entire Chadian cabinet in much the same way as PIRA had attempted to elimin-**

144

COMMUNISM AND TERRORISM

Soviet links with the terrorist movement through Gadhafi. (Top) Brezhnev talks with Gadhafi at Moscow airport. (Centre) Gorbachev seen holding Soviet-Libyan talks with Gadhafi in the Kremlin on 10th October 1985, as a result of which 2,000 Soviet military advisers arrived in Libya (see page 233). (Bottom) Gadhafi raises the hands of Palestinian leaders George Habash (left) and Yasser Arafat (right) in Tripoli. (Photos *Associated Press Ltd*)

The terrorist movement
at work: the planning and
execution of terrorism.
(Top) Gadhafi's number 2,
Jalloud, meets PFLP-GC
leader Jibril, and (bottom)
the leaders of the PLO/
Fatah (Arafat), PFLP
(Habash) and PDFLP
(Naif Hawatima) during a
Palestine National
Council. (Centre) An
Armenian terrorist
atrocity at Esenboga
Airport, Ankara in 1982,
which was assisted by
members of the PLO,
PFLP-GC, PFLP and
PDFLP. The brother of
one of the victims laments
his loss. (Photos
Associated Press Ltd)

The organisation and training of terrorists. (Top left) Philby, who in 1944 recruited into the SIS George Blake (top right), alias George Bihar (see pp 99–100), the Palestinian cousin of Henri Curiel (bottom left), the most important Soviet NKVD agent in Western Europe who first co-ordinated the international terrorist movement in Europe (see p 176). As Philby worked alongside Curiel and Blake in the SIS in the 1940s it is highly likely that Philby and Curiel influenced each other's work with Blake as the conduit and that Philby has a direct link with international terrorism. Curiel was joined as central co-ordinator by Carlos (bottom right), a Soviet KGB agent closely linked with Gadhafi (see pp 125–6). (Centre) PDFLP guerrillas training at a secret camp in Southern Lebanon: leaping over burning rubble while under fire. (Photos *Associated Press Ltd*, bottom left *Agence France Presse*)

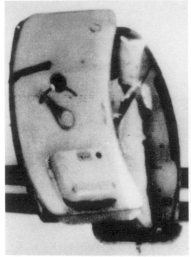

VICTIMS OF TERROR

Victims at the mercy of the terrorist's gun. (Top left) A hooded armed hijacker holds 40 TWA passengers hostage in Beirut. (Centre left) British policewoman Yvonne Fletcher rolls on the ground moments after being shot by a gunman located in the London Libyan People's Bureau (see pp 140–3). (Top right) Photo by a family friend of American Leon Klinghoffer sitting in his wheelchair on the Achille Lauro shortly before he was shot and thrown overboard by Palestinian terrorists. (Bottom) The massacre at Rome International Airport on 27th December 1985, which President Reagan linked with Gadhafi through Abu Nidal's group. (Photos *Associated Press Ltd*, centre left *UPI/ITN*)

ate the Thatcher Cabinet. Weekly consignments of weapons were sent by the truck-load along the 'Gadhafi Trail' to the Polisario guerrillas operating in the Western Sahara. These consignments included Kalashnikovs, Makarovs, RPG-7 bazookas and SAM-7's. The most interesting factor is, however, not where they went, but from where such quantities of sophisticated weaponry came in the first place. After his diplomats murdered a London policewoman in 1984, evidence was uncovered that over a series of years, Libyan envoys had bought thousands of guns on the Western arms markets. One UK arms dealer had sold the Libyans 600 handguns, silencers and ammunition worth £88,000 in 1980, and one of the guns was used to assassinate an anti-Gadhafi dissident in the same year. In 1984, following a European crack-down on Libyan terrorists, a mysterious Libyan military delegation was reported to have stayed in a first-class hotel in Toulon for several days— obviously on an arms buying mission.[24]

The answer lies in Gadhafi's political stance. As a Moslem, he regards Westerners as infidels: as a bedouin Arab he sees his faith more represented in socialism than capitalism. Thus he turns to the socialist world for help. In December 1979, Gadhafi openly expressed solidarity with the USSR's occupation of Afghanistan and, in 1980, Libya, together with the PLO, South Yemen and Syria, were the only states at a protest conference for Moslem states, who refused to condemn Russia's invasion. States at this conference represented more than 700 million Moslems and it is significant that support for the invasion came only from those who represented less than 20 million Moslems. **The previous year had seen Gadhafi urging the more progressive Arab states to join the Warsaw pact countries within the Soviet military bloc and, also suggesting that missiles with nuclear warheads should be placed in North Africa and the Arabian Peninsula 'to defy America's hostile policy towards the Arab nation'.**[25]

If further confirmation was necessary, it was provided by Mohammed Youssouf al-Mougariaf, a former Libyan Ambassador, Cabinet Minister and former chairman of Libya's Watchdog Committee for State Funds. In late 1979, he defected to the West. He confirmed that **Gadhafi was seriously contemplating joining the Warsaw Pact and, that Libya had already become a key Soviet strategic base.** Figures provided by al-

Mougariaf, point to **Libya's expenditure of oil revenues as being currently in the region of 70 per cent on Soviet arms, the funding of international terrorist and subversive operations on a world-wide scale including the training of more than 9,000 terrorists from more than 40 countries.** In fact, so concerned was the late Egyptian President Anwar Sadat, that in October 1979 he ordered a major operation to unseat Gadhafi and was only persuaded from not implementing it, by the personal interference of the then US President, Carter.[26]

3. *The Soviet/Libyan Accord*

The history of Libyan–Soviet accord finally blossomed in **1976** when **Colonel Gadhafi** asked for and **received from Moscow a US$12 billion arms contract.** Deliveries began almost immediately and it was soon realised that **much of the equipment involved, was as yet not available either to the USSR's East European satellites,** nor to her much older and valued Arab clients such as Syria and Iraq. Libya received the staggering amount of 2,800 tanks, 7,000 armoured vehicles and hundreds of MIG 23, 25 and 27 fighters and bombers; Tupolev-B23 supersonic long-range bombers; 25 missile-launching naval craft; surface-to-air missiles and the 190 mile-range Scud ground-to-ground missiles. This fantastic range of weaponry was accompanied by **12,000 Soviet military advisers,** 100 North Korean pilots and 300 Czechoslovak technicians specifically sent to maintain the tanks. What is of the utmost significance, is that the Libyan army in 1976 numbered only 22,000 persons but by 1980 it had risen to about 44,000. Thus the quantities of arms sent, bore no relationship to the size of the Libyan armed forces. However, the picture begins to take on a more clear definition when it is realised that only Soviet personnel flew the latest planes and commanded the missile systems. Nine airstrips had to be built to accommodate the Soviet Antonov transports and a vast construction scheme was implemented to house both the equipment and personnel. It was further agreed between the USSR and Libya, that **1,000 Libyan soldiers were to undergo training annually in the USSR with a further 3,000 going to Bulgaria.** Furthermore, the Soviet advisers were stationed permanently in Tripoli, Benghazi, Tobruk and more importantly at the former US air base at Wheelus Field. **What the Soviets had achieved was a presence which could be determined as being of a permanent nature, on the southern coast of the Mediterranean Sea. Such a presence, bolstered by such a considerable arsenal, could last for the next fifty years** and, it was a prospect which would, as President Sadat of Egypt had foreseen almost a year previously, significantly alter the delicate power balance in the entire Middle East region.[27]

What is absolutely certain is that **Gadhafi's main aim is the total destabilisation of the Middle East** with the two-fold purpose of spreading Islam around the Mediterranean and increasing his Empire at the expense of his neighbours. At present, however, his only successful acquisition has been 30,000 square miles of annexed uranium-rich Chad. Such an attitude is reflective of a man who possesses delusions of grandeur—a 'messiah' who only rules 2.5 million people: a contradiction that the 'desert prince' **must** overcome in order to be treated in a manner that befits his self-appraisal. In an attempt to acquire such status, he consistently backs up his rhetoric by dispensing his country's petro-dollars.

Libya supported Moslem groups in Chad in 1980–1; trained local insurgents in Gambia since 1980; and was responsible for inciting tribal strife in Ghana in 1981. Before 1977, Libyan petro-dollars funded the Eritrean Liberation Movement, but after that year Gadhafi switched his support to Mengistu Haile Mariam's régime. Gadhafi has supported countless plots to overthrow existing Arab heads of state including the 1971 Moroccan plot to unseat King Hassan. Likewise, he was involved in the 1974 plot to overthrow the Sudanese head of state, President Numairy and again in the 1981 campaign to unseat President Mohammed Siad Barre of Somalia.

President Idi Amin Dada was defended by both Palestinian and Libyan soldiers. Prior to Amin's flight from the invading Tanzanian forces in 1979, Gadhafi had sent 2,500 troops to bolster his forces and at least one company of Palestinian soldiers surrendered to Sudanese forces shortly afterwards. Gadhafi's active involvement in Uganda had begun with Amin's decision to expel Israeli advisers from the country shortly after the 1973 Arab-Israeli war. Immediately following the decision, Gadhafi sent a force of 400 troops to Uganda to help train Amin's army. Amin was given refuge by Gadhafi in Libya, for which he was extremely grateful until he realised that Gadhafi had placed him under house arrest. On realising his predicament, he publicly insulted Gadhafi's army, by referring to all Libyan soldiers as 'women'. In retaliation, Gadhafi promptly threw him out. Luckily for Amin, Saudi Arabia was prepared to give him sanctuary (and assistance) in his preparations for a return to power—a threat which still hangs over East Africa. Yet even though Amin was no longer supported by Gadhafi, the latter still interferred in the election of Dr Milton Obote as President in 1980.

On Libya's south-east border with Sudan, Gadhafi has, since 1974, been actively involved in supporting continued insurgency into Sudan with the aim of ensuring constant subversive activity within that country to the detriment of President Numairy. In 1984, Gadhafi ordered a bombing mission to put the Omdurman radio transmitter out of action and stepped up funding to the anti-Numairy, Marxist-oriented 10,000 strong Sudanese People's Liberation Army operating from the south of Sudan. The Libyan-backed guerrillas worked hand-in-glove with Shiite sects and the Moslem Brotherhood to unseat Numairy and, in March 1985, he only just acted in time. He imprisoned about 30 members of the Brotherhood leadership, but, with thousands of Ethiopian famine refugees streaming into the country and sapping its resources, together with an unfavourable economic package foisted on Sudan by the International Monetary Fund and the USA, Numairy was unable to postpone a trip to Washington to plead for the release of already ear-marked funds to alleviate the situation. During the trip, his Commander-in-Chief, General Abdul Rahman Suwar al-Dahab led a bloodless coup d'état which was recognised within hours by Libya as the legitimate Sudanese government. He appointed Dr Guzuli Dafalla as Prime Minister. Diplomatic links were immediately restored with Libya and the Provisional Government expressed a firm intention to establish a mission 'of some considerable size' in Tripoli, and of significantly expanding its representation in the USSR, Syria and Ethiopia. By the same token, Gadhafi's support for the Polisario rebels in Western Sahara had been continuously increasing since 1975, and a further example of his international involvement was his financial backing to Pakistan, in the search for an Islamic nuclear bomb between the years 1975–8.

These incidents apart, Libya attempted to annexe a portion of Niger's territory in 1976 and the following year, induced border skirmishes with Egypt. In an attempt to keep its illegally acquired 30,000 square miles of Chadian territory, Libya pumped money and weaponry into Chad in support of President Goukouni Oueddei's regime and various militant Moslem groups. This desire for more territory, is squarely based on Gadhafi's personal belief that Arab political aspirations can only be achieved under his guidance and leadership. A committed pan-Arabist, he has tried and failed eight times to merge or federate Libya with other Arab nations.

Another country which elicited Gadhafi's interest was the Central African Republic under Emperor Bokassa. In 1976, in an attempt to create some degree of religious unity in northern Africa, Gadhafi futilely tried to persuade Bokassa to convert publicly to Islam with a US$12 million personal gift to Bokassa. When Bokassa was dethroned in 1979, 200 Libyan officers were discovered in the Republic's army and, some 6,000 Kalashnikovs donated by Libya to Bokassa, were found in the royal palace.[28]

Yet Gadhafi's interest in foreign governments stretches across the globe. As recently as April 1983, four Libyan aircraft ostensibly carrying medical supplies for Colombian earthquake victims sought permission to refuel in Brazil. The authorities, cursorily checking the aircraft found not medical supplies, but more than 200 tons of arms, ammunition, explosives and spare parts in the cargo. Following the confiscation of these goods, it transpired that they were *en route* for Nicaragua.

In October 1984, some militant striking British coal miners met members of the PIRA in Dublin. PIRA advised the NUM miners how to employ paramilitary tactics against the police and that Colonel Gadhafi might well be prepared to support them in their 'battle' with Mrs Thatcher and the UK government. Accordingly, Roger Windsor, a member of the NUM executive committee, paid a visit to Libya and received an audience with Gadhafi after holding two days of talks with Libyan trade unionists. The visit arose out of an invitation received by the NUM following their Dublin meetings from the Libyan equivalent of the British TUC, ostensibly to learn the reasons for the dispute. The outcome was that Gadhafi immediately promised money to Windsor. Jack Dunn, Communist member of the NUM stated in early November, that 'We will be getting money from Libya but we don't know how much or when'. The amount was, in fact, **£20 million** and the reason for the vagueness regarding the delivery was due to the UK Government's attempts—eventually successful—to have the National Union of Mineworkers' bank accounts sequestered. In the event, **delivery began in the New Year when students and businessmen brought sums of money from Libya into the UK for distribution to the miners.** Colonel Gadhafi put it thus: that the money was destined for,

... the families of 7,000 miners who have been gaoled in Britain as well as to the families of the 3,000 who have been injured and cannot work and to the relations of five miners who have been 'slain by the police'.

Gadhafi desperately wants to destabilise the UK. He is a Soviet pawn. For many years he has personally funded extreme left-wing publications and organisations in Britain, in order to sow the seeds of disaffection amongst the poor, the deprived and the unemployed. A recent example was the 1985 inner city race riots in London and Birmingham which were organised by a mobile force of agitators acting in concert with their contacts within the local areas, led by a young extremist black woman known only as 'Liverpool Pat'. Its members are drawn from eight different left-wing and anarchist groups with connexions in most of Britain's major towns and cities. **This mobile team** has **also received assistance from** two other extremist groups: **Class War, and the Revolutionary Communist Party, both of which are thought to have received substantial funding from Libya.**[29]

4. *Gadhafi's nuclear dream*

The most dangerous aspect of Gadhafi's power-lust is his seemingly unquenchable desire to possess a nuclear warhead. For such a weapon to be placed in the hands of a man regarded by many as mentally unstable would bring the world to the brink of a nuclear holocaust. Denied direct information, technology and advanced scientific advice by the great powers, Gadhafi, in the quest for a nuclear capability, has exerted every possible

150

means to obtain the necessary raw materials and expertise. More than 10 per cent of Libyan students studying in the United States specialise in the nuclear sciences.[30] A similar figure is also true for both the United Kingdom and France. This raises the spectre that **one day, Libya or some other pro-terrorist government will be in a position to make such weapons.** If this should ever be the case, it must then follow that **such a government will ensure that this weaponry is made available to terrorists.** This hypothesis would simply be a continuation of existing policy exercised by Libya in every other sphere of weaponry, and in April 1979, West German terrorists received training in chemical and biological warfare at PFLP camps in Libya, Lebanon and South Yemen.

In an effort to make his own nuclear weapons, Colonel Gadhafi had made various attempts to acquire such a capability by both surreptitious and clandestine means. Since 1972 Libya has been cooperating with Belgo-Nucleaire, the Belgian state owned company which has acted as a nuclear energy consultant for the Libyan government. Finally, **in 1984, Belgo-Nucleaire began construction of a dual reactor nuclear power station on the Gulf of Sirte.** In 1975 an agreement was reached between Libya and Pakistan under which Gadhafi put up US$100m. to facilitate the creation of an atomic bomb in a nuclear research facility at Chasma in Pakistan. The terms of this agreement were that **Pakistan was to make the bomb, while Libya was to own it.** In the next three years Libya pumped more money into Pakistan for the same purpose, but since 1978, such funding began to decrease until it is now a mere fraction of its 1975 level. The reason for this lies in **Gadhafi's own attempts to manufacture a nuclear bomb.**

Under the guise of space exploration, the West German company OTRAG began testing rocket devices in Libya in 1979. OTRAG is a company in receipt of millions of Deutsche Marks invested by West German businessmen and offered Gadhafi ballistic missiles and tactical weaponry which would put both Cairo and Tel-Aviv well within Tripoli's range. OTRAG had entered the African continent with the intention of launching satellites for politically independent third world countries and, initially, OTRAG was given a rocket-launching area by the government of Zaire which was almost half the size of West

Germany itself. However, OTRAG failed in Zaire mainly because Kayser's terms were too colonial and because Chancellor Helmut Schmidt of West Germany advised President Mobutu of Zaire to rid himself of the company. Kayser then tried to sell OTRAG's holding company. Gadhafi sent three Libyan army officers to Zaire to inspect OTRAG's site and following a favourable report, Gadhafi arranged a meeting with Kayser and other members of OTRAG's board of directors in Munich, West Germany. **Gadhafi offered OTRAG a desert site south of Sebha** and guaranteed the closure of its aerospace. Another incentive was Gadhafi's promise to pay OTRAG a minimum amount of US$250m.

OTRAG had already developed a ground-to-ground missile with a warhead which could travel 2,500 miles. At this point, OTRAG sent one of their directors, Herr Wukasch, to Saudi Arabia, offering that country the facility to develop, on Saudi soil, **a war-headed ground-to-ground missile with an effective range of between 2,000 and 7,500 km.** A consortium was put together by OTRAG under Wukasch's leadership, which offered to supervise and build four missile production plants in Saudi Arabia, stipulating quite categorically, that military warheads would be freely available.

From its medium-sized factories in Europe and the one situated near Munich, OTRAG sends parts manufactured there, to clients all over the world. These parts, are completely compatible with missile systems—something which makes a total nonsense of West German law.

Gadhafi had heard of OTRAG through its activities in Syria in 1976–7. Fred Weymar, the then liaison officer between OTRAG and Zaire, led an all OTRAG negotiating team to Syria in 1976 and early 1977 and subsequent meetings were held in Paris and Geneva, to discuss proposals to provide Syria with liquid propulsion missiles having effective ranges of between 300 and 2,000 km—enough to reach Tel-Aviv and Cairo respectively. The cost, estimated at US$714m. was just too high for Damascus—but not for Colonel Gadhafi. **To this day, airspace over Sebha remains closed and OTRAG is firmly entrenched in Libya.**

Through this connexion **Gadhafi was led to Argentina, where Nazi scientists given refuge after the Second World War, continue their researches begun at Peenemunde**

152

**which produced the dreaded V1, V2 and V3 rockets
which assailed London towards the end of 1943 and 1944.**
The Argentinian government and Libya developed a relationship which is, in fact, much closer than is generally surmised.
The result of this relationship is that **Argentina is prepared
to sell surplus plutonium** not only **to Libya** but also to other
undisclosed countries. Reciprocation occurred during the 1982
Falklands Islands conflict between the United Kingdom and
Argentina, when **Libya helped to channel Iraqi-owned
Exocet missiles to Argentina.** Not only that, but during the
same conflict Libya was supplying Argentina with aircraft
spare parts as well as ammunition. Argentina also asked Libya
to supply her with missiles. In the first week of June 1982, in
response to these requests, Libya sent nine Boeing 707 aircraft
to Buenos Aires packed to capacity with arms and ammunition.
Libya also granted President Galtieri a US$10m. credit in
order that Argentina could buy weapons, but on very stiff
repayment terms. Unhappily, Argentina had to accept Gadhafi's terms in total because she badly needed weapons to resist
the impending UK forces' assault on the islands. At the same
time, Gadhafi also demanded that trade between the two
countries should undergo a significant increase in volume and
suggested strongly that less conspicuous contracts be entered
into between Argentina and Israel. In a final bid to prevent the
recapture of the islands, President Galtieri asked Colonel Gadhafi to purchase 39 Exocet missiles from France and then resell
them to Buenos Aires—France refused and the Argentinian
forces on the Falkland islands surrendered before Gadhafi
could acquire them by less obvious means.

B. SOUTH YEMEN

The transmogrification of a simple tribal revolt into an heroic
ideological struggle was completed when the Dhofar Liberation
Front was renamed the Popular Front for the Liberation of the
Occupied Arab Gulf. This organisation was structured and organised on Marxist-Leninist lines. PFLOAG camps were set up
in South Yemen for both political indoctrination and the military training of recruits. The main camp was situated at Hauf
and arms, supplies and propaganda facilities were provided by
the National Front in Aden. On the third anniversary of inde-

pendence, the National Front politburo changed the country's name to the People's Democratic Republic of Yemen (PDRY), thus aping Naif Hawatima's PDFLP.

Immediately the newly named state condemned the conservative Arab states as being corrupt and reactionary autocracies. With the exception of Libya, it sneered at the 'progressive' Arab states as bourgeois, aligning itself wholeheartedly with the terrorist-oriented 'rejection front' of the Palestinian movement. It established diplomatic relations with North Vietnam, North Korea and Cuba and declared its complete support for liberation movements everywhere. It courted the Chinese People's Republic and the Soviet Union for the economic and military aid they could provide and sought the help of the Cubans and East Germans in order to strengthen its defences and internal security.

By the mid 1970s, South Yemen had created more training camps in order to house personnel from Marxist-orientated terrorist groups. These terrorists came not only from Europe but also from Asia and included members of PIRA, the BMG and the South Moluccans. In 1978, the Cairo magazine *October* wrote of South Yemen, that it: '... has turned the island of Socotra into a stronghold for the Palestinian terror organisations and for the terrorists from many countries.'[31] **George Habash's PFLP were allowed by the PDRY to build extensive camps at Khayat in South Yemen where the PFLP helped to train the JRA.**

Aden, the capital of South Yemen is an extremely advantageous location for both the Soviet Union and the left-wing Palestinian terrorists, not only because it is safe from prying eyes, but also because it is safely distant from Soviet territory. From the early 1970s both George Habash and Wadi Haddad groomed an elite Palestinian-based multi-national terrorist force at Camp Khayat, and **after 1975, these South Yemen camps were being regarded as necessary 'finishing' schools for European terrorists.** At the same time, large numbers of South American terrorists were also undergoing training, all instructed by Cuban specialists.

South Yemen also offered sanctuary to many of the West German terrorists hunted by European police forces and antiterror squads. Although much speculation about South Yemen's role in this sphere had been rife for many years, it was not officially confirmed in the West until May 1980. In the same year, reports emerged concerning the training of international terrorists in South Yemen pointing conclusively to the fact that members of the Red Brigades, ETA and other European terrorists were undergoing training at Hauf, Mukalla and Al-Gheida camps from Cuban and East German instructors, with the full knowledge of the South Yemen government, the Yemeni military forces and the KGB. One of the organisers was George Habash's second-in-command, Bassam Abu Sharif, until 1978 the PFLP liaison officer with the Italian Red Brigades. It was Abu Sharif who had organised the Red Brigades to act as transporters for PFLP weaponry throughout Europe.

Apart from training facilities, South Yemen also provided international terrorists with sanctuary, arms and money, the use of its Embassies, diplomatic pouches and the provision of false documents including passports. South Yemen is also one country with extremely strong and important links with the Soviet Union. Its vital strategic situation facing the Horn of Africa at the mouth of the Red Sea and the Suez Canal, provides the Soviet Union with a warm-water port in the Indian Ocean from which it can radiate its influence throughout not only the whole oil-producing Gulf region, but also north-eastern Africa. In return, the Soviet Union and other Communist countries have provided South Yemen with the internal economic infrastructure it so desperately requires.

The USSR has provided South Yemen with arms and technical assistance vital to its development of the country as a strategic listening-post, whereas the People's Republic of China has been largely responsible for the provision of medical aid and the building of an important road link between Aden and the Hadramaut. Cubans have assumed responsibility for developing South Yemen's agricultural industry as well as providing improved and up-to-date training facilities and programmes for South Yemen's emerging air force. The organisation and implementation of its security system was left to the East Germans who also restructured the police-force. The point of such help and assistance—including the provision of instructors to train international terrorists—is to isolate South Yemen from any dependence whatsoever on the West. At the same time, the presence of so many foreign nationals, many of whom are from countries dominated by Soviet ideology, serves to ensure that

South Yemen will—in as short a time as possible—be possessed of an economic infrastructure, political organisations and security measures all compatible with Marxist-Leninist ideology. Thus, they are also compatible with the needs of the Soviet Union and the remainder of the Communist world in securing the country as a 'permanent' base.

C. IRAQ

Iraq is another Middle Eastern Arab country which, apart from funding and aiding Palestinian terrorist groups, has had an active history of providing commensurate support, including training, finance, sanctuary and diplomatic assistance to terrorist groups from well outside the region. Essentially however, **support for non-Palestinian terrorism has been restricted to those groups connected with George Habash's PFLP. Since the PFLP is the one Palestinian group with world-wide connexions, such 'restrictions' have not prevented any of the important and active European, Latin American or Asian terrorist groups from benefitting from Iraqi government hospitality, PIRA and the JRA in particular have been the recipients of substantial funding from Iraq** over a number of years.

Iraq's forays into the international terrorist scene, began in October 1975 with the appointment of Khali Ibrahim Mahmoud al-Azzawi as the Director of Operations of Iraqi Military Intelligence, who undertook the control and co-ordination of all Iraqi support for terrorist groups, together with Iraqi spy missions abroad. Yet perhaps Brigadier al-Azzawi's greatest contribution was the formulation and creation of the 'Strategic Work Plan'. The plan, first secretly published on 30 May 1976, consisted of instructions to all Iraqi Military Attachés to report on the battle-order, equipment and combat-readiness of the forces of their host-country, including 'mass destruction weapons'. They were also ordered to report on the institutions and personnel who were responsible for carrying out research not only on 'mass destruction' weaponry but also on the military application of such weapons.[32]

Enormous amounts of cash, financed directly out of its oil riches, are used in order to subvert individuals in the UK, Sweden and other Western European democracies, who provide

156

Iraq with intelligence information of the type described above. Much of the intelligence thus acquired enabled Iraq to acquire the technology necessary to build, with French aid, the Osirak Nuclear Reactor. This reactor was intended for the production of atomic bombs. In the early stages of the Gulf War, Iran had attacked the reactor, slightly damaging it. Saddan Hussain, the Iraqi President, immediately following the raid on 27 July 1980, stated that the reactor was aimed solely at Israel and was therefore of no concern or threat to Iran. Thus Israel watched the progress of the reactor with increasing trepidation. **By June 1981, it was clear that the reactor could provide bombs from enriched uranium or plutonium,** of the capability and strength of the one dropped on Hiroshima. This, together with the fact that the reactor would become operational either in late July or early September 1981, prompted Prime Minister Menachem Begin and his Cabinet to instruct the Israel Defence Forces to destroy the reactor. Known as Project Tammuz, the attack on the Osirak reactor had to be perfectly timed. The Israelis could not wait until the reactor was in operation and thus 'hot', because any attack would then have released a huge wave of radioactivity which would have spread out over the whole of Baghdad, killing countless thousands of innocent civilians. On 7 June 1981, Project Tammuz was put into operation and the Osirak Nuclear Reactor completely destroyed by the Israeli Air Force.[33]

Iraq's reaction to the attack was to increase the amount of arms smuggled into NATO capitals by Iraqi diplomats for terrorist groups. (Large quantities of arms are stored in all Iraqi Embassies in basement strongrooms.) Other services included false Lebanese and Iraqi passports, cash and up-to-date information. Indeed, in an interview given by President Saddam Hussein in mid-1978, he explicitly acknowledged the fact that European terrorists had been trained by Palestinians and certainly made no effort to deny that Iraq had played an important part in such training:

Certain Palestinians have trained some of the Europeans outside Iraq under mutual assistance arrangements. Perhaps some may have entered Iraq disguised as Palestinians.[34]

Iraq has never been shy of sending out assassination squads of its own—whether of Iraqi nationals or of rogue Palestinians. Of the former, there are numerous examples but perhaps the most well known was the assassination in London of an exiled former Prime Minister of Iraq, General Abdul Razzal al-Naif. He was cut down by a hail of gunfire on the steps of the Intercontinental Hotel in July 1978. In the same month Iraq backed Abu Nidal's rogue Palestinian outfit which murdered the PLO representative Said Hammami. Hammami's murder in London was directly due to his stated belief that the Palestinians best way forward was to enter into discussions with Israel to achieve a negotiated settlement of the Arab-Israeli dispute. Significantly, Abu Nidal operated out of the Iraqi Embassy in London. **Iraq is also suspected of engineering the 1981 Iranian Embassy siege in London which was ended by the SAS. Similarly, it is also believed to have encouraged Nidal's group to assassinate Israeli diplomats in both Paris and London,** which gave further impetus to discussions within Israel for the 1982 invasion of Lebanon. Iraq, together with Libya, financially supported leftist groups aligned to the PLO because the USSR wanted the Lebanese Christian government of Gemayel overthrown to add to the destabilisation of the region and the loss of Western influence. However, since declaring war with Iran in 1980, Iraq has devoted most of its energies towards containing and repulsing Iranian counter-attacks in an effort to prevent the loss of significant amounts of territory and has thus tended to withdraw from the arena of international terrorism.

D. ALGERIA

Algeria likewise has a history of providing arms, money, sanctuary and training facilities to international terrorists and allowing its embassies in foreign capitals to be used for the provision of false documentation and a distribution point for weaponry and munitions transferred by way of the diplomatic pouch. The story begins in 1968 when Algeria's own guerrilla camps were thrown open to international terrorists.

These terrorists arrived on Algerian soil in order to undergo a course of training in modern guerrilla and insurgency techniques provided by highly skilled KGB instructors, who comprised the entire staff for all the camps. **In 1971, members of ETA and PIRA were introduced to each other by KGB**

instructors as being natural allies—an introduction that was to pay dividends for both terrorist groups in the years following. ETA and PIRA thus signed a formal pact on 1 May 1972, together with the Breton Liberation Front, declaring mutual assistance in a variety of areas. Later the same year, a further formal declaration of alliance was signed by ETA with the Uruguayan Tupamaros, various Kurdish resistance groups and Fatah.

Since 1968, then, Algeria has played willing host to a plethora of international terrorist groups including the Palestinians. These were loosely co-ordinated by the PLO representative in Algiers, who was given ambassadorial status, and who advised the Algerian government on international groups who could also benefit from such training. Apart from better known European terrorist groups, Algerian facilities were also extended to little known groups like the Canary Isles Liberation Movement which was given the added facility of nightly air-time on Algerian radio.[35]

As the provisions for international terrorists waxed in all aspects, the more senior and effective terrorist groups had the privilege of undergoing training together with the regular forces of the Algerian military. Thus **international terrorists were trained alongside regular soldiers in Algerian army camps** in a variety of clandestine techniques, instruction in which was given by Cuban officers often of field rank. Similarly, Algeria opened up its intelligence network to the major international terrorist groups, providing up-to-date information supplied by its Embassies and other agencies which proved to be invaluable when they formulated plans for their next attacks.

Despite all the assistance given to each of the groups that formed the mosaic of international terrorism, Algeria's 'enfant gâté' remained the ETA. When in 1974, ETA joined the Maoist–Trotskyite World Front for the Liberation of Oppressed Peoples, weapons and money flowed freely from both Algeria and Libya to the Front's Headquarters in Brussels. Originating in China, North Korea and Vietnam, many of the weapons were simply transshipped from Algeria to Belgium *via* the former's diplomatic pouch. The following year, 143 ETA terrorists were sent for advanced training from both Algerian and Cuban instructors at the Souma Police Academy, 25 miles outside

Algiers. In the autumn of 1975, Libya and Algeria jointly agreed at a Presidential conference between Colonel Gadhafi and Colonel Boumedienne, to put the venture on a regular footing. **In November 1976,** the two heads of state made a further secret agreement to formulate a joint aid programme specifically designed to assist the European international terrorist network. **Colonel Gadhafi took personal charge of the ETA–IRA connexion while Algeria—financed by Gadhafi—adopted the Bretons and Corsicans.** Training facilities were also agreed upon. The Algerian government removed the training venue from Souma to Blida military camp, just to the south-west of Algiers while Libya agreed to provide specialist training facilities at Az Zarouiah camp in Benina, near Benghazi. The latter became known as 'the Europeans' camp'. **The result was staggering. There was a quantum leap in the number of terrorist attacks perpetrated throughout Europe during the next twelve months.** Yet terrorist attacks in Northern Ireland, the Basque country in Spain, Corsica and Brittany all underwent an increase of geometric proportions. **The French, Spanish and UK security forces were stretched to the limit,** and, unable to cope, began to create unofficial links between themselves and Israel. As the decade drew to a close, the number of terrorist incidents continued to reflect an upward trend. One significant factor did emerge. Increased international co-operation began to reduce the number of multinational operations carried out by terrorist gangs. This, in turn, led to the export of murder-squads from countries such as Libya and Iran aimed solely at the destruction of political dissidents exiled abroad.

*

This is not the whole story. The Arab world on its own is totally incapable of mounting such an attack on the Western democracies, from the single stand-point of technological advance. For the answer to the question of how the Arab states and Palestinian organisations can present such a threat, we must turn away from the Arab world and search the Communist sphere.

160

Communist state support for international terrorism

I ISHUTINISM

THE FORERUNNER OF modern terrorism was the creation in the 1880s of a Russian organisation called the NARODNAYA VOLYA. This organisation was created by the Bolsheviks at their Lipetsk Congress and initiated the whole concept of 'motiveless terror', regarding any murder as a 'progressive action'. The Narodnaya Volya regarded the whole system as the enemy; in this, it was innovative. However, it was superseded by the Social Revolutionaries who adopted Ishutinism in an attempt to break down ties of loyalty between the Czarist monarchy and the people.

Nicholas Ishutin was a Moscow revolutionary, who, in January 1866, conceived the idea of an elaborately contrived apparatus which would operate at two levels, and thus penetrate deeply into Russian Czarist society. Its open level was the political wing which organised insurrectional agitation and also acted as a propaganda machine, working in social clubs, schools, libraries and in the provinces. Its clandestine and covert level consisted of a terrorist wing, completely committed to assassination, robbery, blackmail and other similar acts. Its effect was to bring Russian terrorists and criminals into radical politics for the first time. The Arab terrorist groups of the late 1960s and 1970s moved in the same direction, as did other international terrorist groups simply because **Moscow preferred the Ishutinist principle to be adopted by such groups since it would alleviate potential problems and simplify the means by which the USSR could provide assistance to them.**[1]

In order to anaesthetise moral reflexes and prepare recruits for their tasks, the Palestinians repeatedly subjected their new recruits to rape and forced them to participate actively in com-

A diagram showing that Soviet Nihilism is enshrined in communism and apparent in Terrorism.

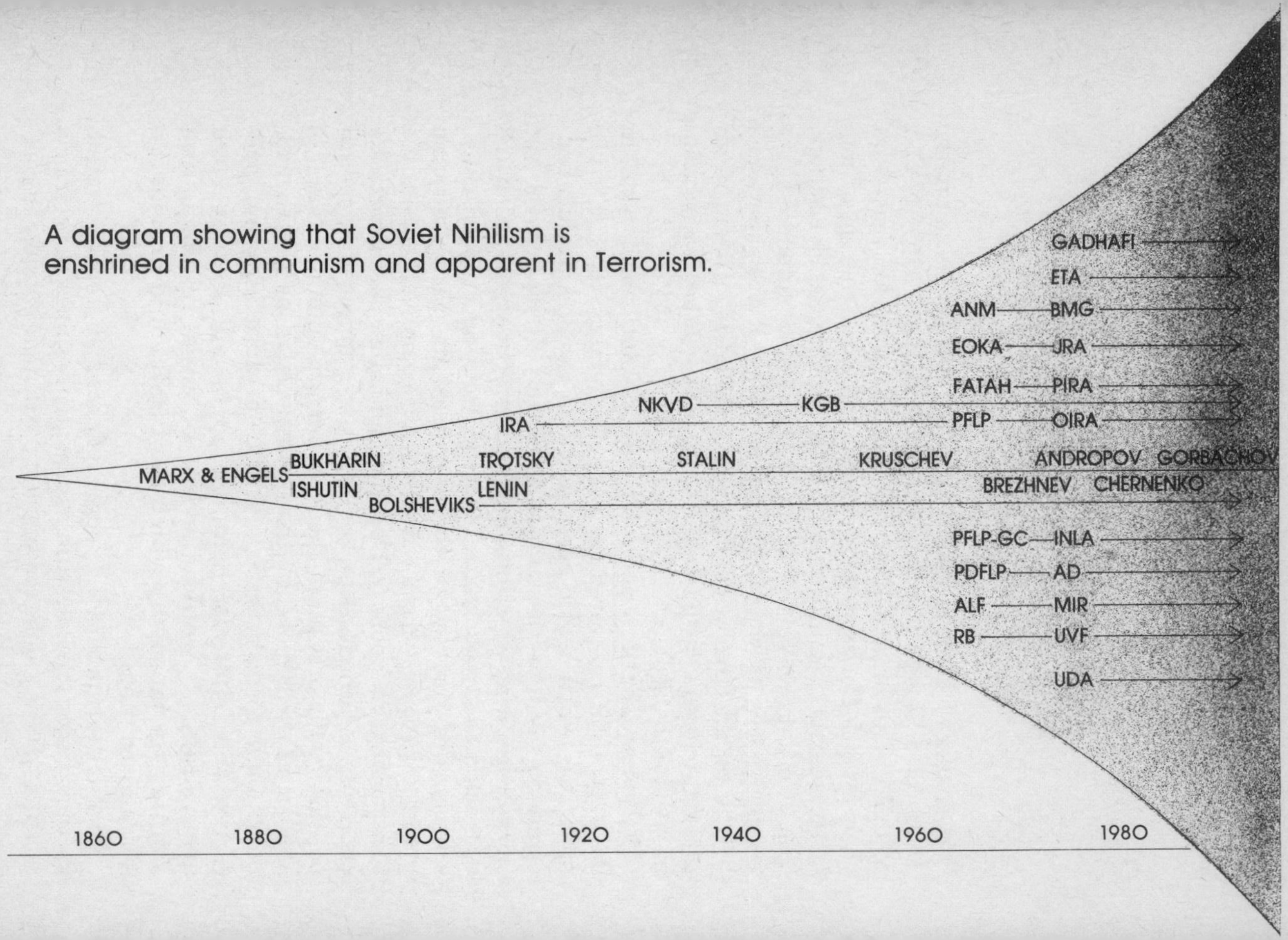

munal sexual acts of depravity. As one commentator on terrorism has succinctly remarked:

The theory is based on the assumption that neither man nor woman can be an effective terrorist so long as he or she retains the moral elements of a human personality.[2]

The same principle was behind the Bolshevik rejection of the Church and the existence of God in 1917 soon after achieving power. In fact, **the basic theory of terrorism** was formulated by the Bolsheviks and thus, over the years, **has become institutionalised within the Soviet political creed.** This helps us understand current Soviet involvement in international terrorism. A startling reappraisal of Soviet foreign policy reveals that

... nearly all the elements of Soviet global strategy are essentially an adaptation to foreign policy of methods which had been learned by the Bolsheviks when they were in the underground.[3]

II   SOVIET SPONSORSHIP FOR TERRORISTS

This situation translates itself into Soviet support for the Palestinian and other terrorist movements. In 1971 two events occurred, the result of which was a wave of international terrorist activity indiscriminately unleashed on the West. Boris Ponomarev, then the Director for International Communist Affairs, outlined the Soviet position with regard to liberation and other movements particularly relating to the Third World, in an article which appeared in *Kommunist*. Coincidentally, the Politburo and Communist Party of the Soviet Union had agreed at a joint meeting to accept KGB advice to accept the Palestinians as a major political instrument in the Middle East and to subsidise them. Yet it is essential to understand that **the USSR** does not mastermind or control individual acts of terror: it **simply offers general sponsorship to terrorist groups.** However, the situation is further complicated by **the use of Cuba and Libya as terrorist conduits** which, as former State Department spokesman, William Dyess, has remarked, provides 'a climate in which terrorism flourishes'.

The CPSU has suffered considerable set-backs through KGB-inspired plots in the years immediately preceding this decision—most notably in Mexico. Nearly 15 years of time and effort had been expended in destabilising the young republic, beginning with the 1959 wild-cat railway strikes. This was an attempt to have the 1968 Olympic Games cancelled by the orchestration of riots and disturbances in urban centres throughout the land. It failed and prompted a concerted and well-planned KGB operation to plunge Mexico into civil war and destroy its government by armed force.

The plan adopted by the KGB involved Cuba, East Germany and North Korea all of whom acted as Moscow's proxies. A terrorist group, Movimiento de Acción Revoluccionaria was created—trained, financed and equipped, by the KGB—and was on the brink of beginning its devastation in earnest when the Mexican Security Services uncovered the plot and on 12 March 1971 presented it to the Government of the day. A similar situation had been uncovered in Ghana during the 24 February *coup d'état* in 1966, involving both the KGB and the East German security services. In April 1968, it was revealed by the Colombian authorities that KGB money had been used to finance the murderous Fuerzas Armadas Revoluccionaria. In 1963 and again in 1970, mass expulsions of KGB personnel posing as diplomats, occurred in the Congo. In July 1970 Sudan expelled hundreds of Soviet personnel after a KGB-inspired coup was aborted. In October 1971, the Dutch authorities intercepted a Czechoslovak arms consignment destined for the IRA. **These are only some of the failures which prompted both the KGB and the CPSU to formally adopt a policy of active support for international terrorism by using surrogates to distance themselves further from these groups and their actions,** thus allowing them to claim non-complicity and even innocence.[4]

The effect of the official Soviet entry into international terrorist circles was quite unmistakable. Terrorist groups formed and functioning toward the end of the 1960s, did so without experience, skills or money and certainly without weapons or international connexions. **The transformation** which occurred within less than a decade **was due almost entirely to the logistical and financial support given to such groups by both Cuba and the Palestinians.** The latter had been wholly armed by the USSR since 1968 and, at least 10 per cent of its fighting force had been trained either in the USSR itself, or in one of the East European countries. The Communist-sponsored revolutionary and national liberation movements have been described as

able to depend on the Soviet Union for substantial financial, military and diplomatic support .... Moreover, they now have the additional benefits of a whole bloc of Soviet allies and client states and proxies which can provide alternative conduits for all kinds of support to client movements.[5]

Whereas this ensured that the weaponry, indoctrination and intelligence made available to such groups were, by the mid-1970s, almost completely pro-Soviet or Communist bloc, it also ensured that the targets of the terrorists were distinctly 'Western' (American or capitalist). This intensification of USSR involvement in and support of international terror thus becomes '... a geographical fact of enormous import for all free societies'.[6]

The international destabilising system comprises the USSR and the East European bloc, Cuba, North Korea, Vietnam and others. In order to allow the USSR to disclaim all responsibility, and all knowledge, four of these countries, Cuba and North Korea, Libya and the Palestinians act as proxies. So concerned were 170 retired US generals and admirals, that they publicly urged President Carter to start taking effective measures against Soviet attempts to dominate the Eastern Mediterranean and elsewhere.[7]

The Soviet Union officially continued to regard terrorism as both counter-productive and harmful to the Arab cause. On occasions it specifically condemned Black September's use of terror, particularly hijacking. Yet despite this, on many specific occasions, the USSR has sought to justify Palestinian terrorism within Israel and the occupied territories since 1967. Official CPSU organs have also often maintained that such terrorism is solely advocated only by splinter groups within the PLO—thus totally ignoring the Fatah–Black September connexion.[8]

The truth is that **the USSR is the ultimate source of international terrorism,** taking a central rôle in 'training, equipping, transporting and protecting' the more infamous and important international terrorists and their organisations. Such a stand-point is adopted because **it is essentially and pri-**

167

marily as interested in disruption, disorientation and chaos among the Western democracies and the Third World as it is in formal occupation or take-over. Thus it regards terrorism as a form of surrogate warfare—a substitute for traditional warfare, which has, in many ways, become both too dangerous and too expensive to use. International terrorism has, therefore, become for the Soviet Union, an extension of state warfare. Together with the Arab countries, the USSR with its Eastern European satellites, Cuba and North Korea have all provided weapons, training facilities, money, organisational and diplomatic support to nullify any attempts made by the democracies to adopt measures against terrorism in international forums. The reasons for such an attitude lie in the fact that the entire Middle East is a region of vital strategic interest to the USSR. Yet the USSR's efforts to become a diplomatic force in the region were lost when its leaders made the monumental error, in 1967, of breaking off diplomatic relations with Israel. This done, the only way in which the USSR can retain a toe-hold of influence in the region, is to back the rejection-front Arab states and the Palestinians against Israel and any US-conceived initiative for peace.

Prior to 1961, however, the USSR never showed any official interest in the Palestinian cause, preferring to confine itself to pronouncements in the UN on the refugee problem. There are good reasons for this stance. The PLO before 1968 was a moribund and ineffective organisation under the control of the Arab League. Thus there was no adumbrative organisation through which the USSR could approach the Palestinians. More importantly though, the KGB was busy building its connexions with the Communist Parties of Jordan, Syria, Egypt and Lebanon and had begun to infiltrate **Soviet-controlled KGB operatives** into the various Palestinian groups **such as Michel Moukharbal and Mohammed Boudia.** This policy was reinforced by a Politburo decision taken in 1964, that spending should be markedly increased on terrorist enterprises undertaken abroad, and that GRU training facilities should be opened up to terrorists of a suitable political complexion. These decisions were taken, in the realisation that **uncontrolled terrorism can seriously debilitate foreign societies because resources are diverted from constructive projects as official repression is invoked.**

This particular period prompted such decisions because of the framework of current Soviet society. In the early 1960s, Soviet mortality rates were already increasing; by 1979, infant mortality had increased to 35.5 per 1000 (a figure which was nearly double that of the mid 1950s). Similarly, adult mortality was inexorably increasing. In 1964, adult mortality stood at 6.9 per 1000. By 1980 it was 10.3 per 1000. Thus the average Soviet citizen's lot continues to grow worse. In order to combat this situation the forces of repression—the KGB—are augmented annually, since Soviet leaders still do not enjoy popular support. The situation is exacerbated by the constant failure of the USSR's agricultural policy. Privately owned agricultural land accounts for only 1.3 per cent of all land under cultivation in the USSR. Yet it provides two-thirds of all the potatoes and eggs and one-third of all vegetables and meat produced in the Soviet Union. Similarly, the Russian birth-rate is the lowest of all Soviet nationalities; this means that the number of Russians of working age will continue to shrink dramatically in the next 15 years. Thus the ruling party of the USSR has to be seen to achieve success outside the country as there is little scope for success within the system.

From 1964 to 1970, the USSR praised the Palestinians more often and continued to encourage the use of violence and to exonerate terrorists. Similarly it began to publish photographs of Palestinian terrorists in training and decided upon Fatah as the leading Palestinian group, blaming Israel for any bloodshed which occurred. A new training centre at Govkovskoye Shosse, 15 miles east of Moscow, was opened up, specialising in sabotage, abduction and assassination training for directly imported Third World students and for those from Patrice Lumumba University. Simultaneously, **contacts with the Palestinians were channelled through the Afro-Asian Solidarity Committee which is controlled by the KGB International Department** and financed by enforced donations from the Russian Orthodox Church, athletes and entertainers. These donations are used to purchase arms and other military supplies for African and Middle Eastern terrorists.

Initially, all the offers of arms and training for the Palestinians emanated from Soviet surrogates, with the East Germans offering to supply arms in 1967 and the Vietcong beginning to train Palestinians in 1966. Subsequent large-scale training was undertaken by, Cuba, Czechoslovakia, East Germany, Hungary and Bulgaria. Only 'selected' terrorists underwent training in the Baku, Tashkent Crimean camps in the USSR. Similarly, although the USSR supported Palestinian hijackings, it referred to two Lithuanian hijackers who had made a bid for freedom as 'criminal murderers' and condemned the Israeli Entebbe raid as 'a vivid example of terrorism'.

After the Munich Olympic massacre, **Moscow was instrumental in creating a public image for the Palestinians based on the Ishutinist principle by disassociating the PLO and Arafat from terrorist acts** and referring to the perpetrators as 'extremists', thus implying that Arafat and the PLO were moderates. The Soviet press continued to stress that the Palestinian Resistance Movement was 'against all forms of terror' and denied any PLO involvement whatsoever in terrorism. Palestinian terrorist leaders added to the fiction by stating that the Palestinians would be prepared to sign an international agreement against terrorism. At the same time **the USSR began to emphasise for the Palestinians a revolutionary policy singling out the USA as the main protagonist,** in the hope that it would have greater global appeal. Thus, by 1978, Palestinian terrorist leaders spoke of 'American Imperialism' as the 'principal enemy' and of the animosity of the Americans for the Palestinian people while entering into a diplomatic offensive **which resulted in the PLO achieving political recognition in a number of countries.**[9]

As one commentator on Soviet foreign policy has put it: 'The USSR does not simply fish in troubled waters: it troubles the waters and then fishes in them.'[10] Once the Palestinians had turned to terrorism, the Soviet Union was then able to cause an escalation of the crisis and, as one Fatah officer who defected publicly commented, 'whenever they are interested in such an eruption, all they have to do is come and give [the Palestinians] instructions.'[11]

Yet in another sense, the USSR has no option but to enlist the Palestinians in their joint cause. **The Soviet Union had begun to view the Palestinians as a revolutionary element which could contribute considerably to unrest and instability within the Middle East.** They would also act as a rallying point for those who opposed ties with the United States, and those who opposed the existing régimes. This was a rôle which

170

the Arab Communist Parties were to adopt, but had proven incapable of doing so. Thus after 1968, their importance was relegated to that of a simple conduit for arms from the USSR and Eastern bloc countries to the Palestinians; however, the Communist Parties of Jordan, Syria, Iraq and Lebanon, established their own terrorist group in November 1969—al Ansar. The acceptance of this group by other Palestinian groups was a condition made by Moscow prior to initiating assistance. **The Palestinians also provided the USSR with the possible facility of blowing-up all the oil-fields in the Gulf-region including those in Iran—something which would, if put into operation, inflict a mortal wound on United States 'imperialism'.**[12]

The serious threat posed by the Palestinians to the leaders of the conservative Gulf Sheikhdoms is another attractive feature to the USSR. Indirect pressure can be brought on these states to toe the radical line or risk a fate similar to that of the Shah of Iran, since the Palestinian movement is an important factor in laying the foundation for leftist revolutions within the Arabian peninsula—particularly the PFLP and PDFLP. This ties in nicely with the USSR's systematic attempt to deprive the West of hitherto automatic access to its major sources of energy in the Gulf region and of strategic raw materials in Central and Southern Africa.

The primary value to the Soviet Union of international terrorism outside the Middle East lies in the terrorists' resolute efforts to weaken, demoralise, paralyse, strike fear into and humiliate the Western democracies, with the sole aim of dismantling them. The raw impotence of Western European Governments was truly exposed by killings in Northern Ireland, Spanish Basqueland, Italy and Turkey. All these,

affected the West's defences against Soviet expansion, the cohesion of NATO, protecting Western Europe and the Mediterranean; the credibility of the United States, protecting oil supplies and routes from the Persian Gulf.[13]

The USSR allocates approximately US$200m. per annum to provide finance alone for national liberation movements, much of which ends up with Fatah and other groups. A symbolic relationship exists between Fatah and the USSR

171

encompassing politics, ideology, military and cultural think-
ing. To this end, **the Palestinians co-ordinate their moves
with the Soviets and serve as the USSR's main link with
more than 30 terrorist organisations throughout the
world.** Much of the initial impetus for this relationship came
from the PNF created by the Jordanian Communist Party from
funds allocated to it by Moscow. But when the PNF did not
achieve the anticipated results, **the KGB began infiltrating
the remaining Palestinian terrorist groups** on a greater
scale in order to ensure an increasing degree of influence.

A number of prominent members of various Palestinian terrorist groups have made public statements concerning the
extent of Soviet aid to them. On 25 September 1976, Zehdi
Labib Terzi, PLO observer at the United Nations, stated specifically that, '...the Soviet Union and all the Socialist countries,
they give us full support—diplomatic, moral, edu-
cational....'[14] This was further amplified by Farook Khaddoumi, in an article published four months later,

> ...The Soviet Union and the Socialist organisations are close friends
> of the Palestinian revolution. The material, moral and political sup-
> port from the Soviet Union is of great importance in the friendly re-
> lations with the Palestinian people.[15]

The itemisation of the sort of support allegedly provided by the
Soviet Union, ensured that the West knew exactly what it was
up against. Significantly no rebuff, denial or comment
appeared in the Soviet press, nor did one Soviet diplomat state
that such comments were untrue. The Soviet silence on this
score was deafening. Not to be outdone, Naif Hawatima, the
PDFLP leader reiterated that:

> The PLO's relations with the Soviet Union are based on political prin-
> ciples, as well as on the basis of the Soviet Union's solidarity with the
> struggle of the Palestinian people.[16]

What in fact this tautological politicism meant was explained
by David Morison,

> Moscow has found that solidarity with the Palestinian cause, as
> expressed by the PLO, serves as a convenient touchstone of Arab 'anti-
> imperialist' sentiment. The Palestinians in their turn can always
> assure Moscow that if they get a state of their own, it will be organised

on the best Marxist model.[17]

The Palestinians were, by 1980, almost totally subservient to Moscow and always responded positively to every whim of Russian foreign policy. Abu Iyad, Arafat's second-in command, openly condemned China for invading Vietnam—even though the latter was the aggressor; on another occasion, Farook Khaddoumi congratulated the Soviet Union for invading Afghanistan whilst Arafat himself told President Bani-Sadr and Ayatollah Khomeini of Iran that the Soviet Union intended to remain in Afghanistan for an 'absolutely temporary' period.

Ham-strung by the increasing tension between Iran and Iraq of the late 1970s in the Gulf of Hormuz, which was threatening to break out into open warfare, the USSR was being castigated in virtually all international circles for its invasion of Afghanistan. They were also being thwarted by continuing internecine warfare in Lebanon, and thus the Soviet Union had to become more open about its relationship with the Palestinians. In November 1980, two press statements were made. 'The USSR ... continues to support the struggle of the Palestinian people for their legitimate inalienable national rights.'[18] The second statement reported that the USSR was 'consistently and firmly supporting' the Palestinian people.[19] One month later Abd-el Muhsin Abu Maizer, a Fatah spokesman for the PLO, was reported as saying that the Palestinians enjoyed the complete support of the Soviet Union in international circles and also that they were continually provided with 'material, economic and military assistance'. It was in July and August, however, that the full significance of these mutual congratulatory statements became obvious. On 2 July, Farook Khaddoumi, head of the PLO's political department, gave a radio broadcast reporting that the USSR had once again emphasised '... its full support, in all realms, for the PLO'. But it was Abu Iyad, the PLO Security Chief, whose *ne plus ultra* crowned the relationship.

If we had the capability of signing a treaty with the Soviet Union, we would have signed a thousand treaties, and if we controlled land we would have allowed the Soviets a thousand bases, because we are dealing with a foe stronger than Israel, the United States.[20]

Thus the symbiosis of the PLO–USSR relationship had, at last been openly acknowledged.

Coupled with all the logistical support, **the USSR entered into a series of disinformation campaigns in a dual attempt to further destabilise the region and to weaken Western resistance to Soviet inspired policies.** The success of many such campaigns initiated by the KGB depends greatly on two factors: the extent to which Soviet agents and sympathisers can influence the Western media and, the extent to which Soviet funded and supported groups can put across the Soviet message. **Apart from the Afro-Asian Solidarity Committee, which provides cover for Soviet dealings with terrorists through its affiliations in over 50 countries, there are a growing number of Soviet-controlled groups.** The most important is the World Peace Council and its affiliates in 135 countries including the US Peace Council.

The US is the host to a plethora of Soviet-inspired groups as the USSR makes every effort to bite into the soft underbelly of US democracy: like the Women's International League for Peace and Freedom; the US Communist Party; and the North American Congress on Latin America; similarly, the USSR actively utilises many of the western Communist Parties. At the same time, **KGB personnel within the UN seek to use that organisation to undermine the West and destabilise the Third World** by utilising disinformation projects, the most notorious of which were: the story floated by a Tokyo newspaper that the CIA intended to hijack an oil tanker in order to induce the Arab Gulf States to agree to the siting of US bases on their land; forging a 'Dissent Paper on El Salvador and Central America' purporting to reflect the views of government officials that support for El Salvador should be reduced; and a KGB campaign to persuade the world that the CIA were implicated in the Aldo Moro kidnapping.

The extent of Soviet penetration may be seen by the number of expulsions of Soviet diplomats which took place between 1980 and 1982 from more than 25 countries, all of them for attempting to suborn nationals of those countries or for supporting terrorist activities.[21]

The usefulness of the Palestinians to the Soviet Union was incalculable. **Through George Habash of the PFLP, the Soviets were able to create chaos and disruption throughout the Middle East for an entire decade. Turkey,** until the

174

military coup in 1971, **had been sliding remorselessly into total lawlessness under Habash's encouragement.** Following the return of civil power, a carbon-copy repetition occurred until General Evren took the reins of government. Yet perhaps Habash's most important sphere was his cultivation of links with other international terrorist groups such as the JRA, the BMG, OIRA and PIRA in Ireland, Spanish ETA and the Italian Red Brigades.

Through the KGB and GRU, the USSR has established direct links with terrorist cells in Saudi Arabia and the Arabian Peninsula by way of South Yemen and also with insurgent groups **in Ethiopia and Angola. Through George Habash and Wadi Haddad, direct links were secured for the KGB and GRU with international terrorists— particularly those of a Marxist-orientation in Italy, Turkey and Ireland. Through the international terrorist network, relations were also established with other African and South American states, mainly by way of the USSR's proxy, Cuba.**

In an attempt **to distance itself from any support that the USSR might have sanctioned to European terrorist groups, the decision had been taken long before, to use the Eastern Satellite states as Moscow's proxies.** A conduit thus having been established, **Moscow began to channel aid to** those terrorist groups of a similar political persuasion and of an effectiveness akin to that of Habash's PFLP. Quite naturally these included **PIRA,** the BMG and RAF, the Italian Red Brigades and the JRA and the Puerto Rican FALN.

It would, however, be totally erroneous to conclude that aid from Moscow to reactionary groups or individuals began with the rise of terrorism in the 1960s.

The forerunner of the KGB, the NKVD, was actively involved in the establishment of foreign networks prior to the Second World War. NKVD Major-General Pavel Sudolplatov controlled the Rote Kapelle network which towards the end of the war was extended to weaken US influence in southern Europe. This group formed part of the Italian Communist Party's partisan organisation which terrorised northern Italy from 1945 until 1949. **In 1950, one of the Communist Party leaders in Italy, Paolo Tedeschi, established a school for terrorist training and,** together with his cousin Raymondo

Aghion, **introduced Henri Curiel** to links within both the French and Italian Communist Parties in 1950 and 1951 **when Curiel shared an apartment with Tedeschi** at 41 via Piavi in Rome. Tedeschi was a colleague of Pietro Secchia who worked under Sudolplatov and fled into exile in Czechoslovakia in 1953. One of Secchia's friends was Giangiacomo Feltrinelli who visited him there many times, undergoing three terrorist training courses at Karlovy Vary and Doupov. It was during these visits that **Feltrinelli met Renato Curcio, another Communist KGB agent and founder of the Red Brigades,** and Carlo Piperno and Toni Negri the founders of Potere Operaio (later Autonomio Operaio). At the same time, some selected Palestinians underwent training, thus opening up possibilities for future linkage between these individuals.

When **Curiel** entered France in 1951, he became actively involved with the Algerian FLN and **linked up with Mohammed Boudia.** Curiel had already hosted Stalin's appointed leader of the Algerian Communist Party, André Marty, in the 1940s and, following the FALN victory, he **set up the forerunner to Aide et Amitié in Paris—Solidarité—which operated on the Ishutinist principle.** It openly operated as a humanitarian organisation but, secretly provided logistical support for French terrorist groups (safe-houses, documents and weapons), later extended to the PLO, Latin American groups, ETA and Italian terrorists. **Curiel now the top Soviet NKVD/KGB agent in Western Europe and sole central co-ordinator of the international terrorist movement, formed a link with Carlos** through his weapons procurement officer, Pereira Carvalho, a Portuguese antique dealer, who lived in rue de Verneuil, Paris VII. When Carlos took over the Boudia operation, he chose as his operational base, rue Toullier, Paris V, only 10 minutes walk from Curiel's apartment at 4, rue Rollin on the other side of the Panthéon. Thus **through Feltrinelli, Carlos, Boudia, Moukharbel and Curiel, the basis for an international terrorist network had been established well before 1968.**[22]

Between 1956 and 1964, the founders of **the BMG,** Ulrike Meinhof and her husband Klaus Rainer Rohl, **had their activities subsidised to the amount of US$250,000 by the Soviets. This money, provided by the KGB, was forwarded to the East German Ministry of State Security** which then acted as paymaster. This was effectively East Germany's initiation into the provision of support for terrorist and reactionary groups.

Apart from providing instructors for PFLP camps in Lebanon and South Yemen during the 1960s and 1970s, the East Germans also provided a degree of pure financial aid. The East Berlin Communist Party, for example, donated 1m. DM per annum to the Palestinians—notably Fatah—*via* the PLO headquarters in East Berlin. These donations began with the 1972 Munich Olympic Massacre and have continued up to the present. Yet the East Germans favoured the PFLP of all the Palestinian groups and, in 1970, set up a rapid-transit system for both terrorists and weapons. Within the next two years, the **PFLP and Fatah had established 22 operative bases in West Germany and used East Germany as a convenient back-door entrance. The Czechoslavakian government and its diplomats assisted the Italian Red Brigades** whereas the East Germans assisted primarily the Palestinians and the BMG. In order **to orchestrate the actions of the various terrorist groups in Western European countries, the KGB set up a control office in Vienna** under a high-ranking KGB officer, Alexander Benyaminov, who was employed at the UN International Atomic Energy Agency. This appointment was to supplement the liaison provided by PLO offices throughout the Eastern Bloc, Vietnam, North Korea, Cuba and the most important of all, Moscow.

III   THE KGB'S ROLE

The use of the KGB to foment internal strife, particularly in Third World countries has been Soviet policy since Stalin's era. Under the auspices of KGB Department VIII, Victor Sakharov was placed in charge of Soviet operations in and out of the PDRY in 1968. His brief was to implement the Soviet Union's three-pronged policy with regard to the Arab states in the Gulf. The prime aim of Department VIII was to dislodge Saudi Arabia's pro-Western monarchy and to make every attempt to sabotage its oilfields. Its second aim was to construct viable and lasting terrorist cells throughout the Gulf area by offering inducements such as scholarships and guerrilla training in the USSR and, lastly, to initiate a campaign of savage urban terror-

177

ism, kidnapping and assassination within Turkey to considerably weaken NATO's East Mediterranean partner. This last aim was important as NATO could effectively bottle up the Soviet Black Sea fleets by sealing off the Bosphorus during a time of war. In order to implement this policy, Sakharov provided Omani Dhofar tribesmen with a special camp in the PDRY; and arranged for Turkish dissidents to be initially trained by the Palestinians in their Syrian camps and then later in their camps in Lebanon, Jordan, Iraq and South Yemen. However, the door to Jordanian camps was firmly shut by King Hussein in 1971. The Turkish dissidents were given financial assistance by East Germany and supplied with arms by the Arab countries.

During 1968, the KGB took over Cuba's intelligence service and began to increase its infiltration of the Palestinian movements, while at the same time repeating its offers to arm and train them. Without Cuba and the Palestinians there would have been no international terrorist network, and both of them are largely dependent on the Soviet Union. **The USSR were able to offer and supply training facilities, weapons and an organisational framework which could be deployed on a world-wide basis.** It was this aspect of the system that led to the creation of **multinational hit teams.**

In an attempt to create Soviet satellites within the Arab world, Mocow made numerous attempts at orchestrating bilateral intelligence pacts. The operative aim behind these was that such countries could act as conduits and proxies for the Soviet Union in the dispersal of Soviet aid to the Palestinians and assist in the implementation of Soviet aspirations for the region as a whole. Perhaps the most successful of these agreements was the Moscow–Baghdad Secret Intelligence Pact concluded between General Yuri Andropov of the KGB (later President of the USSR) and President Saddam Hussain and his Interior Minister Ghaidan Sadoun in 1973. This agreement provided for **the complete re-organisation of Iraq's internal security network along KGB lines** together with the supply of sophisticated surveillance, espionage and interrogation equipment by the KGB. The agreement also stated that the KGB would provide Iraq with aerial surveillance intelligence on military and political developments in the Middle East. In turn, Iraq was to reciprocate, under KGB guidance, by seeking-

178

out intelligence matters of primary interest to the USSR in Western European countries and to assist KGB 'illegals' where the USSR had no diplomatic cover. Simultaneously, **the East German external branch of its Secret Service,** the MSF under General Wolf, **was busy either creating or re-organising the secret services of Angola, Mozambique, South Yemen, Ethiopia and Libya along KGB lines** in order to facilitate the cross-flow of information. **The agents of each of these services were to work closely with the KGB to establish links with international terrorist cells.**[23] **Such linkages considerably enhanced the Soviet Union's world-wide organisation and, by the same token increased its attractiveness to international terrorist groupings.**

Many of the KGB's subversive agents who are put to work in the Gulf Sheikhdoms and in Saudi Arabia are supplied directly by the Palestinians. Having collected information, **the KGB operatives in the Middle East**—whether Palestinian or not—**report their findings to the Soviet Embassy in Nicosia, Cyprus.** The Embassy then forwards all the information to West Berlin where it is channelled to Moscow *via* the East German intelligence organisation. Information which is gathered in Israel is then transferred to the Palestinians and other international terrorists by way of Beirut.[24]

The closeness of the relationship between the Palestinians and the Soviet Union, is exemplified by the level of representation and the frequency of meetings which take place between them. In 1976, Yasser Arafat, and the Soviet Ambassador in Lebanon met regularly each week. Yet for many Palestinians this was not enough, and the PLO observer at the UN stated publicly on US television that, 'sometimes he should meet with him twice a day'.[25] The Soviets determined to fête Arafat as opposed to isolating him and so, after Sadat's historic Jerusalem trip in 1977, Arafat received still more weapons. His diplomatic status was also increased by permitting the PLO to open an office of considerable size in Moscow, and introducing Arafat to senior government personnel as well as the chiefs of staff. On the eve of the 1978 Camp David Agreements it was agreed to send the Palestinians even more advanced weaponry together with the promise that the Soviet Union would not abandon them. The Soviets had succeeded in bolstering Arafat's prestige at a crucial time in the Middle East, but in doing so they had also managed to close down his options by preventing him from declaring for a peaceful solution.[26]

All in all, **between June 1977 and the end of July 1981, the Palestinian leadership and the Soviets and Soviet bloc leadership met more than 140 times** including the Soviet missile experts visiting Palestinian positions in Lebanon on 24 October 1979. The following table indicates the number of political meetings between Palestinian leaders and Soviet bloc government representatives in the Soviet bloc countries during the same period.

	PDSF	SA'IQA	PFLP	PLO	Other Leaders	Arafat	Fatah	PDFLP
East Germany			2	4	7	3		2
Romania		1	1	2	4			
Bulgaria				4	3			2
Czechoslovakia		1	1	2	1	2		1
Hungary	1			2	2			1
Cuba				5	4	3		4
Yugoslavia				2	4	1		
Poland					1	1		
Vietnam				3	1			

Of the 78 meetings held, 34 were with representatives of the East German and Cuban governments—43 per cent of the total. It would seem that the Soviet bloc countries holding meetings with the Palestinians did so frequently, which reflected their strategic value to not only the Palestinians but also the international terror network. Bulgaria and Romania were strategically important because of their geographic location across the Black Sea and the Dardanelles from Turkey, and they were also close to Greece and Yugoslavia, therefore important in the overland transportation of weapons, drugs and supplies. They enjoyed 17 meetings. Czechoslovakia and Hungary were important because the former bordered West Germany and Austria and had a common border with East Germany, whereas

Hungary bordered Austria and was an important country for tank training. Yugoslavia has a common border with both Austria and Italy, which, once again would facilitate weapons and material transportation. The importance of Cuba, lies in its presence as a Soviet proxy throughout the Middle East and Africa and in its willingness to staff training camps and act as a link between European, Middle Eastern and Latin American terrorist groups. It also is of strategic importance located at the southern back-door of the USA.

It is enlightening to note which of the Palestinian groups visited which country. Fatah leaders during this period made ten visits—exactly the same number as the very much smaller but very much more radical PDFLP. Eight of the ten Fatah visits were confined to East Germany, Cuba and Czechoslovakia, whereas more than 50 per cent of the visits made by Arafat were to countries where Fatah had little or no influence. Similarly, with the exceptions of East Germany, Romania, Yugoslavia and Poland, other PLO leaders made the same or more visits to the other countries than Arafat did. Perhaps this may be indicative of Arafat's desire to boost the fortunes of Fatah while leaving others to keep the dialogue flowing between those countries where Fatah and the Palestinian movement as a whole already had influence. Aside from such an analysis, however, the sheer volume of meetings between Palestinians and the Soviet Union and Soviet bloc countries is overwhelming evidence of the existence of a more than friendly relationship.

In 1979 it was abundantly clear that terrorism furthered Soviet diplomacy's attempt to prevent a united and concerted Western effort against Soviet and terrorist excesses. Early that year, the USSR approached the Spanish government with the suggestion that if Spain promised not to join NATO, Moscow would help Spain in its fight against ETA. If Spain refused, then the Soviet Union would refuse any assistance at all to Spain. At this time, **the Soviets had won effective control of the ETA leadership.** Later that year during Arafat's visit to Madrid, **the Spanish government offered to recognise the PLO if the latter stopped helping ETA with weapons,** supplies and training. **A few months earlier the UK government had made a similar proposal to Arafat regarding PIRA. However, the source of heavy Palestinian supply** to both **ETA and PIRA was not Arafat, but George Habash.** The latter of course, did not want a political solution to any terrorist conflict within or without the Middle East. On realising this, the Spanish government deferred to the Soviet Union's suggestion.

Yet another method employed by the USSR to bind the relationship even tighter with the Palestinians, was the use of cultural and other agreements. Between December 1980 and March 1981, five agreements had been concluded: two with organisations in the Soviet Union, and one each with Czechoslovakia, Bulgaria and Yugoslavia. What was important to the Soviet Union in these agreements was that the facility existed for the KGB or other agents to visit the Palestinian camps to assess how the terrorists were deploying the material as well as to what uses the advance training they received were being put.

IV   THE INVOLVEMENT OF THE USSR'S EUROPEAN SATELLITES

Such agreements allowed greater communication with KGB and other East European Security force sleepers who had already infiltrated the Palestinian groups, and this permitted the Soviets, or their East European henchmen, the opportunity of making an on-site evaluation of the situation. Two examples of such visitations were those of Marshall Ogarkov, the USSR Chief of the General Staff, who, in early 1982, visited Cuba and Vietnam among other countries, and Marshall Solokov, who visited both South Yemen and Ethiopia.[27] Little is known of what was discussed at any of these meetings. However, during the Israeli invasion of southern Lebanon in 1982, a document was found which concerned the visit of a Fatah Military Aid Mission to East Germany. On arrival in East Berlin, the Fatah delegation was met by General Fleissner, the East German Deputy Defence Minister; Lieutenant-General Helmuth Borowke, the East German Chief of Staff; Colonel Karl Keides; and Captain Roland Kuchbuch, who acted as translator. At the meeting Lt-General Borowke stated that during a previous meeting between himself and the PLO Deputy Commander[28] in October 1981, **East Germany had agreed to accept PLO trainees into the East German army and attach them to the East German Military Staff College.** What was in fact

182

agreed at this meeting was that the training provided should include political education, technical and tactical training, physical training and courses in Mathematics, Physics and the German language. It was also agreed that **all the training would be based on Marxist–Leninist doctrine.** Much of the rest of the meeting, so far as can be ascertained, concerned the delivery of weapons. The Palestinian terrorists felt that the outstanding feature of help provided by East Germany was the training opportunities it afforded. For the host countries it was a relatively cheap method of ensuring that weapons and ammunition were put to the best use. It was also a product which could easily be passed on to terrorists from all over the world by the Palestinians in their many training camps, **and so hasten the destruction of the West.**

In 1964 the KGB set up training camps at Karlovy-Vary in Czechoslovakia, following a decision by the USSR Politburo to increase its expenditure on terrorism abroad. These camps were solely for the use of the adherents of Third World liberation movements. Within five years, more camps had been provided, particularly in the Crimea region and on the Caspian Sea coast, with other camps in East Germany, Czechoslovakia, Bulgaria and Poland. **By the end of the 1970s, Palestinian terrorists were being trained in command and staff courses in the USSR,** as well as receiving instruction in communications, electronics, engineering, artillery, maintenance, pilot-training, sabotage, the production of incendiary devices and atomic, biological and chemical warfare. These training programmes were being conducted at the Patrice Lumumba University and the Lenin Institute in Moscow, as well as at Baku, Tashkent, Odessa and Simferopol in the Crimea. In Czechoslovakia, apart from the camp at Karlovy-Vary, there were others at Doupov and Ostrava, while the Bulgarian authorities set up a camp at Varna. Hungary created a camp near Lake Balaton and Yugoslavia had one near the Bulgarian border. Military courses in East Germany were held at camps near Pankov and Finsterwald while **Palestinians also travelled under Soviet auspices to train in Cuba.**

Thus the Soviet Union is deeply involved in providing concrete support to terrorist groups, by way of finance, training and weaponry. However, the training forms two distinctly different aspects: academic and practical terrorist training.

Palestinians travel to the Soviet Union on doctored Jordanian, Lebanese and Iranian passports and, on arrival, are usually met by Al-Amid Al-Sha'ar and Hikmat Abu Zaid, the director and deputy-director of the Moscow PLO office. Following this initial meeting, they are then transferred to their assigned camp. The Palestinian trainees are usually subjected to two-hour stints of political studies each day. During these sessions the achievements of the socialist state and the treasures of Marxist–Leninism are expounded. Lectures are organised in order to develop a more complete unerstanding of Israeli expansionist intentions and the relationship between Zionism, Imperialism and, since 1979, 'Egypt's betrayal of the Arab cause by signing the Camp David accords'. At these lectures both Saudi Arabia and North Yemen are presented as further examples of reactionary elements. Normally the courses are intensive six-month affairs, after which accreditation and certification are bestowed upon the successful candidates. During Arafat's visit to Moscow in late 1980, the PLO signed a coordination agreement with the Soviet authorities. One of the immediate benefits derived by the Palestinian terrorists from this agreement was that 200 scholarships were provided for study at Soviet Military Academies and training camps each year. In a radio interview given by Muhammed ash-Sha'er, the PLO representative in Moscow, he categorically stated,

The PLO has a co-ordination agreement with the Soviet Union .... Hundreds of Palestinian officers holding the rank of brigade commander have already been accredited by Soviet military academies, and members of the PLO use arms of Soviet and East European manufacture in their guerrilla warfare against Israel .... The PLO enjoys special diplomatic status in the Soviet Union: the PLO representative is free to travel throughout the country, unlike other diplomatic representatives.[29]

The Soviet Union provided the Palestinians with training facilities in Czechoslovakia and at the same time, delegated to the East German Ministry of State Security the overall responsibility for running terrorist training bases in South Yemen and Iraq as well as handing over one of the Czechoslovakian bases at Karlovy-Vary and a base in Bulgaria. It was not in fact, until 1967 that the USSR began arming and training Palestinian terrorists on Soviet soil, but it was not until early 1975 that the West began to learn of this relationship. Only when the Israeli authorities brought a number of Palestinian activists to trial, did the admission of this training come to light.

The next occasion when the Western security forces were made aware that the Soviet Union was training terrorists came in March 1975. But this time, it became clear that the USSR was providing training and weapons to other Palestinians. Four Syrian terrorists were arrested by Dutch police and freely acknowledged that they had received weaponry, explosives and propaganda training at a camp in a small town near Moscow. Not until 1978 did solid pieces of information become available about Soviet activities in the sphere of international terrorism. Then it became known that the USSR, East Germany and Czechoslovakia had, between them, recently passed out 32 Palestinian pilots and 60 technicians, all of whom had satisfactorily completed their training courses. During the same year, **East Germany, Czechoslovakia and Libya also opened their training camps to Argentinians, Italians, Frenchmen, Germans and the Irish as well as to Palestinians.** From this point onwards, members of the BMG and the Italian Red Brigades were able to receive advanced training at camps in both **Czechoslovakia and East Germany,** while these two countries **granted extensive supplies of Czechoslovakian and Soviet weaponry to the Palestinians for onward distribution amongst the international terrorist community.**

Schools of terrorism have been established on a worldwide basis, not only throughout Eastern Europe, but also in Uganda and Egypt, Kuwait and Libya, Yemen, Iraq, Syria and Algeria as well as Latin America—but most notably Cuba. Instructors at these camps are usually either seconded regular officers from the armies of Libya, Syria and Algeria, or Russian and East German intelligence agents. Russian and Bulgarian psychologists are there to give instruction in the 'fear factor': for example, the greatest terror can be inflicted on adults by explicit or implicit threats against their children. This technique has been employed with considerable success by Palestinian terrorists against Israeli Arabs. In Western Europe, South America and the United States, the same results have been brought about by the use of telephone and/or anonymous letter threats.

To give some idea of the extent of Soviet bloc assistance given to the Palestinians, in the three mainly PFLP camps of Hauf, Mukalla and Al-Gheidha in South Yemen, there are on average 700 Cuban and Soviet instructors present, together with about 115 East Germans whose sole function it is to train international terrorists.

Often when the Palestinians find themselves in real military difficulty, advisers are flown out to extricate them. In January 1981, 50 East German military advisers were suddenly shipped out to Lebanon to bolster the number of instructors. The Palestinians, having invited terrorists from all points of the compass, suddenly found that they had insufficient dry nurses. Two months later, 15 Czechoslovak experts in terror and sabotage arrived in Southern Lebanon to train Arafat's Fatah squads.

V THE USE OF INDIVIDUALS FOR POLITICAL ADVANTAGE

Yasser **Arafat** has been extremely useful to the Soviets. In 1978, he **was invited to play the part of intermediary between the Soviet Union and Ayatollah Khomeini of Iran.** This was quite natural, as on the one hand Arafat was a favourite pawn of the USSR while on the other he has given significant support to some of Khomeini's more fanatical and vitriolic followers. In fact, **Fatah and other Palestinian groups were still training Iranian insurgents ready for the final assault on the Peacock** throne. Once the deed was done, Arafat waited until Khomeini and his followers were installed and then declared whole-hearted support for Khomeini on behalf of all Palestinians everywhere. What Arafat achieved was useful only in the short-term. **In 1979,** however, **a special Palestinian unit, the members of which had been carefully selected by the resident KGB officers in Baghdad and Beirut, was marked out for specialist training at the hands of the very best KGB and GRU instructors at isolated training camps in the Soviet Union. This unit now functions as the nucleus of Khomeini's secret police. Therefore within hours, Moscow is aware of occurrences in Teheran or Qom.** Yet another example of the uses Moscow puts its international terrorist leeches to in order to achieve its considerable long-term goals.

In July 1979, General Shlomo Gazit of Israeli intelligence, was able to quantify the extent of Soviet help to the Palestinians. He stated quite categorically that **more than 1,000 Arab terrorists had undergone training in over 50 different Soviet bloc military schools, at least 40 of which were actually sited within the borders of the Soviet Union itself.** However, Gazit's figures must be regarded as minimal since Soviet-sponsored training schemes have been in continual existence since 1964. It is easier to understand the full impact of Soviet involvement in terrorism, if the career of one individual and his organisation is considered in detail.

Ahmed Jibril, a captain in the Syrian army, leads the Popular Front for the Liberation of Palestine—General Command, a small armed Palestinian group which operates throughout the Middle East. The antecedent of this group is the Palestine Liberation Front, which Jibril and 20 other Syrian army officers founded in 1958. **During 1964, Jibril began to have irregular contacts with the KGB,** which coincided with PLF raids across the Syrian and Lebanese borders into Israel. By the outbreak of the Six-Day War, 95 raids had been completed by the PLF with varying degrees of success. As his contacts with the KGB became firmer and more regular after the Arab defeat, **he was invited to undertake training in KGB camps.** Accordingly, in autumn 1968, he made the first of four lengthy visits to the Soviet Union to undergo training in guerrilla warfare and political subversion. **Within four years, Jibril and his men were among the first 30 Palestinians recruited by the USSR as 'controlled agents'.** The following September, Jibril's Second-in-Command, Abu Bakr, returned from intensive training in the USSR and took charge of Jibril's Ayn Saheb camp in Syria. This camp was the recipient of much of the sophisticated Soviet equipment, but until the 'Yom Kippur' War in October 1973, it was Jibril's command and communications centre.

Jibril was under the command of a KGB controller who worked out of the Soviet Embassy in Beirut. After the 1973 Arab-Israeli War, the Soviet Union's main aim was to prevent any diplomatic gambit analogous to a peace initiative from gaining sway. The task given to Jibril by his KGB controller was to counteract and hinder the efforts of those who were more disposed to raising the curtain on peace negotiations. To this end, he worked hand-in-glove with George Habash and Naif Hawatima, in association with Abu Nidal of Black June. Thus Arafat became isolated with Palestinian circles and Fatah too became impotent. Although able to muster more than 8,500 fighters, compared with Habash's 700, Hawatima's 500 and Jibril's 250, and therefore despite being predominant, Fatah was technically dependent on the Soviet Union both for training and the provision of armature.

To assist Jibril in carrying out his part in the Soviet Union's grand strategy, Moscow enabled him to set up his own support network in Europe based in Bulgaria. Jibril's agent in Sofia was one of his oldest compatriots, Akram Halabi. Halabi created a weapons warehouse to act as a clearing house for weapons sent from the USSR to Lebanon, Libya, Iraq and Syria and re-directed to Bulgaria for trans-shipment and distribution within both Europe and Turkey. Halabi also organised a vehicle refitting operation so that cars stolen within Western Europe could be refitted to allow the carriage of weapons concealed within the bodywork. Between 1972 and 1974, Halabi was personally responsible for the consignment and delivery of more than 65 letter- and parcel-bombs to addresses all over the Western world.

Similarly, **the Soviet Union actively assisted Black September in many of its Western European operations** in order to further its overall strategy. One example is the Schönau Castle Operation in Austria which took place in September 1973. Hassan Salameh, the European director of Black September, ordered six terrorists to infiltrate the Jewish refugee transit camp at Schönau Castle early in 1973. Following the Munich Olympic massacre, the Israeli Mossad had kept a close eye on Schönau Castle and managed to spot the Palestinian insurgents, who barely escaped with their lives. Following Israeli protestations to the Austrian government not long afterwards the six were arrested trying to make their way across the Swiss border to the safety of Salameh's network. During their interrogation, they confessed that they were to determine when the transit camp was full enough to make it a worthwhile target and then telephone a number in Prague or Budapest to trigger the deployment of a 'hit-squad'.

However, because of the Soviet connexion created before his death by Mohammed Boudia, the need for reconnaissance at the camp was nullified. In August 1973, two Palestinians waiting in Czechoslovakia were informed by the Soviet Union of the number of Soviet Jewish emigrés travelling on any particular train. The two terrorists boarded a train in Czechoslovakia and walked along it until they found three Jewish refugees and then held the three—an aged couple and a younger man—at gun-point. Upon reaching Vienna, they made their demands known to the Austrian government. They were given the use of a Volkswagen Komo in which they drove with their hostages to the airport. Twelve hours later, the Austrian Chancellor, Bruno Kreisky, ordered the Schönau camp to be closed permanently, but proceeded to provide the terrorists with a Cessna aeroplane for their escape. By this action, Austria's soft neutrality regarding the Middle East issues was assured and, life for Soviet Jewish emigrés was made more difficult.

VI SOVIET MILITARY AND FINANCIAL AID

In the question of the provision of armaments to the terrorists and acquiescing states in the Middle East, **it was Soviet aid alone which made the three Arab wars of 1956, 1967 and 1973 against Israel possible.** From 1955, the USSR shifted 75 per cent of its foreign economic and military aid to the Middle East with the single futuristic **aim of stopping the flow of oil to both the NATO countries and Japan.** After the Arab defeat in the 1967 war, the Soviet Union's support for the Palestinian terrorists changed from being indirectly channelled through proxy Arab states, into support of a much more direct nature. This alteration in policy was undoubtedly because the USSR wanted to undermine Jordanian and Lebanese stability by utilising Palestinian terrorism. **This might provide the Soviet Union with a possible means of destabilising other pro-Western régimes, thus allowing Soviet control of the Gulf oil-fields.**

In 1969, the Soviet Union began to channel funds and weapons as well as providing other assistance to Palestinian terrorists directly, and it continued its supplies through intermediaries. Yet while seeming to prefer to supply the Palestinians directly, hence reducing its reliance on Arab proxy states, **the USSR began to develop its usage of East European satellite states.** In April 1970, the Bulgarian Ambassador to

Baghdad stated that Bulgaria was arming the Palestinians. This statement confirmed the widespread belief held at that time in the West, that the East European states were acting as third parties for the USSR.[30]

Yet the USSR never completely abandoned using Arab states as proxies in arming the Palestinians. For example, following Arafat's initial visit to Moscow in late July 1972, the USSR specifically chose to use Syria as a conduit for providing the Palestinian terrorists with shipments of light weapons. However, the difference between proxy and direct aid must be understood. By using proxy aid, the Soviet Union would simply indicate that a portion of the supplies sent to an Arab country could be transferred to the Palestinians, whereas with direct aid **all** the shipment went exclusively to the terrorists. Arab countries, however, had to agree to such shipments being made, since their airfields and often their military transportation were being utilised to effect delivery. Direct Soviet aid, totally by-passing proxy Arab states, did not really occur until anarchy prevailed in Lebanon.

With the outbreak of civil war **in 1976** in the Lebanon, **the Soviet Union was forced to use its two major proxy Arab states in order to supply the Palestinians with armature: Syria and Libya** *via* Lebanese ports and airports. Between the end of the Yom Kippur War and 1976, the USSR had provided Syria with arms totalling nearly US$1,000m. each year, much of which went to the Palestinians until Syria intervened in the conflict to prevent the genocide of the Lebanese Christians. When this occurred, **the USSR had no option but to agree to Colonel Gadhafi's request for a shipment of arms totalling US$12,000m.** Such a request was obviously well beyond the needs of Colonel Gadhafi's forces and the surplus was indeed used to equip terrorists—not just the Palestinians. **Most of the weapons provided by the Soviet Union under its contract with Libya, ended up in the hands of Black September, the PFLP, The Arm of the Arab Revolution, PIRA, the BMG, the JRA, as well as other terrorist groups** in the Middle East, Africa, South America and South-East Asia. The Soviets obviously did not object! **By that one shipment of arms, paid for out of Libya's oil revenues, the flame of destabilising chaos and revolution was fanned across two-thirds of the entire globe.**

1976 was also a year which saw the genesis of real Soviet commitment to **the Palestinian destabilising cause.** During that year, military advisers from the Soviet Union actually fought side-by-side, with the Palestinians in Lebanon and Christian Lebanese officers found and killed a Soviet KGB agent at Tel al-Za'atar. Within a year, ship-loads of arms and other materials were arriving at Lebanese ports for the sole use of the Palestinians, and most of the assistance was orchestrated through the Soviet and Cuban Embassies in Nicosia.

During the height of the 1978 Israeli push to the Litani River in Lebanon, the USSR markedly stepped up direct support for the Palestinians. This support was sent through Syrian and Lebanese ports as President Assad was more than content to allow the Palestinians to face the brunt of the Israeli drive into Lebanon. Five ships each day were sent by the Soviet Union in order to ensure that the Palestinian arsenals were fully replenished. The weapons which arrived in Lebanon also included extremely sophisticated armaments which had to be accompanied by Soviet experts so that they could teach the Palestinian terrorists how best to use this new technology.

The Israeli Litani push, provoked a predictable Soviet reaction. Despite Israel's withdrawal, the Soviet Union continued to step up its support programme for the Palestinians who were by now even further entrenched in Lebanon.

At about the same time, the **Soviet Union were supplying Strela ground-to-air missiles to Libya,** to bolster its tactical defence system. **Libya passed a portion of this consignment to the Palestinians** who, in turn, sold several Strela missiles to guerrillas in Zimbabwe. They then used terrorist tactics by aiming the missiles at two civilian airliners from their operating bases in Zambia, one more example of international terrorist support between groups.[31]

However, the Soviet Union prefers not to overtly advertise this direct support unless the situation warrants it. Therefore, Moscow prefers to continue using its Arab proxies, as much for economic as for politico-diplomatic reasons. The Soviet Union would prefer to give weaponry to the Palestinians to retain a hold over them, but as most of the weapons seem to end up in Israel the USSR prefers to supply the Palestinians through proxy states such as Libya and Syria. Then all supplies can be added to the order of the individual country and **the Soviet**

Union appears benevolent, furthers its own global aims, and yet does not pay a rouble towards the cost.

The Soviet connection with Libya is an exceedingly significant one. Libya, for example, has acquired 2,800 Soviet tanks—a number which is almost three times greater than that which the French army possesses. This poses the question, what exactly is the Soviet intention with regard to Libya? A clue perhaps is that in 1980, just prior to the outbreak of the Iran–Iraq War, King Hussein was informed by the Soviet Ambassador to Amman that he could now avail himself of anything Jordan wanted or needed from the Soviet Union's non-nuclear arsenal. (The King had refused to enter into a dialogue with either Egypt or the United States on the basis of the Camp David Agreement.) The Soviet Ambassador, however, pointed out that **if King Hussein should wish to place an order for armaments, he should do so through Colonel Gadhafi of Libya.** By this statement, it would appear that **Libya is effectively a Soviet arms depôt and one which could, if the situation arose, be used as a staging point for a Soviet attack force.** Indeed **Libya could** either by herself or in conjunction with such a Soviet force which would go in from within the Soviet borders or from South Yemen, **mount a concentrated attack on the Gulf oil-fields.**

Naturally, Libya discounts statements such as those which assert that both the Palestinians and the Steadfastness Front countries are in a client–patron relationship with the USSR. However, none of these disclaimers present any kind of proof to the contrary. More usually they are clichés hiding behind the impenetrable shroud of Arab nationalist feeling. As one Libyan publication recently argued: 'To suggest that the PLO is a tool of the Soviet Union contradicts the experience of every Arab.' Yet if one analyses the equipment sent to the Palestinians by the Soviet Union either directly or *via* Syria, Libya and Iraq, immediately prior to the 1982 Israeli invasion of Lebanon, then the only conclusion which can be drawn is that **the Palestinians are in a client–patron relationship with the Soviet Union. In fact the whole history of Palestinian ascendancy and the phenomenal rise of international terrorism points inevitably to the same conclusion.** In 1982, the Soviet Union despatched to the Palestinians, T-34, T-54, and T-55 Tanks, many of which were unloaded at the Lebanese port of

Tyre. Similarly, BTR-152 and BTR-160 Armoured Personnel Carriers were supplied as well as a myriad of anti-tank weaponry including: 57mm anti-tank field cannon; D-44 85mm ATFC; Sagger anti-tank missiles and B-11 and B-14 recoilless cannon. Light weapons consigned to the Palestinians included: Kalashnikov assault rifles, light and medium machine-guns, hand grenades and pistols as well as mortars and a variety of Katyusha rocket launchers. Artillery class weapons included the M-38 122mm (short) cannon and the D-30 122mm and M-46 130mm cannon. Anti-aircraft defence weaponry was staggeringly sophisticated, many times more comprehensive than those found in many small- and medium-sized countries.

Following the cessation of general hostilities between Israel and Syria, the USSR replaced, '. . . aircraft, artillery and SAM missiles lost during the Lebanon fighting, in some cases providing more up-to-date equipment.'[32] Between July and November 1982, military equipment sent from the Soviet Union with an estimated value of several billions of dollars, was unloaded at Syrian ports. The equipment sent included the latest T-72 tanks together with the already proven Sukhoi-22 bomber aircraft[33]. Thus the USSR will continue to do its best to ensure that the *status quo ante bellum* persists. **The USSR has also a long record of supplying certain international terrorist groups with arms, directly** and without the screen of a proxy. **As far back as 1974, the Soviet Union supplied both OIRA and PIRA with RPG-7 hand-held rocket launchers and Soviet AK-47 and SKS carbines.**

The Soviet Union and its Eastern-bloc satellites have also been involved in orchestrating an elaborate weapons delivery plan. Weapons manufactured in Czechoslovakia and East Germany, are delivered to Syria and Libya. From these countries the weapons are shipped in disguised crates to Montreal in Quebec and then re-routed to Le Havre in France by the Marxist Quebec Liberation Front. From Le Havre, they are distributed within France by Breton Nationalist and Corsican Separatist groups. **Finally they are shipped to Ireland (Cork) where they are put to use by the PIRA and OIRA.** Because of a coordinated clampdown between the DST in France, the Royal Canadian Mounted Police and the Garda in Eire, it was discovered that **the French–Irish connexion was handled exclusively by**

members of the Breton Separatists who had taken up permanent residence within Eire after being forced to flee France for their war-time collaboration with the Nazi occupying forces in Brittany. Considerable intergovernmental cooperation, together with international agencies such as Interpol, has meant that such arms-trafficking is considerably reduced although certainly not non-existent. What also transpired from the investigations, was that the Soviet Union and/or its satellite states, usually acted as bankers and financiers for the entire venture.

A further example of Soviet-bloc assistance to terrorist groups concerns the activities of Kintex, the Bulgarian State Trading Organisation. Kintex operates from offices in the centre of Sofia and ostensibly deals in normal manufactured goods and industrial raw materials on an import–export basis. However, Kintex is also a very important dealer in heroin. Buyers and sellers of the drug are brought together in the Kintex main office to effect their transactions from which they take a sizeable commission. They are often a participant in purchasing heroin for export into the West in a further attempt by the Socialist world to undermine Western society by contaminating its youth. One of Kintex's most consistent suppliers are the Turkish left-wing terrorist groups. These groups ship enormous quantities of heroin in to Sofia to exchange them for guns. In its rôle as the state trading organisation, Kintex is in a particularly well-placed position to assist. In fact it has never been known to refuse such offers.[34]

VI   CUBA'S ROLE

One of Moscow's important proxies is Cuba. Fidel Castro's Cuba is not only important to the Soviet Union because of its geographical location, but also because of Castro's willingness to send aid and advisers wherever Moscow thinks they are needed the most. In 1959 Castro sent a full batallion of soldiers, under the cover of being paramedics, to Algeria to assist the FALN in its liberation struggle against the French and, two years later, he won the confidence and allegiance of John Okello, the future Marxist leader of Zanzibar who was to lead a successful coup in January 1964.

Throughout the 1960s, Cuba was involved in the train-

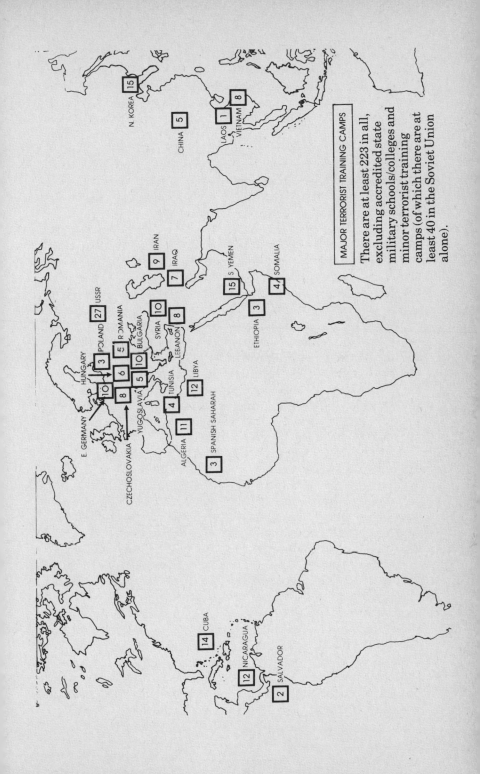

MAJOR TERRORIST TRAINING CAMPS

There are at least 223 in all, excluding accredited state military schools/colleges and minor terrorist training camps (of which there are at least 40 in the Soviet Union alone).

N. KOREA 15

CHINA 5

LAOS 1

VIETNAM 8

IRAN 9

IRAQ 7

S. YEMEN 15

SOMALIA 4

ETHIOPIA 3

USSR 27

POLAND 3

ROMANIA

HUNGARY 10

BULGARIA 5

SYRIA 10

LEBANON 8

E. GERMANY

CZECHOSLOVAKIA 8

YUGOSLAVIA 5

TUNISIA

LIBYA 12

ALGERIA 11

SPANISH SAHARAH 3

CUBA 14

NICARAGUA 12

SALVADOR 2

ing of Palestinian, Italian, German, French and Basque terrorists at camps specially set aside for the purpose in Cuba. Particularly after 1966, Palestinians travelled to these camps in groups of 100. In January that year, Cuba hosted the Tri-continental Conference which was attended by 513 delegates representing 83 revolutionary and liberation groups from all over the world, especially from the Third World. The Conference, held in Havana, declared for close cohesion between socialist countries and national liberation movements in order to devise, 'a global revolutionary strategy to counter the global strategy of American imperialism'.[35]

Towards the end of the 1960s, Western Europe experienced increasing disaffection amongst its radicalised youth, which culminated in the May 1968 riots in Paris. Such young people, were fired by the prospect of a rejuvenation of society through revolution, and Cuba and the Palestinians held much more appeal than that of the Soviet Union. They appealed to romantic radicals and the youth of wealthy Europeans; they appealed to the revolutionary liberation movements all searching for a cause, and the Palestinians fitted the bill much more than the Soviet Union, whose revolution was now more than half a century old. Thus, the USSR capitalised upon this feeling by actively advocating the Palestinian cause and by using Cuban rather than Soviet troops to act as advisers and providers of aid to the Third World.

By 1976, there were always an average of 300 Palestinians training in camps in Cuba, while Cubans acted as instructors in *fedayeen* terrorist camps in the Middle East from the early years of the decade. After the 1973 War, Cuba stepped-up the provision of instructors to the Middle East, sending them to Palestine Rejection Front countries to serve in the camps. Having already achieved a particularly large presence in South Yemen by the end of the 1960s, 40 Cuban experts were dispatched in December 1973 to Naif Hawatima's PDFLP camps within the PDRY.

Once Arafat had secured Castro's permission to set up and maintain a PLO office in Havana in 1974, relations between Cuba and the Palestinians became much more intimate. The Cubans, however, were not just interested in assisting Fatah and accordingly, overtures were made to both Hawatima and Habash who duly visited Havana on 4 January 1977 and 22

April 1978, respectively. On arrival they were accorded a formal military greeting and granted an immediate audience with Fidel Castro.

Part of the formal agreement concerned Palestinian–Cuban cooperation in the training of other terrorists, particularly from the Latin American continent. But it was only at this point that the United States administration became fully aware of the potential threat that such an accord presented to the stability of both Central and South America.

Since the last years of the decade, Castro has been extremely active in his support for the Latin American guerrilla movement and particularly for guerrillas active in Caribbean islands which were in danger of succumbing to the terrorist onslaught. One such country was Jamaica under Michael Manley. Castro identified this as a target and gave orders for it to be infiltrated. The Cuban Embassy in Jamaica was opposite the residence of the UK Consul. It was well documented that within weeks of Castro making this decision, there were more than 1,000 Cuban advisers in Jamaica, all of whom were active in committing acts of violence and terror in a concerted effort to destabilise the country. Had it not been for the far-sightedness of the opposition leader, Edward Seaga, who, prior to the Jamaican elections but following the US Presidential elections (which had seen the defeat of Carter and the victory of Ronald Reagan), met with the incumbent President in Washington and discussed tactics for preventing the creation of another Cuba on the US doorstep, Jamaica might well now be a Cuban-dominated country. Castro at that time could not afford a confrontation, and as Nicaragua was already further along the revolutionary high-road, he could afford to remove his agents provocateurs. A further opportunity presented itself when he managed to infiltrate troops and advisers into the small island of Grenada. Again, had it not been for a swift offensive launched by the USA (notably *not* the UK under Thatcher even though the British government were asked to intervene), yet another island surrogate might have been created.

Cuban involvement in the region has considerably enhanced destabilisation. Towards the middle of 1982, Colonel Gustavo Alvarez Martinez, the Chief of Staff of the Honduran armed forces could offer precise figures relating to **Cuban involvement in Nicaragua** which he asserted was at the root of the border tension existing between the two countries. The figures he gave were: **2,000 Cuban military advisers, 4,200 civilian advisers all from Cuba and 266 specialists from other Communist states, including a sizable number of Palestinians. These figures were not rebutted.**[36] If any recent evidence is required, one only has to refer to the number of so-called Cuban technicians and soldiers repatriated from Belize, following the US invasion of Grenada in 1983.

Other examples of **Soviet use of the Palestinians** as a linking force abound. **In Nicaragua, an extensive PLO training and aid mission has been integrated into the local army framework, with Palestinian instructors teaching the Nicaraguan army the operation of Soviet weapons.** The link between the present Nicaraguan government and the Palestinians stretches back to the early 1970s, when the present Nicaraguan Minister of the Interior, Tomas Borge, was a well-known figure in both Beirut and Damascus. **With Libyan money and Fatah advisers,** he acquired weapons, the transfer of which he then organised to countries in South America for use by terrorist groups. More often than not the transfer was effected in Fatah-owned Lebanese ships. **During the Nicaraguan civil war, contingents of Palestinians** representing the whole gamut of political opinion, **fought alongside the Sandanista rebels against the Somoza régime.** On achieving power at the end of the civil war, the Sandanista openly allied themselves with the Palestinian cause. In return, **Libya partly financed a network of 13 terrorist training camps, built along the north-west coast of Nicaragua to facilitate communications with Cuba.** The Sandanista regime provides political and material assistance to guerrillas in El Salvador and Guatemala and has now become a Cuban proxy within the region. It was also in Nicaragua that a Japanese government envoy was threatened by a Palestinian emissary and told that if Japan did not recognise the PLO forthwith, then a great deal of trouble would be created in Japan itself. Fearing a joint Palestinian–JRA assault, the Japanese Government gave way.[37]

Cuba and the Palestinians have extensive links with South American terrorist organisations, cultivated since the mid-1960s. The Argentine Junta for Revolutionary Cooperation which operated out of Tucumán province and La Plata, moved its organisation to Europe where its most effective terrorist members were under-cover. Once there it formed the Latin America Europe Brigade which was expected to have a strength of 1,500 terrorists. Half of these were inoperative either in Europe or the Middle East, acting as liaison with European terrorists or the Palestinians. The remainder were to undergo training at a 4,000 acre estate at Guanaba in Mexico, and then return to Argentina *via* Cuba. Weapons and armaments, training and some finance, were given by Palestinian groups to Argentinian terrorists. Fatah ably assisted the Argentine Montoneros while George Habash's PFLP and the other Marxist-orientated Palestinian groups gave extensive military assistance to the PRA in Argentina. The Montoneros together with the Uruguayan Tupamaros terrorists, were granted 'winter quarters' near Havana by the Cuban government. There, they can remain in reserve, following spells of intensive training courtesy of the Palestinians.

By 1978, the PFLP had forged extensive links with revolutionary terrorist groups in Brazil, Colombia and Venezuela, apart from those with left-wing Peronist groups in Argentina. Much of the support the Palestinians derive from these countries, is provided in no small measure by the Palestinian communities who live there. Particularly in Brazil and Chile, it is these communities who are *encouraged* by the Palestinian terrorists to provide them with both financial and material aid and, when the need arises, to act as *volunteers*. Faris Sawan, the present PLO chief in Brazil, for example, has organised groups of Brazilians of Arab extraction into cells which are obliged to provide money for the Brazilian Palestinian network. The best of these volunteers are chosen by the local PLO Chief of Operations to undergo further instruction at Palestinian camps in the Middle East, with Brazilian terrorists from the Vanguarda Popular Revolucionara. The Palestinians have had links with the VPR since 1971, when a tactical alliance was formed with the PFLP. It is generally the PFLP which arranges training sessions of between three and six months for the VPR in Libya again *via* Cuba. This is only one example of the links the Palestinians have forged with opposition groups in Latin American countries. These are too extensive to be documented, but suffice to say that strong links persist in Bolivia, El Salvador and Guatemala with locum tenens groups. Significantly, the Palestinians have bureaux but no diplomatic status in Mexico, Peru and Ecuador. The bureau in Mexico City dates from the term of office of ex-President Alvarez (1970–6). The office in Lima was opened in 1979, as a reciprocal gesture on the part of the Peruvian government in response to the siting of the Arlabank headquarters in Lima. The Quito bureau was established without diplomatic status as the Ecuadorian Government were involved in a Middle East balancing act and was thus a compromise. In 1981 they were involved with certain Arab governments concerning Arab investment in their country, while at the same time, negotiating with Israel for the purchase of specific Israeli armature.

VII   THE ROLE OF OTHER COMMUNIST COUNTRIES

The People's Republic of China, because of its very size and potential, is by far the most important of the other Communist countries involved in assisting terrorists. It has also been involved in providing support facilities for the Palestinians for over twenty years. Since 1964 when China became the first country to recognise the PLO following its inception, it has provided arms, training and other assistance at a continually fluctuating rate. Between 1965 and 1969, Chinese aid to the Palestinians totalled a mere US$5m. and the bulk of this went to the PFLP and the PDFLP. Not until Yassir Arafat made his first public official visit to China in 1970, did Chinese involvement in the Middle East assume any really measurable proportion. Later that year, engineers were shipped to South Yemen to assist in constructing a military-economic infrastructure, working alongside Cubans, East Germans and Soviet officials. Simultaneously **China offered training facilities to the PDFLP at bases and camps on the Chinese mainland erected for that very purpose.** Significantly, Fatah terrorists were not invited to attend and the PFLP only begrudgingly so. This may have been because the Chinese could not really comprehend Fatah's allegiance to the philosophy of Nasserism, and regarded the PFLP as ideologically irresponsible and totally irresolute. Yet within two years, China had abandoned these distinctions and permitted a glut of their weapons to enter the Middle East, *via* Iraq and by sea to Lebanese, Syrian and Libyan ports. Over the next few years, **increasing numbers of Chinese instructors were to be seen, in PFLP camps in South Yemen, Baalbeck and near Beirut,** but the honeymoon period was drawing to a close.

In spring 1973, the Chinese government withdrew support from the Popular Front for the Liberation of the Arabian Gulf, due to the growing involvement of the Soviet Union in its insurgency campaign. The USSR were sending PFLOAG guerrillas for instruction to its terrorist camps in the Crimea. This intervention by the Chinese government amounted to a change of heart. Disappointed and disillusioned with the tactics, overall strategy and extremely limited success of the Palestinians, the Chinese reduced drastically its armature supplies to the region. They recognised that to supply the weapons on such a scale was like pouring water through a sieve; Chinese endeavours would no longer be wasted.

North Korea became involved in international terrorism in the early 1960s when it sent out assassination squads to remove the more vocal of its exiled opponents. It was, thus, a short step to providing support services and assistance for independent terrorists. **By 1975,** it was conservatively estimated that **North Korea had been responsible for the training of more than 2,500 terrorists from around the globe at its camps** which were especially designed for this purpose. Similarly, **the North Korean government began sending its own specialist instructors to Palestine camps during the late 1970s.** By the same token, North Korean diplomats became actively involved in orchestrating transnational terrorism throughout Western Europe, by providing safe conduct, false documentation, arms and explosives *via* the diplomatic pouch and in particular by organising contacts with terrorist cells throughout Europe. One example of such assistance concerned the multinational hit-team who attempted to blow up an oil refinery in Singapore. North Korean diplomats organised their safe conduct out of Singapore from their Embassy.[38]

Evidence clearly shows that the Communist states bear a heavy burden of responsibility for the perpetuation of the ugly phenomena of international terrorism. The only recourse for the West to ensure its survival is to present a united front coupled with concerted anti-terrorist action

which can only be born out of intergovernmental cooperation and legislation. Until this is achieved, the West will remain at the mercy of guns and bullets provided by Moscow, bought out of Arab oil revenues, dispersed by Palestinians and fired by unstable youths of little education, poor backgrounds, few prospects and even less hope. The bullets will continue to be fired world-wide at innocent children, the aged and anyone else who happens to get in the way.

PART SIX

Western response to terrorism

I THE TERRORISTS' MANIPULATION OF THE UNITED
NATIONS

The United Nations, through the work of its various agencies, has been directly responsible for swelling the funds of the Palestinian terrorist organisations as well as giving them active military and logistical assistance. It must be emphasised that it is the agency element within the United Nations which must assume direct responsibility for this, although the UN as a body has persistently ignored any damaging evidence which has been placed before it. Thus **the world organisation dedicated to the 'preservation of peace' has perverted its Charter** and principles in order **to give succour to an international terrorist group.** The sole intention of this group, the PLO, is to commit genocide and work towards the total destruction of democracy as we know it. I will now catalogue only a few of the supportive measures which are given to it by the UN.

The United Nations Interim Force in Lebanon was set up by the Security Council on 19 March 1978 following Israel's agreement to withdraw its forces from Southern Lebanon after its succesful invasion. The Israelis had felt the invasion necessary to reduce Palestinian terrorist cross-border infiltration which had reached a height between 1975 and 1976. The terms of reference of UNIFIL and its international legality were embodied in UN Security Council Resolutions 425 and 426. By mid-June 1979 it had become quite apparent that **personnel serving with UNIFIL units had allowed themselves to be compromised by the Palestinians.** Despite their knowledge of the following catalogue of incidents, the UN has not acted to stem the blatant misuse of the UNIFIL's charter.

Colonel Alfred Gow of the Nigerian contingent was arrested by Israeli police after his car was involved in a collision on the Tel-Aviv–Jerusalem road. The car was found to contain three submachine guns and ammunition, as well as two suitcases crammed with explosives and sabotage equipment. Gow and another Nigerian soldier both admitted receiving cash from the PLO for their gun-running activies.

A Senegalese soldier smuggled weapons from Lebanon to Israel in a UN jeep. He received a gaol sentence of ten years from the Israeli authorities.

UNIFIL officers have been caught by the Israeli forces surreptitiously photographing Christian militia positions in order to pass the information on to the Palestinian terrorists.

A UN official attached to UNIFIL had been used by the PLO to smuggle opium into Israel during May 1979.

Direct complicity was established between the Eire contingent and the PLO, giving the latter full freedom of movement and limited support.

UNIFIL commanders allowed the Palestinian terrorists to keep 16 bases and 600 men within the designated UNIFIL area, contrary to the UNIFIL terms of reference.

By May 1980, according to Israel, the Dutch UNIFIL detachment were aware of 44 Palestinian-held strong-points within the UNIFIL area and did not report such a blatant breach of their terms of reference.

UNIFIL commanders allowed the Palestinians to control Tyre as well as two-thirds of the coastal region designated to UNIFIL custodianship.

UNIFIL soldiers returned all intercepted PLO terrorist weapons to the PLO HQ at Tyre.

UNIFIL provided escorts for all the PLO supply convoys.

By June 1982, there were 700 Palestinian terrorists deployed illegally throughout the UNIFIL area.

Between June–December 1980, the Palestinian terrorists made 69 successful infiltrations into Israel through the UNIFIL zone.

UNIFIL troops gave Fatah information about Israeli troop deployments from 1978 onwards.[1]

Apart from these most blatant actions on the part of UN personnel, some of that organisation's agencies have either through crass political naïveté or bias, been actively involved not only in granting the Palestinian terrorist organisations added prestige, but also in supplementing their finances. In all cases, such actions have been in direct contravention of the particular agency's charter.

In 1979, the United Nations Development Programme passed a resolution by 95 votes to 5, agreeing to allocate US$3.5m. for Palestinian projects in the West Bank and Gaza. Although the funds were not to be channelled through the PLO, implicit within the resolution was the stipulation that the projects would be executed in consultation with the PLO. Indeed they had been consulted throughout the preliminary discussions. But in consulting them the UNDP representatives broke their own Charter and Israel quite rightly, refused them entry. The UNDP Charter states that the UNDP should only give assistance to member states through the member states' government.[2]

In an even worse case of political naïveté or blatantly biased decision-making, the **UN has indirectly encouraged Palestinian terrorism by making financial contributions to two Fatah-dominated organisations:** the United Nations Committee of the Inalienable Rights of the Palestinians (UNCIRP) and the United Nations Special Unit for Palestinian Rights (UNSUPR). In 1982 and 1983, the UN granted UNCIRP a budget of US$71,800 and UNSUPR one of US$6,156,500.[3]

Another well-documented example of UN support for Palestinian terrorists—in this case owing to, at best impotence and at worst, political indifference—concerns the United Nations Relief and Welfare Agency, UNRWA. In late Autumn 1969, following the signing of the Cairo Agreement, Palestinian terrorists took over all the refugee camps in Lebanon, even those which were funded by UNRWA. During the Israeli invasion of Lebanon, **extensive arms caches were discovered in UNRWA Palestinian refugee camps and schools.** The latter were used as Ashbal training centres and also as major propaganda production and distribution networks. UNRWA Palestinian employees routinely passed to Fatah reports of Israeli troop movements, and expedited the diversion of UNRWA funds into PLO coffers.[4]

Since 1968, the Arab countries have attempted to manipulate Third World votes in the General Assembly on the Palestinians' behalf and further attempts at politicising the work of UN agencies, although moderately successful, have now been curtailed. The pressure placed by the Arab oil exporting countries on small, developing African nations to break off diplomatic relations with Israel and form an anti-Zionist lobby, were successful only because of their complete dependence on Arab oil and the lack of support from the silent, hypocritical Western powers. This was clearly demonstrated on 13 November 1974 when the culmination of the increasing pressure was finally realised.

On that November day, that august body, representative of nearly every nation in the world, that bastion of democracy—**the United Nations—capitulated to terrorism by inviting Yasser Arafat to address the General Assembly. During his speech Arafat, with submachine gun held aloft, threatened the world with violence.** He held out the promise of peace only if the Assembly acceded to his outrageous demands.

Finally, in 1983, following a series of anti-American and anti-Israeli pronouncements by UNESCO, the largest of the UN agencies, the USA gave notice that it intended to leave UNESCO by the end of the year. This followed the revelations that the Secretariat of UNESCO had indulged in massive extravagances and fiscal misappropriation. The UK also gave notice that it, too, intended to terminate its membership at the end of 1985. This threw the Third World into confusion. The Arab countries were pressed to take up the shortfall in membership costs: The Saudi response was one of total silence. Normally, the USA would pay about US$100,000,000—one-quarter of the annual UNESCO budget. The other Western nations contribute between them about

208

US$134,000,000 leaving less than half the total budget required to be provided by the OPEC countries, the Third World and the USSR and its satellite countries. Since then even tiny Singapore has given notice that it will quit the Agency due to the sharply rising cost of membership.

What, of course, has frightened these countries is, **with the departure of the US and the UK threatened and with the resignations of other Western European countries, they will all now have to foot the bill.** When the time comes, many of their anti-western policies and activities will either have to be cut or curtailed, since the Third World and the USSR will no longer be able to use funds paid by democracies to undermine their own destruction—he who pays the piper will now be seen to call the tune! At the same time the USA has called the bluff of UNESCO's Director-General, Amadou Mahtar M'Bow, who did not think that the USA would set a precedent by opting out of a UN agency. That they have done so, and that others are following in her wake, has raised a spectre. Should the USA opt out of the UN itself at some future time, this would be a shattering blow to the Third World and the USSR for not only does America donate the use of the UN buildings in New York free of charge; it also provides a significant chunk of the UN budget.

In 1981, the USA contributed US$1,098,502,013 to the United Nations and its agencies. This is equivalent to 25 per cent of the total UN budget. In contrast, the USSR pays only 12 per cent of the basic UN budget and NOTHING towards the invididual agency budgets—even so, it is currently more than US$250,000,000 in arrears. The only UN programme to which the USSR provides aid, is the UN Development Programme where 0.7 per cent of its budget comes from Moscow, but where Soviet officials seek to have the money used where it would do the most to help the USSR.

The possibility of an American departure has resulted in much less politicking on the floor of the General Assembly, particularly since the USA announced a 25 per cent reduction in its contributions to the International Development Agency of the World Bank (IDA), and this lead was immediately followed by many other Western nations. Thus Arab influence is significantly waning, not only within the UN and its agencies, but also over small Third World countries, which are by now, tired of being used as pawns in the international power game.

209

To this end, **threats were made that if a UN Security Council resolution was vetoed by the USA, reprisals would be taken against American citizens in Lebanon.** In a strong statement, the then US Ambassador to the United Nations, Jeanne Kirkpatrick, underscored the attitude prevalent in Washington at the time, by urging the UN not to allow the violence in Lebanon to enter its portals. **Threats of violence were made by Shia, Palestinian and Druze groups in Lebanon** in February 1984 against British and American officers serving with the UN Truce Supervision Organisation (UNTSO) should Britain or the USA block the Lebanese draft resolution censuring Israel. **Amal underlined this threat** by issuing a statement through one of its junior spokesmen saying that 'strong problems' would be faced if the USA or UK exercise the veto. By February 1985, the threats had become so numerous that the UN Command made a conscious decision to temporarily withdraw 33 serving American officers from southern Lebanon.[5]

Syria's overt attempts to manipulate and control the Lebanese government, rendered it unable to gather the 9 votes necessary to have the Lebanese resolution adopted. This resolution expressed indignation over Israel's 'iron fist' campaign of reprisals against the Shiite militants who continued to hamper its withdrawal.[6]

The problems experienced by UNESCO and the hard line taken by the USA and to a lesser extent by the UK, has ensured that there was a reluctance among a majority of members to condemn Israel too quickly. This reluctance, however, also reflected the reduction in oil revenues received by the Arab oil-producing states owing to the oil glut and the fact that Western governments were buying less OPEC oil. Similarly, the demise of the Palestinians had taken the steam out of the anti-Israeli lobby. Hence the World forum could debate issues without the emotional irrationality of previous years.

It is little wonder, therefore, that Israel still regards the authority of the United Nations with circumspection and not a little distrust. By actions such as these, together with the lack of administrative oversight, **the UN and its agencies have laid themselves wide open to charges of partisanship** and anti-Semitism, thus effectively reducing their credibility amongst the nations of the world. Each country now realises that political manipulation of the UN is not simply possible but an international fact of life.

II   EUROPE'S REACTION TO TERRORISM

The response of the Western Countries to terrorism has always been dogged with both sluggishness and rampant hypocrisy. The former Chief of USAF Intelligence between 1972 and 1977, Major-General George J. Keegan Jnr, remarked that Israel is

... the only liberal democracy not yet so immobilised by illusion that it cannot still deal effectively with the reality of survival.[7]

Between 8 September 1969 to December 1973 and April 1976 to 3 June 1982, 44 terrorist acts were perpetrated directly at Israeli diplomatic Missions. In Europe alone, there were 29 attacks .

In response to these acts, the free press of the Western world have sensationalised their reporting, employing laudatory romanticisms in describing the perpetrators. This had led, in Alexander Solzhenitsyn's terminology, to the 'heroisation' of terrorists. To rationalise this term we see these terrorist acts being aimed at the people watching, rather than the victims of the acts, and to this end, theatre is employed to increase its news-worthiness to broadcasting journalists. Journalists, politicians and statesmen have urged that the press in the Western world, '... should publish or broadcast minimal, cool factual reports, enough to register the event and limit scare talk but not enough to set up the society-wide vibrations which the terrorist craves. Not a blackout, but a brownout. Publicity is the sea which terrorists fish .... Dry up the sea.'[8]

However, it is further hampered in its effectiveness by the message portrayed by the news media and, in particular, by television. For example, the UK military response to the mindless terror and violence perpetuated by both wings of the IRA and INLA in Northern Ireland is viewed throughout most of the Western world as Westminster treating Ireland as a colony and imposing its will by sheer brute force. Coffins, anguished faces, the menace of masked men and skulking British troops, are images which, over-simplistic in their very nature, falsify the facts by feeding on emotion. Hence the media becomes an awesome propaganda weapon in the battle between the forces of law and order and those who seek to thwart democracy. As one commentator has remarked,

... It is in the nature of the medium to corrupt the message by over-simplification, and by producing the message it wants by its mere presence.

Similarly, government-controlled media permit broadcasts and interviews with terrorists and extremists. In August 1985, the UK government made a stand over the television interview of a PIRA Brigade commander. Journalists at the BBC went on strike, ostensibly because they wished to object to government interference in their reporting. But through their actions they gave the IRA a partial victory. The British government was steadfast and although the programme was later shown, served notice that journalists would not be given a *carte-blanche* to propagate sensationalism.[9]

When Minister for Posts and Telegraphs in Eire, Dr Conor Cruise O'Brien, urged the free Western press to impose its own limitations on reporting terrorist acts. He also complained of the disquieting tendency often present in the Western media, of attaching credence to statements issued by the propaganda wing of various terrorist organisations and, even worse, the continuation of this trend when previous statements issued have been found to be both totally unfounded and bare-faced lies. For example, no Palestinian action emanates from Tunisia since Arafat set up his Headquarters there without his express knowledge and permission. Hence the hijack of the Italian cruise ship the *Achille Lauro* in October 1985 was, indeed, his responsibility despite his repeated denials. Never have hijackers surrendered so quickly and never was Arafat so keen to hog the media limelight, taking as much credit as he could for the succesful outcome in order to bolster his fading and failing international image.

Similarly, the terminology used by the media to describe terrorists has also come under attack. The Honorary Secretary of the Commando Benevolent Fund, Anthony Smith, objected strongly to the term 'commando' when referring to the terrorists. He stated:

212

Those of us who had the honour of serving with them, and as guardians of their honoured and distinguished record, deplore the debasement of the name [commando] as now applied by both the national press and radio to refer to any gang of politically motivated thugs of any nationality who resort to the murder of innocent civilians by the most despicable means.[10]

Apart from the press, **many Western governments have** contrary to what the IRA proclaim **made an abject accommodation with terror.** Abu Daoud, a mastermind of murder has been freed; terrorists have been allowed dignified forums; terrorist leaders have been embraced; terrorist demands have been completely surrendered to; **the demands of the terrorists' pay-masters have been succumbed to as, for example, the West succumbed to the Arab oil governments from 1973 onward.** The worst perpetrators of this capitulation were the governments of France, West Germany and the USA. These governments released Abu Daoud, the perpetrator of the Munich Olympic massacre, and held covert talks with the PLO while at the same time pursuing their own terrorist groups within their sovereign borders: Corsican and Basque terrorists, the Baader–Meinhof Gang and Puerto Rican terrorists.

The bombing of the Conservative Party Conference at Brighton, which left four dead and thirty-two injured, did less to terrorise the British nation and more to anger it. Revulsion and outrage combined to produce a spectacular display of all-party unity. Mr Leon Brittan, the then Home Secretary, stated that the bomb had been 'a calculated attempt to kill the majority of the cabinet.' The bomb consisted of 20 lbs of commercial explosive. New measures were introduced at local and national Party level, but politicians would 'not be bombed into bolt holes by terrorists'. The unity of feeling was expressed by Gerald Kaufman, the Labour Party Shadow Home Secretary,

With Voltaire, we say to the Government we disapprove of what you say but will defend to the death your right to say it.

The government immediately set up a new Intelligence Unit specifically to combat Irish terrorism, and its first major success was to thwart PIRA's 1985 summer seaside bombing campaign. Further protection was afforded to Parliament itself by

213

the installation of a 7-foot high perimeter fence round unprotected areas, X-ray machines at the main entrances of both Houses, an increase of 10 per cent in police and security manpower, the installation of infra-red beams, alarms and cameras within the Palace of Westminster and increased random identity checks. Yet some MPs continued to invite convicted IRA terrorists to meetings within the Palace.[14]

Yet the response of the Western governments is most effective when it is least discussed or revealed. In the abortive coup in the Gambia during August 1981, Senegalese troops were supplemented by at least two SAS officers. The latter freed 41 Britons and others held hostage at a beachside hotel. These officers also freed the wife and four children of the Gambian President, Sir Dawda Jarawa. West German GSG9 troops and special forces from France and Italy have also acted similarly. In February 1982, SAS units were on standby at Stanstead Airport when a hijacked Tanzanian Airlines Boeing 737 carrying 90 passengers was forced to land with an injured copilot and another pilot who had to ingest stimulants in order to keep awake. The plane had been hijacked by members of the Revolutionary Youth Movement of Tanzania which demanded the resignation of President Nyerere. Eventually the hijackers surrendered when they realised that SAS units were in position and would be used by the UK government.[11]

Terrorism poses a double threat to Western society, both overt and external and covert and internal. **Externally, a network of professional terrorists seek to weaken and ultimately destroy democratic societies by attacking not only the institutions within the society but also its citizens and leaders. There is also a significant and covert threat to the internal fabric of the society as internal security is increased to meet the external threat, tension is created raising the level of anxiety.** Both threats, therefore, become curtailments to freedom.

In many countries, two kinds of law operate: the law as applied to ordinary citizens; and the law as applied to the privileged few such as terrorists. Between July 1968 and December 1973, at least 161 people were arrested in connection with international Arab terror, in twelve non-Arab countries and seven Arab countries. Of this number 60 terrorists were set free without trial, 21 were imprisoned but freed due to Arab black-

214

mail, and by December 1973 36 had not yet been brought for trial. Seventeen terrorists completed their prison sentences and were freed, in December 1973 11 were still in prison and the fate of 16 was unknown [in all likelihood they were freed]. The position has not changed much since then.

Perhaps one area which all Western governments have neglected to their continual cost is the manufacture of arms and their eventual distribution to terrorists. **British companies are some of the major culprits.** They are actively engaged in making vital components and spare parts for armies all over the world—making a complete nonsense of government declared arms boycotts and fuelling international political tensions. These businessmen prefer pragmatic hard cash to meeting strategic needs. In 1984, John Berry, a 48-year-old former sales manager for Lotus Cars who lived in Norwich, was accused of supplying electronic timing devices for terrorist bombs to Arabs in Beirut. These timers were uncannily similar to devices used by terrorists in Lebanon and Northern Ireland. The matchbox-sized timers were sold by Berry to an Arab, Monzcr al Kasscr, for £9 a piece. Claiming to be acting for the Syrian government, al-Kasser accompanied Berry to Damascus to discuss specifications. The timers, with a delay mechanism of up to 18 hours, were delivered to al-Kasser at the Metropole Hotel in London. They were manufactured at a small electronics factory in Mildenhall, Suffolk. Berry's conviction, quashed on appeal because of a technicality, was placed before the House of Lords. On realising that things were going badly for him, Berry fled the country and turned up in Malaga. All professional opinion concurs that the only practical use for timers of the kind which Berry produced and sold would be as an integral part of an explosive device.

This activity, *sub-rosa* thought it is, is carried out with the knowledge of the British Ministry of Defence, which itself, sanctions the use of Soviet and Romanian-made bearings in Scorpion tanks and armoured cars. These bearings and other standard items are knowingly bought from European middlemen. The British are not the only end-users. Italy and West Germany use Soviet-made titanium sponge for the manufacture of the Tornado fighter jointly manufactured in the UK. This use of Soviet-bloc parts was first identified by Conservative MP Robin Hodgson, in 1977, but the practice has mushroomed since then.

Firms are able to make any spare part provided that they have the drawings or an original, and provided that the price is right. Thus, **Western armies utilise equipment made within the borders of the enemy they will face should conflict arise in** Europe in the future. This is a dangerous situation as **the mobility of the protectors of Western democracy is dependent**—no matter to what small degree—**on the Soviet Union and its allies.**[12]

In 1980, the Austrian government sold to the PLO, more than 2,000 Armalite-AR180 automatic rifles. In 1981, the West German industrial concern, Rheinmetal, was prosecuted by the Bonn government for obtaining export licences to Italy, Spain and Paraguay but delivering their consignment of 1,000 machine guns to Saudi Arabia, with munitions machinery to South Africa and arms and ammunition to Argentina.[13] The situation will never be resolved until legitimate governments refuse to be intimidated by illegal and callous terrorist groups or until some measure of self-restraint is applied to the entrepreneurial spirit which is so avidly espoused by the industrial and commercial concerns of the capitalist Western countries.

A. EIRE

Other government responses towards combating terrorism have also been arguably inconsistent. Until December 1982, the Irish courts refused to extradite terrorists to Northern Ireland on a warrant charging the terrorists with serious crimes associated with republican violence. The Irish government, by the same token, refused to amend the statute on which the courts based their refusal. **Non-extradition confirmed for the UK the impression that Eire was a sanctuary for PIRA, OIRA and INLA terrorists and a base from which they could launch attacks on Northern Ireland and the mainland,** and underscored the distinct possibility of official condemnation of the crimes. In December 1982, Dominic McGlinchey, the INLA terrorist leader, was extradited from Eire to Northern Ireland because the Irish Chief Justice held that it was no longer sufficient to claim the furtherance of a political aim when conditions of insurrection or organised violent conflict pertained. He stated that modern terrorist violence, '... is often the antithesis of what could reasonably be regarded as political'. He continued that the question was now whether in the particular circumstances, the individual had been engaged in what 'reasonable, civilised people would regard as political activity'. Despite this judgment, the Irish government has maintained an ambivalent attitude towards terrorism. Similarly, it enters into negotiations with the UK government on closer border cooperation and then ineffectively polices the border. It criticises the activities of the Royal Ulster Constabulary and more particularly the RUC E4A Special Anti-terrorist undercover squad, for its effectiveness. Yet, Eire has never made any real effort to clamp down on PIRA, OIRA or INLA activities such as fund-raising, rallies and political meetings. In fact it permits up to 300 known IRA and INLA terrorists to live openly in Dundalk, a town of 27,000 people, only situated five miles from the border with Northern Ireland. Furthermore, it also has a poor record of arresting terrorists—allowing Evelyn Glenholmes, a 26-year-old IRA terrorist wanted in connection with the Brighton bombing to escape on the very day that UK security forces were put on amber alert following information received about a planned IRA/INLA joint bombing campaign.

However, **Eire has outlawed the IRA, making membership of the organisation a criminal offence, which is much more than Mrs Thatcher's posturing government has done—even after the 1984 Brighton bombing!** Yet, the Irish government is continually hampered by its ambivalence between the 'practicalities of partition and the aspirations of unification'. Similarly, rather than produce a coherent security policy of its own, Eire continues to argue that the threat posed to it by the IRA can only be effectively countered by British actions. This arises out of its supposed neutral stance in world affairs. Whilst this can be quite effective in keeping Peter Menten, the 85-year-old Dutch ex-Nazi out of Eire it is adept at permitting extremists time to publicly air their views and seems impotent in the face of the extremism generated by the Irish-American communities in the USA. An example of this was its powerlessness to prevent the New York Emerald Society's Pipe and Drum Band—made up of members of the New York Police Department—joining a parade in County Donegal commemorating ten PIRA and INLA hunger strikers. Those same New York Police, on the one hand are capable of supporting the PIRA and INLA terrorists, whilst on the other have proved incapable of bringing to justice the Wall Street financial district bombers who struck at the end of February 1982. **Responsible for more than 125 bombings since 1974 in downtown New York, as well as Chicago and Washington, the Armed Forces for National Liberation continue to elude the police.** Similarly, Irish government policy takes no account—like most of the world's media—of the positive changes that have taken place in Northern Ireland.

B. WEST GERMANY

The spectre of terrorism has not, however, haunted the ordinary citizens of Western democracies as the terrorists might have hoped. Even after the massacre at the Munich Olympics in September 1972, protection against terrorism came only fifth in the list of voters priorities during the November 1972 Bundestag elections in West Germany. Five years later, prior to the Mogadishu incident, a *blitzumfrage* in mid-September showed that 60 per cent of West Germans were opposed to granting the terrorists' wishes. One month later, in October 1977, another *blitzumfrage* reflected that only 42 per cent were of the same mind while a further 42 per cent would give in to the terrorists' wishes. This last *blitzumfrage* was an aberration and is not reflected in any other poll. Four months later, a disputed poll, showed that 62 per cent of West Germans were prepared to accept curbs on their personal freedom for the sake of combating terrorism, and by October 1978, 63 per cent regarded internal security as being of a higher priority than economic security.[15]

C. FRANCE

In France, one commentator has noted that,

terror still frightens, it still evokes outrage and protest, but it ceases to strike so deeply into the heart; it has a certain air of *déjà vu*.[16]

In all likelihood, this is probably because of the terror which accompanied the French Revolution nearly two hundred years ago and which is totally unmatched by terrorism today in its brutality. It is also probably because the terror of the Revolution is, in France, a revered tradition, hallowed and enshrined in the history and culture of the country. France has, however, been used by foreign terrorist groups both as a base and as a battleground. Such groups have been facilitated in this regard by the tradition of France as a *terre d'asile*. This has meant that France's intellectual life has been leavened by international contacts and ideas, and that clandestine political activity amongst foreign groups is frequent.[17] Commentators on international terror see very good reasons for Paris being the 'world capital of terror':

It has excellent road, rail and air communications with the rest of Europe and the Middle East; it connects with five land frontiers, which ... are difficult to police.[18]

Apart from the geographical aspects, Paris had an almost magnetic charm for armed terrorist groups. As Claire Sterling has noted:

No other Continental capital could match it for freedom to hide, meet, mingle, swap ideas, experience and equipment, plan and organise actions on a continental if not global scale.[19]

Hence, **by the mid-1970s the Palestinians were there in force running a Europe-wide operation under 'Carlos'.** The Palestinians tended to become submerged within Paris's half a million Arabs, giving them a degree of added cover and anonymity which further facilitated the use of the city as a battleground for intra-Arab conflicts.

Acts of violence are continually being perpetrated in France. There were nine terrorist outrages between 1973 and 1977. Orly Airport has been the scene of many attacks; for example, in October 1972 a bomb planted at the El Al desk at the Airport was defused, but in January 1975 there was a rocket attack on a fully-loaded El Al flight and although narrowly missing this plane it blew up an empty Yugoslav jet instead. In the same month there was another failed attack on an El Al plane. This led to passengers being attacked and taken hostage in a departure lounge and an escape flight being negotiated. Yet another incident happened on 31 July 1978, when a terrorist took hostages at the Iraqi Embassy in Paris. Later he surrendered to the police but was shot by snipers from within the embassy as he was being taken to a police wagon. A policeman was also killed in the fusillade from 15 snipers shooting at the terrorist from the Embassy windows. All the snipers had diplomatic immunity and the most the French Government felt itself capable of doing was to expel three of the so-called diplomats for carrying arms. In the furore which followed, Raymond Marcellin the former Minister of the Interior, claimed that France was unable to counteract the terrorist menace due to a lack of police preventative capacity and the present legal provisions. This latter point is important. The preamble to the 1946 Constitution, still in effect today, states that 'Any person prosecuted because of his action in favour of liberty has the right of asylum on the territories of the Republic.' Similarly, the Geneva Convention of 1951 which, by the Bellagio Protocol of 1967, was extended to cover all countries, also applies in France. Thus asylum is usually granted automatically as a person sets foot on French soil.[20] This was essentially France's dilemma in the case of Abu Daoud.

Abud Daoud is alleged to have organised the Munich Olympic massacre in September 1972. Paradoxically, his arrest in no way compromised the Constitution or the 1951 Geneva Convention. In fact, the decision to release him was neither within the spirit of the extradition treaties France had signed with both West Germany and Israel, nor the European Convention on the Suppression of Terrorism which France had recently signed but not ratified. Essentially, at the time Abu Daoud was released France was courting the Arab countries. President Giscard d'Estaing was due to pay an official visit to Saudi Arabia to discuss oil supplies, while a US$150m. defence agreement was pending with Egypt. France, too, was secretly negotiating through Libya for the release of an anthropologist, Mme. Claustre, who was being held by Chadian rebels. It is thus not difficult to imagine that **some political influence was brought to bear on the controversial decision to release Daoud. Whether such influence or pressures were explicit or implicit is of no concern. That they existed and were succumbed to, is enough.** France had bowed to external pressures which had, indeed, compromised its principles. As one analyst has remarked, a state

...may not wish to become involved in the trial or imprisonment of a terrorist for fear of reprisal or for political or even economic reasons. If ... terrorist activities were directed at foreign nationals a state may wish to maintain a neutral stance.[21]

Other states are in an entirely different situation. As far as Italy is concerned, there is little other than its own dissolution to offer the terrorists. The same is true of Spain, which has more of a chance of reducing terrorism by adopting some form of federal system.

Spain has tried to ignore the use of its territory by Syrians, Libyans, Palestinians and other Arabs who, since 1981, have carried out murders, assassinations and shootings as an extension of the Middle East conflict. Instead Spain has concentrated on reducing ETA's threat to her new-found democracy. However, on 12 April 1985, a bomb in a restaurant near the US base at Torrejon killed 18 people and wounded a further 80. This event has radically changed the Spanish approach. Since then, increased collaboration with the Israeli Mossad and with the French authorities has significantly reduced the threat. Spanish police together with MI5, MI6, the SAS and US Special Forces have also made increasing use of mercenaries who will eliminate known terrorists with bullet or bomb. One such mercenary is a UK company director who was paid more than £250,000 by the Spanish government.[22]

E. THE UNITED KINGDOM

The United Kingdom is almost totally ambivalent in its attitude towards terrorism. Whereas government ministers whether Labour or Conservative will rail against the IRA and the security forces will use every device to hunt its members down, **their attitude towards other terrorist groups operating in other countries is to question whether or not the terrorists may have some justification for their actions.** Fair-minded though this attitude may appear, there is a danger that in the end one can manufacture justification for any act—an attitude that can be summed up as viewing terrorists acts, extra-territorial to one's sovereign soil, as being only the concern of the government on whose territory the act is perpetrated. Such an attitude is viewed by terrorists as weakness and it is an attitude commensurate with that held by France. With regard to the UK, the absurdity of such an attitude was frankly shown in the summer of 1981, when the then Foreign Secretary, Lord Carrington quite bluntly retorted that he did not believe the PLO to be a terrorist organisation![23]

The British government had shown firmness at the time of the Iranian siege of 1978. Following the April 1984 murder of a policewoman by Libyan 'diplomats', the Thatcher government was stung out of its ambivalence. It finally disregarded the lives of the 8,000 UK citizens living in Libya, forgot that UK exports to Libya in 1983–84 amounted to £274m. and ignored the worries of the CBI and other bodies who urged restraint. In turn it drew up a black list of so-called diplomats and circulated the list around the Western intelligence services. It was this list which enabled Dr Omar Sodani, the former spokesman for the Libyan Peoples' Bureau in London, to be identified as a killer and assassin. Suspected of being promoted to head Gadhafi's network to eliminate dissident Libyan opinion, he turned up in West Germany in early April 1985, where he seems to have participated in the murder of a Libyan dissident, Jabril Denani on 6 April. He then entered Belgium under the name of Omar Ehmeida.[24]

Mrs Thatcher must alter either her own attitude or her advisers. She cannot afford to rail against the IRA and INLA and yet agree to meet a Jordanian delegation made up of two Palestinian Fatah terrorists. That this meeting was cancelled at the last minute because of internal PLO differences is beside the point. Similarly, President Mitterand cannot expect to stamp out terrorism and yet grant a full posthumous reinstatement to Henri Curiel at the same time as he unconditionally pardoned Jean-Marc Rouillon and Nathalie Menigon of Action Directe.

European reaction to the terrorist threat has been somewhat different from that of the United States but has relied on increased co-operation between the various national security forces. Two of the French security forces, the DGSE and the DST have given conferences and lectures in Tunis to Saudi Arabian and Tunisian agents as well as those from other Arab countries—particularly the Gulf. Similarly, in order to ensure greater cohesion between the French security services, a plan is afoot to create an all-Party Permanent Security Committee under the authority of the Prime Minister.

F. THE UNITED STATES OF AMERICA

In considering the defence of Western democracy against the
ravages and in-roads of terrorism, George Shultz the US Secretary of State, argued that the West would have to adopt an
'active' defence, including pre-emptive measures against
known terrorist groups. This statement was made in the aftermath of new agreements between the United States and the Italian governments. It was followed by closer relations between
the Italian and the British and between the UK and Spain with
the increased momentum of talks on the Spanish/Gibraltar
border question. In the wake of the London Libyan Bureau
fracas, surveillance of Libyans living in Britain was substantially increased. By the same token, following the assassination of Indira Gandhi, there were calls to increase UK court
penalties for convicted terrorists including the reinstatement
of the death penalty. **The successful attempt on Mrs
Gandhi's life revealed the emerging links between Sikh
terrorism and various Palestinian and other Arab factions.**[25] This acted as another spur to inter-governmental security cooperation, which resulted in the Italian–USA capture
of the *Achille Lauro* hijackers.

The United States, although having begun a clampdown on
international terrorist activities, **must bear a large measure
of responsibility for more than 2,400 killings of UK
soldiers and civilians perpetrated by the IRA since 1969.
It has persistently turned a blind eye to the activities of
NORAID** and its personnel. NORAID has been a continuous
source of overseas funding and weapons for the IRA. Martin
Galvin, its Publicity Director, has been the focus of riots in
which a number of people have died and many more have been
injured. Persistently, he has illegally and clandestinely
entered Northern Ireland from Eire in defiance of a UK government order denying him permission to enter any part of the
UK. The United States authorities have done nothing to assist
in his apprehension—even though he is a foreign national med-
dling in the affairs of a so-called friendly power.

NORAID sends money to Republican charities, to help the
dependents of terrorists imprisoned for their crimes. Two of the

major recipient charities are the Green Cross situated in West Belfast, which received a reckonable total of £20,000 in 1981 and, Cumann Cabrach in Dublin, which receives substantial but undisclosed amounts. Significantly **in 1981, the RUC seized 8,400 weapons, and in that year more than 85 per cent of the arms captured, originated from the USA.** NORAID has also been involved in laundering IRA and INLA money.

One of the great breakthroughs came when Dr Fitzgerald called the Dail into emergency session in order to obtain permission to freeze an IRA bank account in February 1985. The account held the equivalent of £1,750,816. Information concerning this account had been uncovered by US Customs agents. The money was initially banked in a variety of amounts in Eire and then transferred to the Irish branch of a Swiss bank. This money was then retransferred to the Swiss bank's branch in New York. From there it was rebanked at the New York branch of the Allied Irish Bank and then transferred back to Eire. The proceeds of extortion, this money was urgently required by PIRA in order to purchase weapons to replace the US$1m. in military equipment seized on board the trawler *Marita Anne* in September 1984.[26] This seizure was a considerable success and came as a severe blow, not only to the PIRA and INLA but also to the other European terrorist groups who depended on them. Greater cooperation between the Red Army Faction, Action Directe and the Fighting Communist Cells had been established **in November 1984,** with PIRA and INLA as associate members. In that month **a European alliance was formed to orchestrate attacks on NATO installations across Europe. By early January 1985, 30 bomb and shooting outrages had been perpetrated.** In mid-January, Action Directe and the RAF finally announced the formation of a 'political-military front in Western Europe' in furtherance of declared policy to continue attacking NATO targets.

Yet Action Directe with an active membership of about 30 (of which 19 are in gaol) and the RAF, with only about 20 activists at large, require the support of other groups in order to make their policy work. Prima Linea, the Italian left-wing terrorist group, Onkruit and the Red Resistance Front from Holland and the Portuguese FP25, have thus also been enrolled. This will

require a stepping up of surveillance and security by the security forces of the Western democracies at border crossings and
airports. Western governments will have to learn to follow policies more reflective of consistency than appeasement[27]

III   THE CHURCH

**The voice of the Western world's religious leaders has not
been heard condemning terrorism. The worst offender is
the Vatican** headed by the present Pope. In 1982, he received
Farouk Khaddoumi, the foreign affairs spokesman of Fatah
and the PLO. Some weeks later, **the Pope publicly embraced
Yasser Arafat** after giving him a private audience. The same
year, and several times since, he has made no effort to disci-
pline Cardinal O'Fiaich, the Primate of Ireland, for remarks
supportive of Irish republican nationalism. Pope John Paul II
himself elevated O'Fiaich to the Cardinalcy. Again, the Vatican did not suspend Fr Patrick Fell, a Coventry priest, from his
clerical duties when he was arrested, convicted and sentenced
in 1973 for conspiracy to cause criminal damage and arson and
for having plotted to cause terror and destruction. This is reflective of the impotence of the Catholic church when it comes to
dealing with terrorism—particularly Irish terrorism. By the
same token, not one Vatican voice was raised in protest at the
slaughter of the Lebanese Christian communities by Moslems.
Even the Archbishop of Canterbury's Middle East spokesman
Terry Waite, could refer to the deported PLO terrorist Bishop
Khoury as 'a man of God, committed to peace'—showing that
the Anglican church is little better than its more orthodox
rival.[28]

IV   THE EUROPEAN PARLIAMENT

If each of the European states individually prove to be disin-
clined in taking on the terrorist, the situation may yet be
redressed but only if some degree of collective action is implemented. Until the Israel Defence Force's action and the release
of the hostages at Entebbe, the considerably worsening problem of terrorism was astutely ignored. However on 6 July 1976,
the European Parliament approved a comprehensive resolution to combat international terrorism, advocating action in

respect of Third World countries. This was followed up a year later, when one of the Christian Democrat members for Italy, Sgr. Vernaschi, reminded the Parliament that many countries linked to the EEC by association agreements tended to shelter terrorists. Where this was so, he urged for the suspension of trade agreements. During the same debate on terrorism, a French Liberal Democrat member, M. Durieux, tabled an amendment to a resolution concerning terrorism, in which all countries which aided and abetted international terrorism whether by direct participation, or indirectly by allowing their territories to be used as bases or places for receiving hostages, were condemned. The following April, Herr Siegler Schmidt, a West German socialist urged for a simplification of procedures to facilitate police cooperation and also argued that the sale and supply of arms by EEC members to countries that trained and financed terrorists should be curtailed[29]—needless to say these questions were evaded.

Following the expulsion of the Palestinians from Jordan and the adoption of increasingly effective Israeli security measures across the Syrian and Lebanese borders, the Palestinian terrorists internationalised their conflict. They targeted Israel's communications with the outside world, European countries who had diplomatic relations with Israel, together with the most vulnerable means of transport—air travel. **Israel retaliated by attacking terrorist bases on the soil of Arab states,** particularly in Lebanon and Syria and more recently, Tunisia[30]. **Had the European countries replied in as positive a way to the spectre of international terrorism, then much of its bite would have been prevented.**

It is essentially the Western democracies' failure to acknowledge the collective nature of the terrorist problem that is the root cause of the West's seeming inability to respond resolutely to the situation. Sanctions against countries providing sanctuary to international terrorists must be applied collectively as must the institution of effective measures to combat and counter terrorism. To some extent this last proposal has been somewhat implemented. **The formation of the GSG9 unit in West Germany and GIGN in France, together with the UK's increasing use of the SAS has severely curtailed terrorist acts.** Coupled with tough anti-terror legislation already in force in France, West Germany and the UK, a meaningful and determined response to terror has been initiated. **Yet not one Western government has confronted either the PLO or the USSR with the evidence of their heavy and central involvement in terrorism. Both organisations have thus remained beneficiaries in the attempt to dismantle the Western democracies** and attain a limited goal as a stepping-stone to a long-term gain: the PLO to attain a state within geographical Israel as a stepping-stone to the spreading of the Marxist revolution.

The view of the PLO held by various governments is constantly in a state of flux. In 1980 the United States saw it as being a monolithic entity closely associated and fully committed to terrorism and violence in order to disrupt the global balance of power. However, by early 1982 the Administration's view had reverted more to the Carter belief that it constituted a heterogenic pluralistic movement incorporating diverse interests and groups.[31] This change of view did not herald a diminishing in the understanding of the PLO's central role in international terrorism. In May 1981, the US National Security Adviser, Richard V. Allen stated that

We must identify the PLO as a terrorist organisation... The Soviet involvement is organic ... training African terrorists [and] Latin American terrorists.[32]

Other governments and leaders continued, however, to display a singular reticence on this point. For example, Prime Minister Thatcher along with the British and French Foreign Ministers at the time, Lord Carrington and Jean-Francois Poucet, suggested to the US Administration on 24 February 1981 that the PLO should be included in any Middle East peace initiative. Such suggestions were sharply rebuked with a reiteration that the PLO was a terrorist organisation. Two years previously, it had been pointed out that **if the PLO's aim of an independent state in the West Bank and Gaza Strip were to be achieved, it would not only mean the creation of another terrorist state, but would ensure a quantum leap in the capability of the international terrorist movement.** Such a state would be, in effect, the first step in realising the PLO's original aims against both Jordan and Israel; having realised this, King Hussein severed all political relations with the PLO

227

on 19th February 1986—*l'appetit vient en mangeant.*[33]

V CONCLUSION

This global crisis of terrorist action must be understood for what it is: **the final battle** for the preservation of man's dignity, his freedom and that of the democracy in which we all share. To underestimate either the exigency or the level of response necessary to overcome this evil will precipitate dire consequences for us all. Because it affects us all the Western nations must unite and approach this threat together. But first we must understand precisely who we are fighting. A terrorist is a person who employs terror, violence and intimidation as a political weapon and for his organisation's own political gain. If his organisation is seeking to overthrow a democratically elected state then they are terrorists, whether they call themselves the PLO, the IRA or the Red Brigades.

The **Soviet Union as part of its policy of destabilising the West, supplies arms and training under KGB control to Palestinian terrorists, who in turn co-ordinate international terrorism. Arab oil states with their wealth contribute money,** aid, and sanctuary for the Palestinian terrorists to **form a deadly alliance made up of oil and terror, a Terror Triangle. At the head of this triangle is the Soviet Union aided by its Libyan and Cuban satellites. Their aim is to destroy Western democracy and sow the seeds of a Third World War.**

This book has shown just how far the terrorists and their supporting host countries are prepared to go in order to gain ground. They manipulate world organisations and encourage the destruction of smaller countries by determined insurrection.

The leaders of the West, need to recognise the potency and deadly force of international terrorism and deal firmly and ruthlessly with it. Should the West's leaders capitulate or fail in their response, then these terrorists will achieve their aim— the destruction of the very fabric of Western society.

These pillars of insurrection have been built up over the years, they have not suddenly sprung up. Block by block they were built as we gave ground to the Soviet demands first at Yalta and then by leaving open the Middle East by disbanding both the Ottoman and the British Empires. **This vacuum presented the anti-Western outlook with an ideal opportunity,** and a hitherto unstable area became the tinder-box of insurrection that we now know.

During the times when the West, America in particular, has stood firm over important territorial issues, over Berlin, over the Russian supply of weaponry to Cuba, and even the current stance taken by America over its defence of Israel, we have shown that **we can push back the anti-Western forces.** The Israeli envoy at the UN summed up the situation during the last veto against this small country (a veto called by the Saudis): '... a country has the right to defend itself against aggressors, no matter who they are or where they are....' **To resist the terrorist threat Western governments need to join together to form a Western Pact which should be agreed and ratified by all democratic countries.** Twelve general recommendations should be brought into force by the Pact countries and *must* cover trade and retaliatory actions. The terrorists have shown us the loopholes they exploit and these recommendations take this into account. Should such an agreement be ratified based on this 12-point Action Plan, then it would form an effective barrier against terrorism.

VI   GENERAL RECOMMENDATIONS

1   Airports
Airports in all Western countries should up-grade their security by using 3-dimensional scanners along with systematic baggage and personal searches, particularly at airports operating international flights. Only passengers should be allowed to enter any waiting area, thus reducing the possibility of further attacks such as those at Vienna and Rome airports in late December 1985. All airport personnel should undergo security clearance checks. On-board searches of ALL hand luggage would reduce the risk of an airport worker assisting terrorists to smuggle weaponry aboard.

2   Airlines
Western airlines who insist on flying to dangerous airports such as Beirut, Athens, Karachi, Manila, New Delhi and Tripoli, should be ordered by the airline's own government to effect

adequate high-risk insurance for each and every passenger carried on any part of that flight. Similarly, the airline's own government should exact a levy from such airlines in order to underwrite such insurance in case the airlines themselves are unable to find insurers. This may have the effect of raising the cost of tickets to dangerous airports.

3 Exit visas
These should be introduced for all those individuals wishing to visit states such as Libya, Lebanon, Cuba, Iran, USSR and the Eastern Bloc and all countries involved in terrorism. Western nationals arriving back from those countries should be personally screened and nationals of those countries should undergo questioning.

4 Skymarshals
All flights should have skymarshals to increase on-board security. They should be armed with disabling darts which could be fired inside the planes without endangering the pressure level. Low velocity, small hand guns could also be considered for use.

5 Safeguarding of targets
All Western embassies, consulates, trade, cultural and other centres should, where appropriate, have barriers against car bombers erected. There should be a substantial increase in the installation of detection devices and, where necessary, an increase in military and/or security personnel.

6 The Hague Treaty of 1970
The reaffirmation of the Hague Treaty concerning the apprehension and extradition of aeroplane hijackers should be extended to include other hijackers of trains, buses, cars and ships. Those countries reaffirming the treaty must comply with its provisions and begin to isolate others which do not. Western governments should review their own policies towards terrorism and actively expose leaders of terrorist states who lie and protest their non-involvement.

7 Retaliatory action
All Western governments should seriously consider retaliatory action in order to intensify pressure upon the terrorists. In

cases where specific countries such as Libya can be clearly identified as instigators of specific terrorist acts, Western governments should consider bombing specific military targets in those countries as both a reprisal and a deterrent. **They should not be dissuaded by Gadhafi's threats of 'interminable war' made at the beginning of January 1986, and consideration should be given to toppling Gadhafi.** All Palestinians, Shiites or Sikhs should, when a terrorist act is perpetrated by any of these factions against a Western democracy, stand guarantor and undergo thorough security screening. No funds from any of these nationals should be allowed to be transferred abroad until prior permission has been granted. All vehicles and all personnel should be searched and identified at each border crossing of each subscribing Western democracy. Capital Punishment should be reintroduced for all perpetrators of terrorist acts, involving loss of life. Security forces should be placed on a 'search and destroy' footing regarding known terrorists who refuse to give themselves up, and there should be a system of rewards for information provided.

8 Diplomatic and other government personnel
Any country which supports terrorism should have its diplomatic missions reduced or recalled. The same should apply to other government personnel. Similar reductions should also take place in the diplomatic personnel representing those countries in the West. Since Robert Kennedy's assassination in 1968 by the Palestinian Sirhan Sirhan, world leaders have been imperilled, a process that culminated in Olaf Palme's murder on 28 February 1986. This was ordered by Abu Nidal and the Rejection Front to curtail Palme's Middle East peacemaking.

9 Trade: economic sanctions
Western governments should cut trade to those countries who aid and abet terrorism. Export grants should be withdrawn from companies trading with the USSR, Eastern Bloc countries, North Korea, Vietnam and Libya. Companies continuing to trade in violation of a government directive should be fined a total of ten times the value of the order. A total Western ban should be placed on the issue of certificates of origin and any company found supplying them should be wholly investigated and fined.

231

10 Security liaison

A central national databank on terrorism should be created with an international link between countries mutually agreeing the extradition of terrorists for offences in any of the Pact countries. There should be a greater flow of information between the security forces of the West, and in turn these security forces should increase attempts at infiltration of terrorist organisations. At the same time increased security screening should be employed by the services in order to root out those who collaborate with known terrorists. **There should also be a significant increase in the use of the 'military option'** where a successful operation is thought to be possible such as that carried out in December 1985 by Egypt in Malta. Crack Western military units should increase the amount of joint operation exercises undertaken, in order to present a co-ordinated anti-terrorist front.

11 The Press

Where terrorism is concerned, the press should be restricted in their reporting. It is simply not good enough for journalists to argue that censorship is being employed where terrorism is encouraged by free publicity. No one argues that news must be reported: it is the often hysterical way in which it is reported that fuels the terror of acts committed in the hope that democracy will be destroyed. Simple, factual reporting—restricted in length, and giving the minimum of facts—in the newspapers, with a partial television and radio blackout, only while negotiations are taking place, is not too much to ask of journalists when the very fabric of the society they supposedly avow is under critical threat. Procedures on the present UK system of the D-notice should work effectively. Offending newspapers and journalists should be reprimanded and their reporting rights curtailed.

12 Western governments

Most importantly, Western governments must act consistently and in concert. They must organise an Anti-Terror Summit of world Pact leaders in order to agree firstly, that hijackers will be extradited to their country of origin or tried in the country of arrival; secondly, that individual governments will not enter into agreements or accommodations with terrorists; thirdly, that no policy is enacted that will encourage terrorists, for example those convicted and imprisoned for terrorist crimes should *not* be considered for remission of sentence.

A firm policy regarding criminal acts linked to terrorism (bank robberies to acquire money to purchase weapons) should be formulated. Searches should also be continuously made to track the funding arrangements of terrorist groups and, where specific bank accounts can be traced, these should be seized.

If the USSR and other Third World countries continue to use the UN and its agencies in an improper fashion, then the Western democracies should reduce their contribution. In addition, they should give notice of withdrawal from those agencies most abused. **The USA should assert its sovereignty over the New York UN Headquarters and should warn the KGB that spying and disinformation activities will not be tolerated. On 7th March 1986 the US finally made a start by ordering the Soviet Union to cut its diplomatic mission to the UN from 275 people to 170 by April 1988. If necessary, the West should withdraw** *en bloc* **from the UN** or, at the very least, give notice that such a decision is on the table for serious consideration.

*

These proposals, enforced together, would reduce the terrorist menace to little more than the harmless baying of caged wolves and yet, they represent the minimum level acceptable to all truly democratic societies and as such, are easily attainable. To this end, I charge the leaders of each Western government to begin their response to the terrorist threat by implementing these twelve points. It is their elected duty to protect us: it is unacceptable that they should not know how.

Unless these points are implemented, leaders of the world's democracies will be directly responsible for the entire collapse of Western civilisation at the hands of some 50 centrally co-ordinated anti-Western terrorist movements with their 2 million trained and armed destabilisers. The gravity of the situation cannot be emphasised too strongly, particularly since more than 2,000 Soviet military advisers have been sent by Gorbachev to bolster Gadhafi's régime since Gadhafi met Gorbachev in Moscow in Ocober 1985. Some of the things this book warns against have come to pass since the book was finished: how much more will come to pass? Now that the facts have been clearly stated, and the many foregoing revelations show a pattern, **the West *must* stand up to the anti-Western terrorists.**

*

Postscript, 21st April 1986. Since this book was finished, the Americans have bombed Libyan targets on 15th April, and Mrs Thatcher has allowed F111s to take off from American bases in Britain. **Both the US and Britain have shed their ambivalence and have come down firmly against terrorism,** and the European countries are being dragged along in their wake even though France and Italy made secret deals with Libya in the 1970s to spare their citizens from attack in return for allowing terrorists sponsored by Gadhafi freedom to travel throughout Europe, and even though France made a similar deal with the PLO (as reported in the Daily Telegraph of 5th April 1986). At last the West has begun to realise there is a war on.

NOTES AND REFERENCES

PART ONE

1 Maxime Rodinson, *The Arabs* (1981) p 95.
2 Cit. in J. B. Kelly, *Arabia, the Gulf and the War* (1980) p 16.
3 J. B. Kelly, op. cit. pp 17, 240–41.
4 Ibid, pp 17, 24.
5 See William R. Polk, *The Arab World* (1980) pp 236–7; John Laffin, *The PLO Connections* (1982) pp 24–9, 31; Thomas Kiernan, *The Arabs: Their History, Aims and Challenge to the Industrialised World* (1978) p 430.
6 On the Arafat–Suwaidani connextion, Ya'acov Caroz, *The Arab Secret Services* (1978) pp 292–3; Ehud Ya'ari, *Fatah* (1970) p 39.
7 See Gerard Chaliand, *Palestine Resistance* (1972) pp 56–8.
8 J. Laffin, op. cit. p 34.
9 J. B. Kelly, op. cit. pp 215–45.
10 Ibid p. 129; F. Ajami (1981) Introduction.
11 Quandt, William, Jabber, Fuad and Lesch, Ann Mosely, *The Politics of Palestinian Nationalism* (1973) esp pp 52 ff.
12 J. B. Kelly, op. cit. p 135.
13 Harkabi, Yehoshafat 'Fedayeen Action and Arab Strategy' in *Adelphi Papers* no 53 (1968); J. B. Kelly, op. cit. pp 129, 130; W. R. Polk, op. cit. pp 240–2.
14 Bard E. O'Neill, *Armed Struggle in Palestine: A Politico–Military Analysis* (1978) pp 112–96; W. R. Polk, op. cit. pp 236–45; and J. B. Kelly, pp 126–36.
15 *The Times* (London); *Le Monde* (Paris); and *The New York Times* (USA) 21 May 1970.
16 *New York Times* (USA) 11 June 1970.
17 F. Ajami, *The Arab Predicament* (1981) p 9.
18 *Al-Jumhur* (Beirut) 20 February 1972.
19 *Settembre Nero: A cura di Berghamaschi, Laurora, Salvatore e Trovatore* (1972) *passim*; Vittoria Lojacomo, *I Dossiere di Settembre Nero* (1974) pp 202–4; Andrea Jarach, *Terrorismo Internazionale* (1979) esp. intro.; Y. Caroz, op. cit. pp 413–17.
20 Adam B. Ulam, *In the Name of the People* (1977) pp 154–8. Sterling op. cit. pp 202–4. Philip G. Cerny, 'France: Non-Terrorism and the Politics of Repressive Tolerance' in J. Lodge (ed.) *Terrorism: A Challenge to the State* (1981) p 93.
21 *Al Nahar* (Beirut) 27 November 1972; *Al Anwar* (Beirut) 28 November 1972.
22 S. A. Ibrahim, 'Anatomy of Egypt's Militant Islamic Groups' in *International Journal of Middle East Studies*, November 1980, pp 423–53 and Ibrahim (1982) op. cit. p 21.
23 Y. Caroz, op. cit. pp 417–18; also *Falastin Thawra al-Mukawama* (Baghdad)

3 June 1975.

24 Peter Mansfield, *The Arabs* (1981) p 421, and Ibrahim (1982) op. cit. p 95.
25 D. Holden, and R. Johns, *The House of Saud* (1981) p 442. Mansfield op. cit. pp 414–15.
26 Ibrahim (1980) *passim*; Ibrahim (1982) op. cit. pp 93–4, 115–16; Kelly op. cit. pp 270–1; *The Middle East Monitor* IX nos 22 and 23, December 1979; *The Sunday Times* 8 January 1984.
27 *Annual of Power and Conflict 1974–5* and *1978–9*. *New York Times* 28, 30, 31 January 1980; *The Times* (London) 28, 31 January 1980.
28 David Pryce-Jones in *New Republic* December 1980.
29 Harkabi Yehoshofat, *The Palestinian Covenant and its Meaning* (1979) p 95.
30 *Free Palestine* (London) May 1981; Laffin (1982) op. cit. pp 38, 46–7; also *The Middle East* (London) March 1979.
31 Walter Laqueur (ed) *The Terrorism Reader: A Historical Anthology* (1978) p 259.
32 Michael Walzer, *Just and Unjust Wars* (1978) p 217.

PART TWO

1 *Ar-Rai al-A'am* (Kuwait) 17 August 1981.
2 *Jamahiriya Review* (London) August 1982.
3 Rober W. Tucker, 'Lebanon: The Case for the War' in *Commentary* October 1982. Christian Kind, 'The Ousting of Arafat' in *Swiss Review of World Affairs* XXXII no 7 October 1982.
4 Ezer Weizman, *The Battle for Peace* (Bantam Books: New York 1981) p 271. Kind, loc. cit.
5 *Plain Truth* August 1980 and *Britain and Israel* no 62, October–November 1976; Everett Mendelsohn *A Compassionate Peace* (Penguin: Harmondsworth 1982) p 44.
6 *Cairo Radio* 25 December 1969. *Britain and Israel* no 38, *November 1974; David Holden and Richard Johns, The House of Saud* (Sidgwick and Jackson: London 1981) p 371; Mahmoud Riad, *The Struggle For Peace in the Middle East* (Quartet Books: London 1981) p 283; Laffin, op. cit. p 133.
7 *The Palestine Liberation Organisation: Liberation or Liquidation* (Israel Information Centre Information Briefing: Jerusalem, November 1979) p 6. Riad, op. cit. p 334.
8 Claire Sterling, *The Terror Network: The Secret War of International Terrorism* (Weidenfeld and Nicolson: London 1981) p 281; *Information Briefing* (Nov 1979) loc. cit; *The Middle East* December 1978, March 1979; David Gilmour, *The Dispossessed: The Ordeal of the Palestinians 1917–80* (Sidgwick and Jackson: London 1980) p 157.
9 *Britain and Israel* loc. cit.; *Plain Truth* loc. cit.; *The PLO in Lebanon* (Ministry of Foreign Affairs Information Division: Jerusalem, August 1982) pp 30–31.
10 *The Spectator* (London) 30 August 1975; *Britain and Israel* no 62, *October–November 1976; Information Briefing* (1979) loc. cit.; Gilmour op. cit. p 157; *The Middle East* (London) November 1981.
11 *Falastin ath Thawra* (Beirut) March 1976.
12 Haled al-Azm, *The Memoirs of Haled al-Azm* (Arabic) (Beirut: 1973) Part I, pp 386–7.
13 *Al-Nahar* (Beirut) 15 May 1975.
14 *Associated Press* 12 April 1948; *Britain and Israel* no 109 September–October 1980.

15 *Arab Report and Record* (USA) 1–15 January 1969; *Time* (USA) 18 April 1969. *Middle East Journal* (USA) Winter 1969; *New York Times* (USA) 18–19 October 1969; John K. Cooley, *Green June, Black September* (Frank Cass: London 1973) p 5.

16 Arnold Hottinger, 'Jordan and the Palestinians' in *Swiss Review of World Affairs* XXXII **no. 9,** December 1982.

17 *The Middle East* March 1979, Hani al Hassan's comment. *Trouw* (Netherlands) 31 March 1977, Zuhair Mohsin's comment. See also Aumann op. cit. p 14. Hottinger, loc. cit.

18 *Die Zeit* 14 February 1977.

19 In *Merkur* (Munich) 28 October 1980.

20 *Britain and Israel* loc. cit.

21 Hottinger, loc. cit.

22 *The Economist* (London) 11 January 1980; *Britain and Israel* **no 109,** September–October 1980.

23 *Al Nahar* (Beirut) 24 August 1980. King Hussein's Autonomy Plan included: federal union between Jordan, the West Bank and Gaza Strip; the latter two to have their own government, parliament and judiciary with the capital in East Jerusalem; Amman to be the federation's capital and to control all foreign policy and defence; the federation to be called the United Arab Kingdom and to have its own central parliament and government with equal numbers of MPs from Jordan, the West Bank and Gaza Strip elected by secret ballot. See *Financial Times* (London) 18 June 1980; *Yorkshire Post* 19 June 1980; *Britain and Israel* loc. cit.

24 *Al-Ahram* (Cairo) 5 January 1970.

25 *Le Monde* (Paris) 11 January 1971.

26 *Al-Ahram* (Cairo) 9 June 1972.

27 *The Times* (London) 7 March 1983.

28 *El Hayat* (Beirut) 29 January 1970 and *Britain and Israel* **no 18,** November 1972; *Accessories to Terror* . . . op. cit. p 21; Maxime Rodinson, *Israel and the Arabs* (Penguin: London 1982 edn) p 148.

29 *Syrian Arab News Agency* 12 February 1971; *Accessories to Terror* . . . op. cit. p 23.

30 *Daily Telegraph* (London) 28 September 1972 reported that the USSR had flown a consignment of mortars and machine-guns to Damascus and handed them over directly to Fatah. See also *PLO in Lebanon* op. cit. p 14 and *Britain and Israel* **no 18** November 1972.

31 *Irish Times* (Dublin) 2 October 1978.

32 Letter to the *Church Times* (London) 1 May 1981.

33 *The Times* (London) 7 March 1983.

34 J. B. Kelly, (1980) p 220.

35 *The Spectator* (London) 30 August 1975.

36 William W. Haddad, in *Current History Journal* (US) January 1982.

37 *Al-Hayat* (Beirut) 22 January, 4 November 1971; *MENA* (Damascus) 15 February 1971, 14 January 1972; *Al-Nahar* 10 August 1971, 20 June, 4 July 1972, *Al-Anwar* (Beirut) 2 June 1972; *Radio Sa'ut Falastin* (Dera'a) 23 June 1972; *BBC Arabic Service* 30 June 1972; *Al-Jarida* (Beirut) 30 June 1972; *Newsweek* 21 June 1982; *New York Times* 30 June 1982; *Jerusalem Post* 18 July 1982; *PLO in Lebanon* op. cit. pp 14, 28; Laffin, op. cit. pp 110–11; Tal, op. cit. pp 14–16, 33, 39.

38 *Al-Amal al-Shahri* (Beirut) 2 April 1977.

39 Fouad Ajami, (1981) p 157; Laffin, op. cit. pp 9, 11.

40 *New Republic* (USA) 10 March 1982; *Daily Telegraph* (London) 15 July 1981; *AP* 30 July 1981; *International Herald-Tribune* (USA) 25 February

1982. For atrocities, see *Los Angeles Herald-Dispatch* (USA) 5 June 1980; *Evening Standard* (London) 10 October 1978; *PLO in Lebanon* op. cit. pp 15, 21–2; *Britain and Israel* **no 135** September–October 1982.

41 *AP* 1 January 1981; *An-Nahar* (Beirut) 4 January, 2 June 1982.

42 Peter Mansfield (1981) pp 403–4.

43 O'Neill op. cit. pp 187–8; *New York Times* 16 August 1970, 18 January 1971; *Mid-East* June 1970; *Daily Star* (Beirut) 21 December 1970.

44 Holden and Johns, op. cit. pp 435–7.

45 Arafat made this statement at the 14th National Council meeting at Damascus in January 1979. *The Middle East* (London) March 1979; *Information Briefing* November 1979 p 6.

46 Laffin (1982) p 174.

47 *The Middle East* (London) August 1982; *Britain and Israel* **no 18** November 1972; *PLO in Lebanon* op. cit. p 14.

48 *Monday Morning* (Beirut) 22 November 1981.

49 *An Nur* (Baghdad) 4 September 1969; *Accessories to Terror . . .* op. cit. p 37.

50 *Britain and Israel* loc. cit.; Laffin (1982) p 138.

51 *Now!* (London) 14–20 September 1979; *The Middle East* (London) September 1981.

52 *Tripoli Radio* (Libya) 31 March 1970. *The Spectator* (London) loc. cit.; *Libya–PLO Relations* loc. cit.; O'Neill, op. cit. pp 191–2; *A.P.* 3 July 1973; *Denver Post* (USA) 4 July 1973; *The Times* (London) 6 July 1973; *Britain and Israel* loc. cit.

53 Brian Crozier, 'Libya's Foreign Adventures' in *Conflict Studies* **no 41** December 1973; Sterling op. cit. p 259; *The Spectator* (London) loc. cit. *New York Times* (USA) 16 September 1975; Sterling op. cit. p 260.

54 *Information Briefing* (November 1979); *Libyan–PLO Relations* op. cit. p 10; *Al-Ushbua al-Arabi* (Beirut) 18 June 1979. Mudar Badran, the Jordanian Prime Minister, has been quoted as saying that a Palestinian organisation of only 30 people had received US$6m. from Libya in 1980. *As-Said* (Beirut) 26 December 1980. *An-Nahar al-Arabi w'al-Dauli* (Beirut) 29 June 1981; *The Middle East* (London) October 1981.

55 Abu Iyad, in an interview with *Al-Maukaf al Arabi* (Lebanon) 22 June 1981; *Libyan–PLO Relations* op. cit. pp 5–7. *Jamahiriya Review* (London) April 1982.

56 *New York Times* (USA) 9 June 1980; *Annual of Power and Conflict 1978–9* p 348. *Al-Kifak al-Arabi* (Lebanon) 8 June 1981; *As Sapir* (Lebanon) 19 July 1981.

57 *Jamahiriya Review* (London) October 1982.

58 *Britain and Israel* **No 18** November 1972; *Jamahiriya Review* September 1981, *As Sapir* (Lebanon) 19 July, 3 September 1981; *Al-Kifak al-Arabi* (Lebanon) 8 June 1981; *Tripoli Radio* (Libya) 16 September 1981; *Accessories to Terror . . .* op. cit. p 37. *Jamahiriya Review* (London) January, October 1982; *TV Eye* (IBA London: Thames Television) 10 December 1981; *The Middle East* (London) February 1982; *MENA* (Cairo) 8 June 1981; *Now!* (London) 24–30 October 1980; Sterling op. cit. p 260; *Al-Zahaf al-Akhdar* (London) 25 February 1983; *Jamahiriya International Report* (London) 4 March 1983.

59 O'Neill, op. cit. pp 188–9; *Britain and Israel* **no 62** October–November 1976.

60 J. B. Kelly, op. cit. pp 172–6. O'Neill op. cit. p 167; Sakharov, Vladimir with Tosi, Umberto *High Treason: Revelations of a Double Agent* (Robert Hale: London 1980) p 197; Barron op. cit. p 78.

61 *Near East Report* (USA) 30 January 1981; see also Arafat's statements in *El Sha'ab* (Algiers) 19 November 1979.

238

62 *A.P.* 29 November 1979. *Sunday Times* (London) 8 and 15 January 1984, 10 March 1985; *Daily Express* (London) 15 December 1984; *Time* (USA) 6 February, 15 and 29 April 1984, 1 July 1985; *The Times* (London) 9 March, 4 September, 19 November 1984, 26 February, 29 April 1985, *Foreign Affairs* Spring 1985; *Le Point* (France) 4 March, 1, 8 and 22 April 1985; *The Listener* (UK) 27 June 1985; *The Economist* 29 June 1985.

63 *The Middle East* (London) November 1981; Laffin op. cit. p 153. *The Spectator* (London) 30 August 1975; *The Middle East* (London) February 1981.

64 *Beirut Radio* 30 October 1976; *Information Briefing* (1979) p 7; *The Observer* (London) 5 September 1982.

65 *Information Briefing* (1979) pp 6–7; *The Middle East* (London) August 1981; *The Mail on Sunday* (London) 24 October 1982.

66 Sayigh, Rosemary *Palestinians: From Peasants to Revolutionaries* (Zed Press: London 1979) pp 174–5, 200; *The Middle East* (London) November 1981; Laffin op. cit. p 54. *Information Briefing* (1979) p 6; *The Middle East* (London) loc. cit.; *Yorkshire Post* (UK) 7 June 1982.

67 *AP* 21 May 1981; *Lebanese Television* 16 February 1982; *New York Times* 18 May 1982; *Monte Carlo Radio* 30 July 1981; *Al-Rai* (Amman) 20 April 1982; *PLO in Lebanon* op. cit. pp 16–17. *The Listener* (London) 27 June 1985.

68 *Britain and Israel* **nos 131, 132** August–September 1982, **no 135** September–October 1982; *Newsview* 6 July 1982, *Jerusalem Post* 14 July 1982; Salim (1982) *passim*; *Daily Telegraph* (London) 17 June 1982; *Yorkshire Post* 16 June 1982; *The Sun* (London) 18 June 1982; *Davar* (Tel-Aviv) 25 June 1982; Laffin op. cit. pp 18, 19; *PLO in Lebanon* op. cit. p 16; Weizmann (1981) p 270.

69 Tucker (1982).

PART THREE

1 *New Statesman* (London) 31 October 1975.

2 Claire Sterling (June 1981) pp 5–7.

3 *International Terrorism: The Darkening Horizon* op. cit. p 20 and p. 42.

4 Boyes loc. cit. and W. Boyes, 'The Financing of Terror: Terrorism and Organised Crime' *Contemporary Affairs Briefing* II **no 7** (April 1983) pp 2–3.

5 *International Terrorism: The Soviet Connection* op. cit. p 33.

6 Cit. C. Dobson, and R. Payne, *Terror! The West Fights Back* (London 1982) pp 197–8.

7 *Tages Anzeigen* (Berne) 14 May 1979; *A.P.* (Qatar) 15 May 1979; *Al-Medina* (Saudi Arabia) 13 November 1979; *Reuters* (Beirut 6 April 1980; *Reuters* (Damascus) 14 January 1980.

8 D. R. Divine, in Migdal, S. Joel (1980) p 228; P. J. Vatikiotis, (1971) p 162. Robert B. Betts (1979); Tareq Y. Ismael (1976); W. W. Kazziha (1975) *passim*.

9 *Newsweek* (USA) 19 July 1982; *The Times* (London) 11 May 1978; *New York Times* (USA) 26 June 1978. Russell stated that the PFLP had received assistance from nationals of the Netherlands, Brazil, France, Venezuela, the UK, Colombia, Italy, Turkey, Algeria, Egypt, Libya, Jordan, Lebanon and West Germany.

10 Laffin op. cit. p 100; *Annual of Power and Conflict 1977–8*; Sterling op. cit. p 17, p. 311.

11 Sterling, op. cit. pp 117–18, p 274, pp 338–9; J. Laffin (1978) p 79 and (1982 edn) op. cit. pp 161–3, pp 166–7; C. Dobson, and R. Payne (1978) op. cit. pp

28–9; C. Smith p 101; Demaris, *idem* (1978) pp 34–5.

12 Sterling op. cit. pp 116–17; Lojacomo op. cit. p 64.

13 Cit. P. Wilkinson, *Terrorism: International Dimensions* in 'Conflict Studies' **no 113** p 8; Sterling op. cit. p 122.

14 Sterling op. cit. pp 196–7; Robert F. Lamberg, (March 1982) p 11.

15 *International Herald–Tribune* (USA) 7 & 9 June 1980; Tal op. cit. p 69; *Frankfurter Allgemeine Zeitung* (West Germany) 3 August 1981.

16 Laffin (1982) op. cit. pp 17–18, 123, 125.

17 Ibid pp 102–4; *Daily Telegraph* (London) 6 June 1980; *The Times* (London) 27 August 1982; *The Sun* (London) 29 August 1981; *Daily Telegraph* 29 August 1981.

18 Boyes (April 1983) op. cit. pp 2–4.

19 Sterling op. cit. pp 43, 44, 219, 314; Lojacomo op cit. p 146; S. Possony, F. Bouchey (1978) p 143; *La Stampa* (Turin) and *Corriere della Sera* (Italy) 29 December 1979; *La Republica* (Rome) 29 December 1979.

20 *Panorama* BBC1 TV (UK) 3 December 1979.

21 Dobson and Payne (1978) pp 36–40; C. Smith, op. cit pp 78, 103; *Annual of Power and Conflict 1973–4* p 8. 1976–7 pp 16–17. Sterling op. cit. p 135 *Lotta Continua* (Italy) 6 October 1978; Demaris op. cit. p 34; *Washington Post* (USA) 7 September 1975; Sterling op. cit. pp 136–9; Laffin (1978) p 149.

22 Sterling op. cit p 74; Goren (1984) p 146; *Le Point* (France) 28 June 1977; *Economist Foreign Report* 21 June 1978.

23 Ibid pp 129, 59–65, 54, 55–57, 74–5, 141; *Le Point* (Paris) 21 June 1976 and 6 June 1977; *International Terrorism: The Darkening Horizon* op. cit. pp 21–22.

24 *Lotta Continua* (Italy) loc. cit.

25 *The Middle East* (London) June 1981.

26 *The Spectator* (London) 30 August 1975; *US Congress: House Committee on International Security* (Committee Print) 1 August 1974; Sterling op. cit. pp 124, 155–9; *Christian Science Monitor* (USA) 14 March 1977; *UP* 22 January 1974; *Politique Hebdo* (France) June 1972; *Die Zeit* (West Germany) 7 December 1974; Ortzi, Francisco Letamendia, *Historia de Euskadi* (Barcelona 1978) p 391; P. Wilkinson, *Terrorism: International Dimensions* loc. cit.; Possony and Bouchey op. cit. pp 35–8; Laffin (1982) pp 102–3, 122–3; *Daily Telegraph* 29 September 1978. In March 1977 the PIRA and PFLP signed an agreement initiating joint terrorist operations on the UK mainland against Zionist organisations and personnel.

27 Boyes (June 1981) p 6; Tal op. cit. p 52; *Daily Telegraph* (London) 19 July 1978; *The Times* (London) 27 August 1982; *The Times* (London) 29 October 1982, 22 March, 29 April 1984; *Sunday Times* (London) 7 November 1982; *Sunday Telegraph* (London) 14 November 1982.

28 Tal op. cit. p 52; *Boston Globe* (USA) 26 October 1977; *Time* (USA) 24 October 1977; Sterling op. cit. pp 39, 91; M. Funke (ed.) *Terrorismus: Untersuchungen zur Strategie und Struktur Revolutionärer Gewaltpolitik* (Bonn 1977) pp 278–9; Demaris op. cit. p 286.

29 Laffin (1978) p 149; Tinnen and Christensen op. cit. p 46, pp 96–8; Sterling op. cit. pp 98, 118; Lojacomo op. cit. p 119; *CIA International and Transnational Terrorism* op. cit. p 14.

30 Sterling op. cit. p 146; Dobson and Payne (1978) p 233; *Boston Globe* (USA) 26 October 1977; *International Terrorism: The Darkening Horizon* op. cit. pp 21–2; Y. Ofer (1979); Laffin (1982) pp 97–8; Tal loc. cit.

31 Tal loc. cit.; *International Terrorism: The Darkening Horizon* loc. cit.; Pridham op. cit. pp 34–5.

32 Tal loc. cit; *The Observer* (London) 20 September 1981; *The Times* (London)

17 November 1982, 31 December 1984; *Daily Express* (London) 30 January 1985, 2 February 1985.

33 *Jewish Chronicle* (London) 11 March 1983.

PART FOUR

1 C. Sterling, *The Terror Network: The Secret War of International Terrorism* (1981) pp 70–3.

2 Ibid p. 170; *La Republica* (Rome) 24 October 1979 and 16 April 1980; *La Stampa* (Italy) 19 April 1980; *Corriere della Sera* (Italy) 16 April 1980. *Washington Star* (USA) 22 August 1978; *New York Times* (USA) 17 August 1975, 20 December 1977, 26 May and 4 June 1977; *Christian Science Monitor* (USA) 14 March 1977.

3 W. Boyes (June 1981) p. 3; Sterling (1981) pp 126–7; *New York Times* (USA) 18 September 1972.

4 Sterling (1981) pp 159–61; O. Demaris (1978) p. 370; *Daily Mail* (London) 2 April 1973.

5 *Christian Science Monitor* (USA) 14 March 1977; *An Phoblach* (Dublin) 20 February 1976; *Daily Telegraph* (London) 3 September 1979.

6 Sterling (1981) p. 161. *The Times* (London) 24 April 1984; *Le Point* (France) 4 March 1984; *Economist* (London) 29 June 1985.

7 *New York Times* (USA) 12 June 1972; *Newsweek* (USA) 21 December 1981.

8 *Epoca* (Italy) 2 November 1974. Dobson and Payne (1978) p 40.

9 *Der Spiegel* 7 August 1978; Klein (1979) *passim*; *New York Times* (USA) 17 September 1976; Sterling (1981) pp 145–7; *Le Figaro* (Paris) 15 December 1979; *al-Watan al-Arabi* (Paris) 1, 7 December 1979; *Newsweek* (USA) 20 July 1981; *Lotta Continua* (Italy) 5 October 1978.

10 Sterling (1981) p 254; *ABC* (Madrid) 13 October 1979; *Corriere della Sera* (USA) 22 october 1979; Kaufman (1976) p 277; *International Herald-Tribune* (USA) 20 August 1980; *Journal de Genève* (Switzerland) 21 January 1979. *Washington Post* (USA) 13 May 1977; *Al-Anwar* (Lebanon) 22 May 1976.

11 *Foreign Broadcast Information Service* 18 January 1978. *The Times* (London) 17 November 1982; *The Guardian* (London) 26 February 1985.

12 *Newsweek* (USA) 20 July and 21 December 1981; Boyes (June 1981) p 3; Laffin (1982) p 123; *International Terrorism: The Darkening Horizon* (1979) p 19; *New York Times* (USA) 25 July 1976. Libyan funding of United States organisations has ceased since the closure of the Libyan Embassy in 1983 by order of President Reagan, until Colonel Gadhafi can find another conduit.

13 *CIA International and Transnational Terrorism* (1976) p 20.

14 *Corriere della Sera* (Italy) 6 August 1980; *Il Giornale Nuovo* (Italy) 9 August 1980.

15 *International Terrorism: The Soviet Connection* (1979) pp 31–2; Sterling (1981) p 270; *BBC Monitoring Service* (UK) 4 February 1979.

16 *The Middle East* (London) October 1981. *L'Espresso* (Rome) 19 October 1981. *New York Times* (USA) 9 August, 2 November 1975, 16 July 1976; *Christian Science Monitor* (USA) 3 May 1976; *Washington Star* (USA) 22 August 1976, 28 January 1977; *The Times* (London) 15 December 1976; *US News and World Report* 10 April 1978; *Foreign Broadcast Information Service* 24 March 1978.

17 *News at One* (IBA ITN UK) 4 February 1982; *The Times* (London) 1 February 1982. Mansfield (1981) p 462. *Newsweek* (USA) 20 July 1981; 'The Most Dangerous Man in the World' (*IBA:ITV Central:UK*) 5 January 1982;

'Trading in Terror' *Panorama* (BBC1-TV:UK) 23 November 1981; *News At Ten* (IBA:ITN:UK) 29 January 1982; *Now!* (UK) 24–30 October 1980. *Jeune Afrique* (Paris) 13 February 1980; *L'Europa* (Italy) 1 April 1980; Sterling (USA) (1981) pp 260–1. *The Guardian, The Times* (London) 10 January 1984. *Newsweek* (USA) 1 February 1982; *The Mail on Sunday*, (London) 20 June 1982.

18 *The Middle East* (London) October 1981.

19 *Time* (USA) 23 November and 21 December 1981; *Newsweek* (USA) 9 November 1981; *The Guardian* (London) 5 January 1982.

20 *News at Ten* (IBA:ITN:UK) 29 January 1982; *The Times* (London) 8 May 1981, 13 March 1982; *The Observer* (London) 21 March 1982.

21 *Foreign Broadcast Information Service* 1 February 1979.

22 Laffin (1982) p 139; *Spectator* (London) 30 August 1975; *Times* (London) 19 April 1983; *The Times* (London) 8, 12–14 March, 19, 25, 30 April, 1 May, 12, 18–21, 29 November, 31 December 1984; *The Guardian* (London) 13 March, 24 April, 1 May, 26 November 1984, 26 February 1985; *Daily Express* (London) 21 January, 8, 21 February 1985; *Daily Telegraph* (London) 23 April 1984; *Sunday Times, The Observer* (London) 22 April 1984; 25 November 1984. *Jewish Chronicle* (London) 23 November 1984; *Mail on Sunday* (London) 25 November 1984.

23 *Jamahiriya Review* (London) April 1982; *Daily Star* (London) 31 October, 20 November 1984; *Newsweek* 11 February 1985; *Le Point* (Paris) 8 April 1985.

24 Sterling (1981) p 261; *Daily Telegraph* (London) 23 April 1984; *Le Point* (Paris) 31 December 1984.

25 *Newsweek* 18 June 1979.

26 *Now!* (UK) 24–30 October 1980.

27 *Corriere della Sera* (Italy) 31 March 1979, 21 July 1980; *Washington Post* (USA) 25 May 1976; *Miami Herald* (USA) 24 April 1977; *Christian Science Monitor* (USA) 21 June 1977; *L'Espresso* (Italy) 1 June 1980; *New York Times* (USA) 29 May 1975, 12 January 1979; Crozier (February 1978) p 4; *Annual of Power and Conflict* 1976–7 p 14; Sterling (1981) p 268.

28 Sterling (1981) p 263; *Neue Zürcher Zeitung* (Switzerland) 22 June 1979; *Newsweek* (USA) 20 July 1981; Mansfield (1981) p 462; IBA:ITV:UK *Central Documentary* 5 January 1982; *International Herald-Tribune* (USA) 13 October 1979; *Daily Telegraph* (London) 23 April 1984; *The Guardian* (London) 12 March 1985; *Time* (USA) 15 April 1985; *The Times* (London) 11, 25 April 1985; *L'Evènement du Jeudi* (Paris) 4–10 April 1985.

29 *The Times* (London) 21 April 1983. *The Times* (London) 20 November 1984; *Mail on Sunday* (London) 11 November 1984; 24 December 1984. *Daily Mail* 3 October; *Mail on Sunday, Sunday Times* 6 October 1985.

30 *The Observer* (London) 9, 16 December 1979. *International Terrorism: The Darkening Horizon* (1979) pp 29–30; *Panorama* BBC-TV:UK 17 June 1980, 1 June 1981; *The Times* (London) 4 August 1981; *The Middle East* July 1982; *Germany and the Argentine Bomb* (BBC2-TV:UK Newsnight Production) 19 April 1982; *The Guardian* (London) 8 June 1982. *Arabia: The Islamic World Review* December 1984. The full name of the company whose acronym is OTRAG is Orbital Transport Rocket AG.

31 *October* (Egypt) 16 May 1978.

32 *Now!* (UK) 14–20 September 1979.

33 Perlmutter et al. (1982) *passim*.

34 *Newsweek* (USA) 17 July 1978. *The Times* (London) 15 December 1976; *Now!* (UK) loc. cit.

35 *Foreign Broadcast Information Service* 2 November 1977.

242

1 Ishutin called his overt wing 'The Organisation' and his covert wing 'Hell'. Ulam (1977) pp 154–8; Sterling (1981) pp 203–4. Goren (1984) pp 108, 116, 131, 136, 147, 169.
2 Johnson (1979) loc. cit.
3 *International Terrorism: The Soviet Connection* (1979) pp 11–14 and *Internationald Terrorism: The Darkening Horizon* (1979) p 13.
4 *Washington Star* (USA) 5 March 1970; *Washington Post* (USA) 20 November 1963, 20 September, 5–7 October 1968; 19 March, 24 March, 7, 27 July; 6, 27 September 1971; *Christian Science Monitor* (USA) 31 March, 7 April, 10 July, 29 September, 20 October 1971; 14 December 1972; *New York Times* (USA) 30–31 July, 2, 4 August, 9 September, 1–5, 7–8 October 1968; 18 April, 23 June, 27 July, 3, 20, 26 September 1971; *Wall Street Journal* (USA) 2, 16 October 1968. *Time* (USA) 19 April 1971. Barron (1975:1979 edn) pp 298–334; *The Times* (London) 7 June 1967; *Guardian* (Manchester) 30 July, 19 October 1971, 28 August, 8 December 1972. *Daily Telegraph* (London) 29 April 1971, 14 December 1972. *The Observer* (London) 28 March 1971.
5 Wilkinson (1981) p 148.
6 *International Terrorism: The Darkening Horizon* (1979) pp 14, 12 and *International Terrorism: The Soviet Connection* (1979) pp 19–22.
7 *New York Times* 23 January 1979; as-Sufi (1979) App. B pp 54–6.
8 *Radio Moscow* 15 November 1976; *New Times* 21 May 1974; Gurewitz (1979) p 257.
9 *Middle East Record* v.2 (1961). Goren (1984) pp 96, 100, 102; *Il Giornale Nuovo* (Milan) 1 January, 22 May, 18 September 1980; *US Congress Judiciary Committee: Senate Hearings on Terroristic Activity* Pt 4 94th Congress 14 May 1975; *Pravda* 6 February 1965. Barron (1975:1979 edn) p. 34. *Pravda* (USSR) 19 June 1981; *Izvestiya* (USSR) 18 January 1981; *Washington Post* (USA) 3 October 1982; *New York Times* (USA) 24 January 1982; Barron (1985) pp 23–4, 28, 29; M. Feshbach (1982). *Trud* (Moscow) 26 January, 21 October 1969; *Pravda* (USSR) 30 January, 28 February 1969; *Middle East Record* v. (1969–70) pp 415–16; *TASS* (USSR) 20 February 1970; *Daily Star* (Beirut) 26 April 1970; *NYT* 17 January, 7 February 1970; *New Times* (Moscow) 24 September 1969; *The Observer* (London) 20 April 1969. Barron (1985) pp 21–2, 60. *Radio Cairo* 16 May 1967; *Int.Her.Trib.* 9 August 1968; *Middle East Record* v (1969–70) p 258; *Ha'aretz* (Israel) 11 May, 12 June 1969. *BBC* 19 December 1970; *IHT* 16 October 1970; *Radio Ankara* 15 October 1970; *Middle East Record* op. cit. p 57; *Radio Moscow* (Arabic and English) 5 July 1976. *Izvestiya* (USSR) 8, 16 September 1972; *Pravda* 11 September 1972; 5, 9 March 1973; *Trud* 16 September 1972; *Radio Moscow* 3 March, 14 April 1973; *FBIS* 5 March, 10 August 1973; *Radio Moscow* (Arabic) 16 August 1975; *Daily Telegraph* (London) 18 February; 1 March, 1 June, 4 December 1979; 18 July 1980, 4 July 1981; *IHT* 6 March, 23 July 1980; 13, 27 April 1981; *Jerusalem Post* 16, 24 July 1979; *Newsweek* 5 March, 23 July 1979; *The Times* (London) 21 October 1981; *Al Dustur* (London) 30 April 1979; *AP* (Qatar) 15 May 1979.
10 T. B. Millar (1981) p 77.
11 *New York Times* 20 December 1979, my words in brackets.
12 *al-Watan al-Arabi* (Paris) 1, 7 December 1979; *Le Figaro* (France) 15 December 1979. *Pravda* (USSR) 16 January 1968; *Le Monde* 9 December 1968; *New Times* (Moscow) 26 June, 20 October 1968. *Middle East Record* v

(1969–70) p 285; The Jordanian Communist Party later created the PNF in 1973, many leaders of which, achieved high positions in the PLO:

13 Sterling (1981) p 295.
14 *US:PBS-TV* 25 September 1976.
15 *Rose al-Yusuf* (Egypt) 8 January 1977.
16 *As-Siyasah* (Kuwait) 7 May 1977.
17 Morison (1978); See also *International Terrorism: The Darkening Horizon* (1979) p 18.
18 *Izvestia* (Moscow) 26 November 1980.
19 *Pravda* (Moscow) 27 November 1980.
20 *Radio Moscow* 14 March 1981. Beirut Radio *The Voice of Palestine* 2 July 1981; See also *PLO . . . USSR* p 7.
21 *Ar-Rai al-A'am* (Kuwait) 17 August 1981. Barron (1985) pp 45–7, 169–71, 242–8, 256–7, 259, 262, 265, 266; *HCIS* April 1978, February 1980, July 1982; *Atlantic* November 1980; *Wall Street Journal* 10 December 1982; Goren (1984) p 102; *Shukan Gendai* (Tokyo) 23 August 1979; *NYT* 6, 9 March 1981; *Radio Moscow* 19, 23 March, 2 April 1978; *El Triunfe* (Madrid) 23 September 1978.
22 Goren (1984) pp 146–7, 161; *Le Matin* (France) 3 October 1978; *Paese della Sera* 4 May 1982; *Rude Pravo* (Prague) 3 February 1981; *Guardian* (Manchester) 22 June 1976, 26 September 1978; *Ma'ariv* 1 April 1970; *Middle East Record* (1969–70) p 259; *Le Point* 21 June 1976; *IHT* 29 June 1976; *Der Spiegel* 24 October 1977.
23 *Now!* (UK) 14–20 September 1979; 24–30 October 1980.
24 Laffin (1982) p 121; *Commentary* June 1980. Palestinian terrorists also assisted Soviet intelligence in Pakistan throughout the 1970s. *Daily Telegraph* (London) 16 September 1979.
25 *US:PBS-TV* 25 September 1976.
26 *al-Sayif* (Beirut) 13 August 1978; Sterling (1981) pp 277, 339. When Arafat was next in trouble, in 1981, the USSR made considerable noises about the possibility of upgrading the status of the PLO representative in Moscow to that of Ambassadorial level. When some of the anti-Arafat factions within the PLO were apprised of this, there was a considerable reduction in anti-Arafat lobbying. *Palestine News Agency WAFA* 2 July 1981. The Soviets, however, could not come to his assistance in 1983 when Arafat faced a successful revolt by his more hard-line lieutenants, in the pay of Syria.
27 Kux (1982).
28 Probably Abu Iyad of Fatah.
29 *Radio Monte Carlo* 17 February 1981.
30 O'Neill (1978) p 195.
31 *Die Welt* (Hamburg) 31 January 1978; *Al-Azmal* (Beirut) 9 February 1978; *Al-Mandar* (London) 12 February 1978; also Sterling (1981) p 278.
32 *Jamahiriya Review* April 1982.
33 Hottinger (January 1983).
34 Boyes (April 1983) p 4.
35 Possony & Bouchey (1978) p 47; *Le Monde* (Paris) 27 October 1967.
36 Lamberg 'Notes from Honduras' (June 1982) pp 8–9.
37 Guapp (March 1983) p 9; Laffin (1982) p 56.
38 *US Congress: Senate Committee on the Judiciary:Terroristic Activity Hearings* (May 1975) part 4, 14 May 1975 p 194; *Phalangist Radio* (Lebanon) 25 November 1979, 23 June 1981; *Washington Post* 7 September 1975; *Christian Science Monitor* 5 March 1977; *al-Anwar* (Beirut) 9 April 1978; *Conflict Studies* **no 69** (1976) pp 9–10.

1 *Britain and Israel* **no. 96** July–August 1979, **no. 110** November–December 1980; *Sunday Times* 25 May 1980; *PLO in Lebanon* op. cit. pp 19–20; *Fatah Document* dated 26 May 1981.

2 *The Middle East* August 1979.

3 *The Free Nation* July 1982.

4 *International Herald-Tribune* 23 June 1972; *Het Volk* (Belgium) 2 June 1972; *Montreal Star* 1 June 1972. *New York Times* 30 June 1982; *PLO in Lebanon* op. cit. p 14; Laffin op. cit. p 58.

5 *Le Point* 31 December 1984, March 1985; *The Times* 12 February 1985; *Plain Truth* July–August 1985.

6 *The Times* 9 March 1985.

7 *International Terrorism: The Soviet Connection* op. cit. p 36.

8 Stephen Rosenfeld of *The Washington Post* cited in *International Terrorism: The Darkening Horizon* op. cit. pp 26–7.

9 David Wood in *The Times* 11 May 1981; *Jewish Chronicle* 14 September 1984; *Le Figaro* 10 August 1985.

10 *The Times* 17 April 1973.

11 *The Sunday Telegraph* 9 August 1981, 21 february 1982; *The Times* 2 March 1982.

12 *The Observer* 14 and 21 March 1982; *Sunday Times* 23 November 1984.

13 For the wider implications of this, see Boyes, W. (June 1981) op. cit.

14 *The Times* 2 March 1982, 11 January, 18 and 20 March 1984, 10, 19 and 21 November 1984, 19 March and 25 April 1985; *Daily Telegraph* 1 June 1984; *Sunday Times* 11, 18 and 25 November 1984; *Mail on Sunday* 18 November 1984; *Newsweek* 24 December 1984; *The Times* 8 April 1985. *The Guardian* 23 October 1984; *The Times* 25 March 1985.

15 J. W. Falter, 'Die Bundestagswahl vom 19 November 1972' in *Zeitschrift für Parlamentsfragen* (March 1973) pp 128–29; Pridham, Geoffrey 'Terrorism and the State in West Germany during the 1970s: A Threat to Stability or a Case of Political Over-Reaction?' in Lodge, J. (1981) op. cit. p 43; *Stern* 20 October 1977. N.B. A. 'Blitzumfrage' is a flash-poll; compare our straw-poll. *Frankfurter Allgemeine Zeitung* 10 February 1987. Ibid, 10 March 1978. *Frankfurter Fundschau* 30 October 1978.

16 P. G. Cerny, 'FRANCE: Non terrorism and the Politics of Repressive Tolerance' in Lodge, J. op. cit. p 94.

17 Ibid p 105; C. Dobson and R. Payne *The Carlos Complex: A Study in Terror* (London, 1978) p 81; *Le Monde* 26, 27, 28 and 29 November 1976.

18 Dobson and Payne loc. cit.

19 Sterling op. cit. pp 52–3, 232.

20 *Le Monde* 2 August 1978. Dobson and Payne (1978) op. cit. pp 55–6; *Le Figaro* (Paris) 22 May 1978. *Le Monde* 2 August 1978; *Le Figaro* 3 August 1978. A similar event occurred at the UK Libyan Embassy in April 1984. *Le Figaro* 9 August 1978. P. G. Cerny, op. cit. p 113 *et seq.*

21 David Freestone, 'Legal Responses to Terrorism: Towards European Cooperation' in J. Lodge, op. cit. p 200. See also T. E. Carbonneau, 'The Provisional Arrest and Subsequent Release of Abu Daoud by French Authorities' in *Virginia Journal of International Law* **XVII** (1977) and D. C. Rapoport, 'Between Minimum Courage and Maximum Cowardice: A Legal Analysis of the Release of Abu Daoud' in *Brooklyn Journal of International Law* **III** (1977).

22 *The Observer* 22 April 1984; *Le Point* 31 December 1984, 4 March and 22

April 1985; *Mail on Sunday* 24 February 1985; Rivera (1985). *Passim.*
23 Quoted in full in *The Middle East* August 1981.
24 See note 22.
25 *The Times* 13 March 1982, 5 April, 1 May and 29 November 1984; *The Economist* 29 June 1985; *Mail on Sunday* 11 November 1984.
26 *The Sunday Telegraph* 14 November 1982; *The Times* 27 August 1984; *Newsweek* 11 February, and 4 March 1985; *Daily Express* 21 and 22 February 1985. *The Times* 13 March 1982, 5 April, 1 May, 29 November 1984; *The Economist* 29 June 1985; *Mail on Sunday* 11 November 1984.
27 *Newsweek* 11 February 1985; *The Times* 21 September 1985. *The Daily Telegraph* 12 April 1982. *IBA:ITN News at One* 15 October 1985. *The Times* 16 October 1985.
28 *European Parliament: Working Documents* no. **222/76.** *Debates of the European Parliament* no. **223,** 15 November 1977, p 70.
29 Ibid, **no. 223,** 16 November 1977, p 135; **no. 229** (April 1978) pp 139, 149–52.
30 *Britain and Israel* no. **18** (November 1972).
31 Ben-Zvi, Abraham 'The Reagan Presidency and the Palestine Predicament: An Interim Analysis' *CSS Paper* **no XVI** (Tel-Aviv University September 1982) pp 1–2, 10.
32 *Newsweek* 11 May 1981.
33 *Yediot Aharanot* (Israel) 24 February and 5 May 1981; *Los Angeles Herald* (USA) 11 April 1981; *Ha'aretz* (Israel) 25 February 1981; *Jerusalem Post* (Israel) 12 April 1981; *New York Times* (USA) 11 April 1981; *Washington Post* (USA) 8 April 1981; *Middle East Policy Survey* **XXX** 24 April 1981. *International Terrorism: The Soviet Connection* op. cit. p 27.

BIBLIOGRAPHY

DOCUMENTS

European Parliament, STRASBOURG
Debates of the European Parliament
European Parliament Working Documents.

United States Congress, Washington
House COMMITTEE on International Security 1 August 1974
Senate COMMITTEE on the Judiciary : Terroristic Activity Hearings May 1975
Senate COMMITTEE on Foreign Relations : International Terrorism Hearings 14 September 1977.

Fatah Documents provided by Israeli Information Ministry in facsimile esp. *Report of the Fatah Military Aid Mission to East Germany* (N.D.).

NEWSPAPERS, MAGAZINES AND JOURNALS (by country)

Algeria	*Al Sha'ab*		*Le Matin*
Austria	*Die Presse*		*Le Monde*
Belgium	*Het Volk*		*Le Nouvel Observateur*
Canada	*Montreal Star*		*Le Point*
Czecho-	*Rude Pravo*		*Politique Hebdo*
slovakia		Iraq	*An Nur*
Denmark	*Kristeligt Dagblad*		*Falastin Thawra al-*
Egypt	*Ahar Sa'a*		*Mukawama*
	Al-Ahram	Israel	*Davar*
	Al-Gumhuriyya		*Ha'aretz*
	Al Hayat		*Jerusalem Post*
	October		*Ma'ariv*
	Rose al-Yusuf		*Yediot Aharanot*
Eire	*An Phoblacht*	Italy	*Corriere della Sera*
	Irish Times		*Epoca*
France	*al-Watan al-Arabi*		*Gente*
	Alliance		*Il Giornale Nuovo*
	France-Soir		*Il Manifesto*
	Jeune Afrique		*Il Messaggero*
	L'Aurore		*L'Espresso*
	L'Evènement du Jeudi		*L'Europa*
	L'Express		*La Republica*
	Le Figaro		*La Stampa*

	Lotta Continua	Switzerland	*Journal de Genève*
	Paese-Sera		*Neue Zürcher Zeitung*
	Panorama		*Swiss Review of World*
Japan	*Shukan Gendai*		*Affairs*
Jordan	*Al-Aqsa*		*Tages Anzeigen*
	Al-Dustur	Syria	*Al-Anwar*
	Al-Quds		*Al-Hayat*
	Al-Rai		*Al-Mussawar*
	Amman al-Masa	Turkey	*Hurryet*
Kuwait	*Al-Qabas*		*Ortam*
	Ar-Rai al-A'am	U.K.	*Al Dustur*
	As-Siyasah		*Al Mandar*
Lebanon	*Al-Ahad*		*Arabia: The Islamic*
	Al-Amal		*World Review*
	Al-Amal al-Shahri		*Ash-Shark al-Awsat*
	Al-Anwar		*Britain and Israel*
	Al-Azmal		*Church Times*
	Al-Hawadeth		*Daily Express*
	Al-Hayat		*Daily Mail*
	Al-Jadid		*Daily Mirror*
	Al-Jarida		*Daily News*
	Al-Jumhur		*Daily Star*
	Al-Kifah		*Daily Telegraph*
	Al-Kifak al-Arabi		*Economist*
	Al-Liwa		*Economist Foreign*
	Al-Nahar		*Report*
	Al-Maukaf al Arabi		*Evening Standard*
	Al-Sayif		*Financial Times*
	Al-Usbu al-Arabi (Al-		*Free Palestine*
	Ushbua al-Arabi)		*Glasgow Herald*
	Al-Watan al-Arabi		*Guardian*
	An-Nahar		*Jewish Chronicle*
	As-Said		*The Listener*
	As Sapir		*Middle East*
	As Sayad		*International*
	Daily Star		*Middle East Monitor*
	El Hayat		*New Statesman*
	Falastin Ath-Thawra		*Now!*
	Fatah		*Observer*
	Monday Morning		*Plain Truth*
	Sha'un Falastinia		*Spectator*
Libya	*Al-Zahaf al-Akhdar*		*Sunday Express*
	(London)		*Sunday Telegraph*
	Jamahiriya		*Sunday Times*
	International Report		*The Mail on Sunday*
	(London)		*The Middle East*
	Jamahiriya Review		*The Sun*
	(London)		*The Times*
Netherlands	*Trouw*		*Yorkshire Post*
Saudi Arabia	*Al-Medina*		*8 Days*
	Al-Riyadh	USA	*Arab Report and*
Spain	*ABC*		*Record*
	El Pais		*Arab World*
	El Triunfe		*Atlantic*

Boston globe
Christian Science
  Monitor
Commentary
Congressional Record
Current History
  Journal
Denver Post
Far Eastern Economic
  Review
Foreign Affairs
International Herald-
  Tribune
Life
Los Angeles Herald-
  Dispatch
Los Angeles Herald-
  Examiner
Los Angeles Times
Miami Herald
Mid-East
Middle East Journal
Middle East Policy
  Survey
Middle East Record
Near East Report
New Republic
Newsview
New York Times

Newsweek
The Free Nation
The Nation
US News and World
  Report
Wall Street Journal
Washington Post
Washington Star
Time

USSR
Aziia i Afrika
  Segodnia
Izvestia
New Times
Pravda
Trud

W. Germany
Der Spiegel
Deutsche Nazional und
  Soldaten Zeitung
Die Welt
Die Zeit
Frankfurter
  Allgemeine Zeitung
Frankfurter
  Rundschau
Konkret
Merkur
Rheinplatz
Süddeutsche Zeitung

Yugoslavia
Borba

NEWS AGENCIES

Agence France Press
Arab News Agency
Associated Press
BBC Monitoring Service
Foreign Broadcast Information Service
Kuwait News Agency
Middle East News Agency
Novosti
Palestine News Agency
Reuters
Tass
United Press

RADIO AND TELEVISION TRANSMISSIONS
FROM THE FOLLOWING STATIONS

Amman Radio
Aukara Radio
BBC Arabic Service
Beirut Radio (Phalangist)

Beirut Radio (Voice of Lebanon)
Beirut Radio (Voice of Palestine)
Cairo Radio
Damascus Radio

Dera'a Radio (Sa'ut Falastin)   U.K.:BBC1TV *Panorama*
Jerusalem Radio (Kol Yisroel)   U.K.:BBC2TV *Newsnight*
Lebanese Television   U.K.:IBA:ITN *News*
Monte Carlo Radio   U.K.:IBA:ITV *Central*
Moscow Radio   U.K.:IBAITV *Thames*
Tripoli Radio (Libya)

BOOKS AND ARTICLES

Ajami, F. *The Arab Predicament: Arab Political Thought and Practice Since 1967* (CUP) Cambridge 1981.

Amin, S. *The Arab Nation: Nationalism and Class Struggles* (Zed Press) London 1978.

Arblaster, A. 'Terrorism—Myths, Meanings and Morals' in *Political Studies* XXV no. 3 (Sept. 1977).

Aumann, M. *The Palestinian Labyrinth* (Israel Academic Committee on the Middle East) Jerusalem (1982).

Ayoob, M. (ed.) *The Middle East in World Politics* (Croom Helm) London 1981.

al-Azm, Haled *The Memoirs of Haled al-Azm* Beirut 1973 (Arabic).

al-Azm, Sadeq *A Critical Study in the Thought of the Palestinian Resistance* Beirut 1973 (Arabic).

Baker, B. *The Far Left* (Weidenfeld & Nicholson) London 1981.

Barron, J. *K.G.B.: The Secret Work of Soviet Secret Agents* (Transworld) London 1979 edn.

Bell, J. Bowyer *Transnational Terror* (AEI-Hoover Institute) Stamford 1978.

K.G.B. Today: The Hidden Hand (Coronet) London 1985 edn.

Ben-Dor, G. 'The PLO and the Palestinians' in *The War in Lebanon* C.S.S. Memorandum no. 8. Tel-Aviv University (Feb. 1983).

Ben-Zwi, A. *The United States and the Palestinians: The Carter Era*. C.S.S. Paper no. XIII Tel-Aviv University (Nov. 1981).

The Reagan Presidency and the Palestinian Predicament: An Interim Analysis. C.S.S. Paper no. XVI Tel-Aviv University (Sept. 1982).

Bertram, C. (ed.) *Arms Control and Military Force* (Gower Press) Farnborough 1982.

Betts, R. B. *Christians in the Arab East* (S.P.C.K.) London 1979.

Birks, J. S. and Sinclair, C. A. *International Migration and Development in the Arab Region* (ILO) Geneva 1980.

Blancpain, J. P. 'Cracks in the International Credit System' in *Swiss Review of World Affairs* XXXII no. 3 (June 1982).

Borkin, J. *The Crime and Punishment of I. G. Farben* (Andre Deutsch) London 1979.

Boyes, W. 'The International Arms Trade and the Terrorist' in *Contemporary Affairs Briefing* I no. 7 (June 1981).

—'The Financing of Terror: Terrorism and Organised Crime' in *Contemporary Affairs Briefing* II no. 7. (April 1983).

Bradley, P. 'The Oil Syndrome: Its False Foundations and Their Consequences'

BIPAC Paper no. 1 (August 1980).

Bulloch, J. *Final Conflict: The War in the Lebanon* (Century Press) London 1983.

Burton, A. *Revolutionary Violence* (Leo Cooper) London 1977.

Caroz, Y. *The Arab Secret Services* (Corgi Books) London 1978.

Cerny, P. G. 'France: Non-Terrorism and the Politics of Repressive Tolerance' in Lodge, J. (ed.) *Terrorism: A Challenge to the State* (Martin Robertson) Oxford 1981.

Chaliand, G. *Palestine Resistance* (Penguin) Harmondsworth 1972.

Cooley, J. K. *Green June, Black September* (Frank Cass) London 1973.

Crozier, B. 'Libya's Foreign Adventures' in *Conflict Studies* no. 41 (Dec. 1973).

—'The Surrogate Forces of the Soviet Union' in *Conflict Studies* no. 92 (Feb. 1978).

—*Strategy of Survival* (Arlington House) New Rochelle N.Y. 1978.

Cudsi, A. S. and Dessouki, A. (Eds.) *Islam and Power* (Croom Helm) London 1981.

Dayan, M. *Breakthrough: A Personal Account of the Egypt-Israel Peace Negotiations*. (Weidenfeld & Nicholson) London 1981.

Deacon, R. *The Israeli Secret Service* (Sphere) London 1979.

Demaris, Ovid *L'Internationale Terroriste* (Olivier Orban) Paris 1978.

Divine, D. R. 'The Dialectics of Palestinian Politics' in Migdal, J. S. (ed.) *Palestinian Society and Politics* (Princeton U. P.) Princeton N. J. 1980.

Dobson, C. and Payne, R. *The Carlos Complex: A Study in Terror* (Coronet) London 1978.

—*The Terrorists: Their Weapons, Leaders and Tactics* (Facts on File) New York 1979.

—*Terror! The West Fights Back* (MacMillan) London 1982.

Eaks, Louis *From El Salvador to the Libyan Jamahiriyah—A Radical Review of American Foreign Policy Under the Reagan Administration* (Third World Reports) London 1981.

Eickelman, D. F. *The Middle East: An Anthropological Approach* (Prentice-Hall) Eaglewood Cliffs N.J. 1981.

Eisenberg, D., Dan, D. and Landau, E. *The Mossad: Israel's Secret Intelligence Service* (Corgi) London 1979.

Evron, Y. 'The Role of Arms Control in the Middle East' *Adelphi Papers* no. 138 (1977).

Fallaci, O. *Interviste con La Storia* (Rizzoli) Milan 1974.

Falter, J. W. 'Die BUNDESTAGSWAHL Vom 19 November 1972' in *Zeitschrift für Parlamentsfragen* (March 1973).

Feldman, S. *Israeli Nuclear Deterrence: A Strategy for the 1980's* (Columbia UP.) New York 1982.

Feshbach, M. 'The Soviet Union: Population Trends and *Dilemmas' Population Reference Bureau* XXXVII no. 3 (August 1982)

Freestone, D. 'Legal Responses to Terrorism: Towards European Cooperation' in Lodge, J. (1981).

Fromkin, D. 'Die Strategie der Terrorismus' in Funke, M. (ed.) *Terrorismus* (Althäum Verlag) Düsseldorf 1977.

Funke, M. (ed.) *Terrorismus: Untersuchungen zur Strategie und Struktur Revolutionärer Gewalt-Politik* (Bundeszentrale für politische Bildung) Bonn 1977.

—(ed.) *Terrorismus* (Althäum Verlag) Düsseldorf 1977.

Furlong, P. 'Political Terrorism in Italy: Responses, Reactions and Immobilism' in Lodge, J. (1981).

Gilmour, D. *The Dispossessed: The Ordeal of the Palestinians 1917–80*

(Sidgwick & Jackson) London 1980.

Golan, G. 'The Soviet Union and the P.L.O.: *Adelphi*

Goren, R. *The Soviet Union and Terrorism* (Allen & Unwin) London 1984.

Grollenberg, L. *Palestine Comes First* (SCM Press) London 1980 edn.

Guapp, P. 'Notes from the "New Nicaragua"' in *Swiss Review of World Affairs* XXXII no. 12 March 1983.

Gurevitz, B. 'The Soviet Union and the Palestine Organisations' in Ro'i, Y. (1979).

Haddad, W. W. Article in *Current History* Jan. 1982.

Halliday, F. *Arabia Without Sultans* (Pelican) Harmondsworth 1974.

Harkabi, Y. 'Fedayeen Action and Arab Strategy' *Adelphi Papers* no. 53 (1968).

—*The Palestine Covenant and Its Meaning* (Valentine-Mitchell) London 1979.

Heller, M. 'Politics and Social Change in the West Bank Since 1967' in Migdal, J. (1980).

Heradstveit, D. *The Arab-Israeli Conflict: Psychological Obstacles to Peace* (Oslo UP and Global Books) Oslo and London 1979.

Hirst, D. *The Gun and the Olive Branch: The Roots of Violence in the Middle East* (Futura) London 1978 edn.

Holden, D. and Johns, R. *The House of Saud* (Sidgwick & Jackson) London 1981.

Hottinger, A. 'Syria: On the Verge of Civil War' *Swiss Review of World Affairs* XXXII no. 4 July 1982.

—'Jordan and the Palestinians' *Swiss Review of World Affairs* XXXII no. 9. (Dec. 1982).

—'Syria After Lebanon' *Swiss Review of World Affairs* XXXII no. 10. (Jan. 1983).

Hottinger, A. & Nogues, A. 'Rebuilding Beirut' in *Swiss Review of World Affairs* XXXII no. 12 (March 1983).

Hudson, M. 'The Palestinian Arab Resistance Movement: Its Significance in the Middle East Crises' in *The Middle East Journal* XXIII (1969).

—'The Palestinian Resistance Movement since 1967' in Belling, Willard A. (ed.) *The Middle East* (SUNY Press) Albany 1973.

Hurni, F. 'Partial Peace in the Middle East' in *Swiss Review of World Affairs* XXXII no. 3 (June 1982).

—'Middle Eastern Knots' in *Swiss Review of World Affairs* XXXII no. 4 (July 1982).

Hutchinson, M. C. 'The Concept of Revolutionary Terrorism' in *Journal of Conflict Resolution* XVI no. 3 (Sept. 1972).

I.D.F. Spokesman (Israel) *Libyan-PLO Relations* (IDF) Jerusalem n.d.

—*The PLO and International Terror* (IDF) Jerusalem (March 1981).

—*PLO Ties with the USSR and Other Eastern Bloc Countries* (IDF) Jerusalem (Sept. 1981).

Ibrahim, S. A. 'Anatomy of Egypt's Militant Islamic Groups' in *International Journal of Middle East Studies* (Nov. 1980).

—*The New Arab Social Order: A Study of the Social Impact of Oil Wealth* (Croom Helm) London 1982.

Ismael, T. Y. *The Arab Left* (SUP) Syracuse 1976.

Issawi, C. *An Economic History of the Middle East and North Africa* (Methuen) London 1982.

Itayim, F. 'Strengths and Weaknesses of the Oil Weapon' *Adelphi Papers* no. 115 (1975).

Jarach, A. *Terrorismo Internazionale* (Valecchi) Florence 1979.

Jenkins, B. *International Terrorism: A New Mode of Conflict* (Crescent) Los Angeles 1975.

Johnson, P. *The Seven Deadly Sins of Terrorism* (Jonathan Institute) Jerusalem 1979.

Kaufmann, J. *L'Internationale Terroriste* (Libraire Plon) Paris 1976.

Kazziha, W. W. *Revolutionary Transformation in the Arab World* (Charles Knight) London 1975.

Kedourie, E. *Islam in the Modern World* (Mansell) London 1980.

Kelly, J. B. *Arabia, The Gulf and the West: A Critical View of the Arabs and their Oil Policy* (Weidenfeld & Nicholson) London 1980.

Kemp, G. 'The Military Build-up: Arms Control or Arms Trade' *Adelphi Papers* no. 114 (1975)

Kerr, M. *The Arab Cold War 1958–67* (O.U.P.) London 1967 Second edn.

Khoury, F. J. *The Arab-Israeli Dilemma* (S.U.P.) Syracuse 1968.

Kiernan, T. *The Arabs: Their History, Aims and Challenge to the Industrial World* (Sphere) London 1978 edn.

Kind, C. 'The Ousting of Arafat' in *Swiss Review of World Affairs* XXXII no. 7. (Oct. 1982)

Klein, H. J. *Rückkehr in die Menschlichkeit* (Rowohlt) Hamburg 1979.

Kux, E. 'The Soviet Marshals and Kremlin Politics' in *Swiss Review of World Affairs* XXXII no. 3 (June 182).

Lacey, R. *The Kingdom* (Hutchinson) London 1981.

Laffin, J. *Fedayeen* (Cassell) London 1978.

—*The Israeli Mind* (Cassell) London 1979.

—*The Dagger of Islam* (Sphere) London 1979.

—*The PLO Connections* (Corgi) London 1982.

Lamberg, R. F. 'The Long Arm of Cuban Subversion' in *Swiss Review of World Affairs* XXXI no. 12 (March 1982).

—'Notes from Honduras' in *Swiss Review of World Affairs* XXXII no. 3 (June 1982).

—'The PLO in Latin America' in *Swiss Review of World Affairs* XXXII no. 3 (June 1982)

Landau, J. M. *Radical Politics in Modern Turkey* (E. J. Brill) Leiden 1974.

Laqueur, W. *The Road to War* (Penguin) Harmondsworth 1968.

—*Terrorism* (Weidenfeld & Nicholson) London 1977.

—(ed.) *The Terrorism Reader: A Historical Anthology* (Signet) New York 1978.

Lewis, B. 'The Palestinians and the PLO' in *Commentary* (Jan. 1975).

Lodge, J. 'The European Community and Terrorism: Establishing the Principle of "Extradite or Try"' in Lodge, J. (1981).

—(ed.) *Terrorism: A Challenge to the State* (Martin Robertson) Oxford 1981.

Locjacomo, V. *I Dossiere di Settembre Nero* (Bietti) Milan 1974.

Mack, A. 'The PLO and the Prospects for Peace in the Middle East' in Ayoob (1981).

Mansfield, P. *The Arabs* (Penguin) Harmondsworth 1981 edn.

Mauz, M. *The Soviet and Chinese Relations with the Palestine Guerrilla Movement* (Davis Institute) Jerusalem 1974.

Maull, H. 'Future Arab Options' *Adelphi Papers* no. 114 (1975).

Mendelsohn *A Compassionate Peace* (Penguin) Harmondsworth 1982.

Migdal, J. S. *Palestinian Society and Politics* (Princeton U.P.) Princeton N.J. 1980.

Millar, T. B. *The East-West Strategic Balance* (Allen and Unwin) London 1981.

Morison, D. 'The Soviet Bloc and the Middle East' in *Middle East Contemporary Survey* (1978).

Mowat, R. C. *Middle East Perspective* (Blandford Press) London 1958.

Nahas, D. *The Israeli Communist Party* (Croom Helm) London 1976.

Nixon, R. *The Real War* (Sidgwick & Jackson) London 1980.

O'Brien, C. C. *Herod: Reflections on Politial Violence* (Hutchinson) London 1978.

Oded, A. 'Slaves and OIL: The Arab Image in Black Africa' in *Wiener Library Bulletin* n.s. 27 no. 32 (1974).

Ofer, Y. *Operation Thunder: The Entebbe Raid* (Penguin) Harmondsworth 1979.

O'Neill, B. E. *Armed Struggle in Palestine: A Political*-Military Analysis (Dawson) Folkestone 1978.

Ortzi, F. L. *Historia de Euskadi* (Ruedo Iberico) Barcelona 1978.

Ott, D. H. *Palestine in Perspective: Politics, Human Rights and the West Bank* (Quartet) London 1980.

Perlmutter, A., Handel, M. and Bar-Joseph, U. *Two Minutes Over Baghdad* (Valentine Mitchell) London 1982.

Pisar, S. *Of Blood and Hope* (Cassell) London 1980.

Podhoretz, N. 'J'Accuse' in *Commentary* (Sept, 1982).

Polk, W. R. *The Elusive Peace: The Middle East in the Twentieth Century.* (Croom Helm) London 1979.

—*The Arab World* (Harvard UP) London 1980.

Possony, S. and Bouchey, F. *International Terrorism—The Communist Connection* (American Council for World Freedom) Washington 1978.

Pridham, G. 'Terrorism and the State in West Germany During the 1970's: A Threat to Stability or a Case of Political Over-Reaction' in Lodge, J. (1981).

Quandt, W., Jabber, F. and Lesch, A. M. *The Politics of Palestinian Nationalism* (U.C.P.) Berkeley 1973 and 1974 edns.

Quandt, W. *Decade of Decisions: American Policy Toward the Arab-Israeli Conflict 1967–1976* (U.C.P.) London 1977.

—*Saudi Arabia in the 1980's: Foreign Policy, Security and Oil* (Blackwell) London 1982.

Rafael, G. *Destination Peace: Three Decades of Israeli Foreign Policy* (Weidenfeld & Nicholson) London 1981.

Rapoport, D. C. 'Between Minimum Courage and Maximum Cowardice: A Legal Analysis of the Release of Abu Daoud' in *The Brooklyn Journal of International Law* III (1977).

Riad, M. *The Struggle for Peace in the Middle East* (Quartet) London 1981.

Rivers, G. *The Specialist* (Sidgwick & Jackson) London 1985

Rodinson, M. *Israel and the Arabs* (Penguin) Harmondsworth 1982 edn.

—*The Arabs* (Croom Helm) London 1981 edn.

Ro'i, Y. (ed.) *The Limits to Power: Soviet Policy in the Middle East* (Croom Helm) London 1979.

Rubinstein, A. Z. *Soviet Foreign Policy Since World War II: Imperial and Global* (Winthrop) Cambridge Mass. 1981.

Sadat, A. el. *In Search of Identity: An Autobiography* (Fontana) London 1978.

Safran, N. *From War to War* (Pegasus) New York 1969.

Said, E. W. *The Question of Palestine* (Routledge) London 1980.

Sakharov, V. and Tosi, U. *High Treason: Revelations of A Double Agent* (Robert Hale) London 1980.

Salim, W. *Views of a Christian Lebanese* (Aid For Christian Lebanon) London & Beirut 1982.

Sampson, A. *The Arms Bazaar* (Coronet) London 1978.

Sayigh, R. *Palestinians: From Peasants to Revolutionaries* (Zed Press) London 1979.

Servier, J. *Le Terrorisme* (Presses Universitaires de France) Paris 1979.

Settembre Nero A cura di Berghamaschi, Laurora, Salvatore e Trovatore (Stampa Club) Milan 1972.

Sharabi, H. 'The Arab-Israeli Conflict: The Next Phase' *Adelphi Papers* no. 114 (1975).
Shamir, Shimon. *Communications and Political Attitudes in West Bank Refugee Camps* (Shiloah Centre) Tel-Aviv 1974 edn.
—'West Bank Refugees: Between Camp and Society' in Midgal (1980).
Shimoni, Y. *The Arabs of Israel* (Am-Oved) Tel-Aviv 1947 (Hebrew).
Shoukri, G. *Egypt: Portrait of A President 1971–81* (Zed Press) London 1981.
Sid-Ahmed, A. 'L'économie arabe à l'heure des surplus petroliers' in *Economies et Sociétés*. IX no. 3 (March 1975).
Sidler, P. 'Jordan Between Hammer and Anvil' in *Swiss Review of World Affairs* XXXI no. 11 (Feb. 1982).
Sloan, S. 'Conceptualising Political Terror: A Typology' in *Journal of International Affairs* 32 (1978).
Smith, C. *Carlos: Portrait of a Terrorist* (Sphere) London 1976.
Sterling, C. *The Terror Network: The Secret War of International Terrorism* (Weidenfeld and Nicholson) London 1981.
Steven, S. *The Spymasters of Israel* (Hodder and Stoughton) London 1981.
as-Sufi, Sheikh 'Abd al-Qadir *Resurgent Islam : 1400 Hijra* (Dirwan Press) Norwich 1979.
Tal, E. *P.L.O.* (W.Z.O.) Jerusalem 1982.
Tibawi, A. L. 'Visions of the Return: The Palestine Arab Refugees in Arabic Poetry and Art' in *The Middle East Journal* XVII (1963).
Tigay, A. M. *Myths and Facts: A Concise Record of the Arab-Israeli Conflict* (Near East Report) Washington 1980.
Tinnen, D. and Christensen, D. *The Hit Team* (Dell) New York 1977.
Tomlinson, J. *Left, Right: The March of Political Extremism in Britain* (John Calder) London 1981.
Tsur, J. *Zionism: The Saga of a National Liberation Movement* (Transaction Books) New Brunswick, New Jersey 1977.
Tucker, R. W. 'Lebanon: The Case for War' in *Commentary* (Oct. 1982).
Ulam, A. B. *In the Name of the People* (Viking) New York 1977.
Vatikiotis, P. J. *Conflict in the Middle East* (Allen and Unwin) London 1971.
Vocke, H. *The Lebanese Civil War* (Hurst) London 1978.
Walzer, M. *Just and Unjust Wars* (Allen Lane) London 1978.
Weinstock, N. *Zionism: False Messiah* (Ink Links) London 1979.
Weizmann, E. *The Battle for Peace* (Bantam) New York 1981.
Whetton, L. L. 'The Arab-Israeli Dispute: Great Power Behaviour' *Adelphi Papers* no. 128 (1976–7).
Wilkinson, P. *Political Terrorism* (Macmillan) London 1974.
—'Terrorism: International Dimensions' in *Conflict Studies* no. 113 (1979).
—*The New Fascists* (Grant McIntyre) London 1981.
Wolf, J. B. 'Controlling Political Terrorism in a Free Society' in *Orbis* 19 (1975–6).
Ya'ari, E. *Strike Terror!* (Sabra Books) New York 1970, also known as *Fatah*.
Yodfat, A. Y. and Arnon-Ohanna, Y. *PLO Strategy and Tactics* (Croom Helm) London 1981.
Yodfat, A. Y. *The Soviet Union and the Arabian Peninsula* (Croom Helm) London 1983.
Zelniker, S. and Shalom, Z. *Co-operation Between Israel and Egypt : Positions and Trends* C.S.S. Paper no. IX Tel-Aviv University (Oct. 1981).

OTHER PUBLICATIONS

Information Division of Ministry of Foreign Affairs, Jerusalem, Israel.
Accessories to Terror: The Responsibility of Arab Governments for the Organisation of Terrorist Activities (1973 edn.).
The Treatment of Arab Terrorists (1974).
The Palestine Liberation Organisation: Liberation or Liquidation (1979).
The PLO in Lebanon (1982).
Information Division of the Foreign Information Department, Tripoli, Libya.
Libya : A Case to be Heard. (1981).
Jonathan Institute, Jerusalem, Israel.
International Terrorism: The Darkening Horizon (1979).
International Terrorism: The Soviet Connection (1979).
Institute for the Study of Conflict, London.
Annual of Power and Conflict 1972–81 Vols.
National Foreign Assessment Center, Central Intelligence Agency of the U.S.A.
International and Transnational Terrorism (Washington 1976).
International Terrorism in 1977 : A Research Paper (1978) Reference no. RP 78–102 554.
Embassy of Israel (London) (various) *Information Briefing*.

APPENDIX

ABBREVIATIONS USED IN THE TEXT

AAF	Arab Assistance Front.
AAR	Arm of the Arab Revolution.
AD	Action Directe
AGLF	Arab-German Liberation Front.
ALF	Arab Liberation Front.
ANM	Arab Nationalist Movement.
AOLP	Arab Organisation for the Liberation of Palestine.
AONL	Arab Organisation for National Liberation.
APPU	Arabian Peninsula Peoples Union.
ASALA	Armenian Secret Army for the Liberation of Armenia.
BMG	Baader-Meinhof Gang.
CCC	Fighting Communist Cells.
CEDADE	Circle of Spanish Friends of Europe.
CIA	Central Intelligence Agency.
CPSU	Communist Party of the Soviet Union.
DGI	Dirección General de Intelligentsia.
DLF	Dhofar Liberation Front.
DST	Direction de Surveillance de la Territoire.
EEC	European Economic Community.
ETA	Euzkadi Ta Askatasuna.
FANE	Fédération d'Action Nationale et Européen.
FBI	Federal Bureau of Investigation.
FDFAP	Federation of Democratic Forces of the Arabian Peninsula.
FLN	Front Liberation Nationale.
FSLN	Frente Sandinista de Liberacion Nacional.
GIGN	Groupe d'Intervention de la Gendarmerie Nationale.
GPMG	General purpose machine-gun.
GRC	German Revolutionary Cells.
GSG9	Grenzschutzgruppen 9.
IDF	Israel Defence Forces.
ILO	Islamic Liberation Organisation.
INLA	Irish National Liberation Army.
IRA	Irish Republican Army.
JCR	Junta de Coordinacion Revolutionara.
JRA	Japanese Red Army.
MIR	Movimiento de la Izquierda Revolucionara.
NAYLP	National Arab Youth for the Liberation of Palestine.
NDFLOAG	National Democratic Front for the Liberation of the Arabian Gulf.
NFLP	National Front for the Liberation of Palestine.

NFLSA	National Front for the Liberation of Saudi Arabia.
NLFSY	National Liberation Front of South Yemen.
NORAID	The support group of PIRA active in N. America.
OIRA	The Official Wing of the IRA.
OPEC	The Organisation of Petroleum Exporting Countries.
OTRAG	Orbital Transport Rock AG.
PASC	Palestine Armed Struggle Command.
PDF	Popular Democratic Front.
PDFLP	Popular Democratic Front for the Liberation of Palestine.
PDRY	Peoples Democratic Republic of Yemen.
PFLOAG	Popular Front for the Liberation of the Arabian Gulf.
PFLP	Popular Front for the Liberation of Palestine.
PFLP-GC	Popular Front for the Liberation of Palestine: General Command.
PIRA	Provisional Wing of the IRA.
PLA	Palestine Liberation Army.
PLF	Palestine Liberation Front.
PLO	Palestine Liberation Organisation.
PNC	Palestine National Congress.
PNF	Palestine National Front.
PPSF	Palestine Popular Struggle Front.
PRA	Peoples Revolutionary Army.
PRSY	Peoples Republic of South Yemen.
PSF	Popular Struggle Front.
RAF	Red Army Faction.
RASD	The Surveillance and Intelligence Agency of FATA.
RB	Red Brigades.
RHF	Repentance and Holy Flight.
RPG's	Rocket-propelled grenades.
SAM	Surface-to-air missile.
SAMED	Sons of the Palestinian Martyrs Society.
SAS	Special Air Service.
SBS	Special Boat Squadron.
SMG	Sub-machine gun.
SOSL	Sons of South Lebanon.
SS	Schutzstaffel.
SSF	Somali Salvation Front.
TPLA	Turkish Peoples Liberation Army.
UDA	Ulster Defence Association.
UNCIRP	United Nations Committee of the Inalienable Rights of the Palestinians.
UNDP	United Nations Development Programme.
UNIFIL	United Nations Interim Force in Lebanon.
UNRWA	United Nations Relief and Welfare Agency.
UNSUPR	United Nations Special Unit for Palestinian Rights.
USAF	United States Air Force.
UVF	Ulster Volunteer Force.
VMO	Vlaamse Militante Orde.
VPR	Vanguarda Popular Revolucionara.
WAFA	Palestinian News Agency.

INDEX

260

262